ENHANCING COMPUTER SECURITY WITH SMART TECHNOLOGY

ENHANCING COMPUTER SECURITY WITH SMART TECHNOLOGY

Editor

V Rao Vemuri

Auerbach Publications
Taylor & Francis Group
Boca Raton   New York

Published in 2006 by
Auerbach Publications
Taylor & Francis Group
6000 Broken Sound Parkway NW, Suite 300
Boca Raton, FL 33487-2742

International Standard Book Number-10: 0-8493-3045-9 (Hardcover)
International Standard Book Number-13: 978-0-8493-3045-2 (Hardcover)
Library of Congress Card Number 2005047840

Library of Congress Cataloging-in-Publication Data

Enhancing computer security with smart technology / editor, V Rao Vemuri.
     p. cm.
  Includes bibliographical references and index.
  ISBN 0-8493-3045-9 (alk. paper)
   1. Computer networks--security measures. 2. Computer Security. 3. Artificial intelligence. 4. Machine learning. I. Vemuri, V Rao.

TK5105.59.E62 2005
005.8--dc22   2005047840

Taylor & Francis Group
is the Academic Division of T&F Informa plc.

Visit the Taylor & Francis Web site at
http://www.taylorandfrancis.com

and the Auerbach Publications Web site at
http://www.auerbach-publications.com

Contributors List

Ajith Abraham
School of Computer Science and
  Engineering
Chung-Ang University
Seoul, South Korea

Roshen Chandran
Paladion Networks
Vashi
Navi Mumbai, India

Dipankar Dasgupta
Intelligent Security Systems Research
  Lab
The University of Memphis
Memphis, Tennessee, U.S.A.

Stephanie Forrest
University of New Mexico
Albuquerque, New Mexico, U.S.A.

Fabio A. González
Profesor Asistente, Departmento de
  Ingeriera de Sistemas e Industrial
Universidad Nacional de Colombia
Bogota, Colombia

Kenneth Ingham
University of New Mexico
Albuquerque, New Mexico, U.S.A.

Abhishek Kumar
Paladion Networks
Vashi
Navi Mumbai, India

Khaled Labib
Department of Applied Science
University of California at Davis
Livermore, California, U.S.A.

Yihua Liao
Department of Computer Science
University of California at Davis
Davis, California, U.S.A.

Srinivas Mukkamala
Department of Computer Science
New Mexico Institute of Mining and
  Technology
Socorro, New Mexico, U.S.A.

Sanjay Rawat
Artificial Intelligence Laboratory
Department of Computer and
  Information Sciences
University of Hyderabad
Hyderabad, India

Challa S. Sastry
Artificial Intelligence Laboratory
Department of Computer and
  Information Sciences
University of Hyderabad
Hyderabad, India

Andrew H. Sung
Department of Computer Science
New Mexico Institute of Mining and
  Technology
Socorro, New Mexico, U.S.A.

Vinod Vasudevan
Paladion Networks
Vashi
Navi Mumbai, India

V Rao Vemuri
Department of Applied Science
University of California at Davis
Livermore, California, U.S.A.

Contents

Preface

This book is about enhancing computer security through smart technology. This is compiled with the intention of bringing together two groups of people: those coming from a computer security background and those from an artificial intelligence and machine learning background. Toward this objective, this book is organized into two parts. The first part provides tutorial introductions to some of the challenging problems in computer security to students and researchers coming from the area of machine learning. The second part introduces some of the more important machine learning concepts to students coming from the computer security area. Space here is not adequate to cover the entire range of issues pertaining to machine learning and computer security. Emphasis is therefore placed on problems related to the detection of intrusions by using machine learning methods. Although complexity issues (sample complexity and computational complexity) play significant roles in the computational learning theory, much of the emphasis here is on practical algorithmic aspects of machine learning and its role in computer security.

This book is conceived as a collection of tutorial chapters. Each self-contained chapter is written by a specialist in the subject field. A reader who has a basic background in computer science, such as that represented by a B.S. degree in computer science, but not necessarily some background either in security or in machine learning, should be able to read, understand, and benefit from this book. This book is not about recipes to secure your computer from attacks.

That there is a need for such a book can be easily seen. After two decades of computer security research, are we better off today than we were 25 years ago? The answer is an emphatic "no." People who routinely use computers to check their e-mails, pay bills, and make travel reservations are being inundated with spam (unsolicited e-mail messages), phishing attacks (a sort of identity theft), and so on, in addition to viruses and worms. If this trend continues, people may begin to lose their trust in conducting business transactions online — a not-so-desirable conse-quence. Cyber-security and cyber-trust are two issues that are likely to dominate research in the next decade.

To address these difficult problems, we have chosen to draw from a broad spectrum of views, expertise, and experience. Chapter 1 by Vemuri is a tutorial introduction to the general issue of cyber-security and cyber-trust. Chapter 2 by Ingham and Forrest provides a comprehensive survey of the state-of-the-art in firewall technology, the first line of defense. Anyone familiar with the spate of phishing attacks since early 2004 will appreciate the relevance of Web application security, discussed by Kumar, Chandran, and Vasudevan in Chapter 3. These three chapters constitute an introduction to the issues facing our cyber-society.

The rest of the book is on the use of machine learning methods and tools and their performance. In Chapter 4, Vemuri gives a very brisk introduction to machine learning and computational learning theory. In Chapter 5, Liao and Vemuri provide a basic introduction to the exciting field of machine learning as it applies to intrusion detection.

Chapter 6 by Mukkamala, Sung, and Abraham delves into computer attack taxonomy; gives specific examples of common attack signatures; and presents feature selection, extraction, and ranking algorithms. This chapter concludes with a discussion of the limitations of current anti-virus tools in detecting malware variants, with emphasis on obfuscated (poly-morphic) malware and mutated (metamorphic) malware.

In Chapter 7, Dasgupta and Gonzalez introduce the immune system metaphor to solve a variety of problems relevant to computer security. Chapter 8 and Chapter 9 belong to a category that can be dubbed as "methods in the making." In Chapter 8, a relatively small chapter, Challa and Rawat explore the potential of wavelets in detecting attacks in their early stages by monitoring and analyzing network traffic. Finally, in Chapter 9, Labib and Vemuri propose the use of a statistical toolbox and environment to streamline the computational steps common to many security-related applications. Results reported in these two chapters are recent and tentative, and need the scrutiny of time for their acceptance.

The maxim that "an author does not write a book alone" is even truer for an editor. This book would not have taken this shape without the untiring effort of each and every author who contributed. I thank all of them for responding in a timely fashion to my requests. However, I would like to single out a few individuals. It was V. Sreeharirao of the Jawaharlal Nehru Technological University, Hyderabad, India, who planted the idea of writing this book in my head after I conducted a one-day seminar on machine learning and computer security. I thank Arun K. Pujari and B.L. Deekshatulu for arranging my sabbatical at the University of Hyderabad and making all the arrangements for the said seminar, and finally, my doctoral student, Yihua Liao, who not only maintained the Web site but also acted as a sounding board for many of the ideas that shaped this book.

V Rao Vemuri

About the Editor

V Rao Vemuri, Ph.D. received his doctoral degree from the University of California, Los Angeles, and currently holds appointments in the Department of Applied Science and in the Department of Computer Science at the University of California, Davis. He also holds an appointment as a Computer Scientist at the Lawrence Livermore National Laboratory in Livermore, California.

Prior to his current appointments, Dr. Vemuri taught at Purdue University at West Lafayette, Indiana, SUNY at Binghamton, New York, and worked at TRW at Redondo Beach, California.

At TRW, he worked on a variety of projects including the MX missile and Hubble Space Telescope. Dr. Vemuri co-founded and acted as the CEO of Smartifacts, LLC and worked on the development of Web-based smart artifacts. He is also the founding president of Eco Foundation, a non-profit foundation.

Dr. Vemuri served as the editor-in-chief for CS Press, associate editor for IEEE *Transactions on Neural Networks*, and as a member of the editorial board of *Differential Equations and Dynamical Systems*. He delivered several keynote addresses at international conferences and authored or edited ten books and published well over 100 papers in reviewed journals.

Dr. Vemuri's teaching and research interests are in artificial intelligence and machine learning. He applies these technologies to a variety of problems including computer security, knowledge discovery, data mining, and information filtering. Some of his major contributions in the recent past include the development of a neural network technique for the Comprehensive Test Ban Treaty Verification Project and a genetic algorithm method to support the Human Genome Project.

Chapter 1

Cyber-Security and Cyber-Trust

V Rao Vemuri

1.1 Introduction

History is undergoing the third in a succession of great changes in technology and cost of transportation. The 19th century was characterized by the falling cost of transporting goods; the 20th, by the falling cost of transporting people; and the 21st century will be dominated by the falling cost of transporting ideas and information. "Death of distance" is very much here.

The last two decades of the 20th century witnessed a steep increase in the pervasiveness and ubiquity of digital technologies in our lives. The trip from mainframes to personal computers, laptops, and PDAs took place at breathtaking speed. The radio frequency identification tag (RFID), embedded in everyday objects from smart toys to smart clothing, is another journey that has already begun. Indeed, much of what we do is getting inexorably tied to digital technologies.

With the declining costs of Internet access and information processing, more and more people are beginning to use computers. The rank and file of these users is not the literati of cyber-world; it is the ordinary person who is seeing the desktop computer, connected to the Internet, as another utility outlet — just plug in and use the services. And these folks are expecting a quality of service (QoS) that is commensurate with the QoS they are accustomed to with other utilities such as electricity, gas, and telephone. People expect such service to be continuously available anytime and anywhere — reliable, secure, and easy to use.

Nowadays, computers are being sold in department stores along with microwave ovens, television sets, and music players. Many households (in the United States) that own an automobile also own a computer. Just like getting behind the wheel, turning the key, and driving to the grocery store, people are expecting to get in front of the terminal, fire it up, log on, read mail, make reservations, find driving directions, play games, and pay the bills. With the advent of wireless technologies, people are able to perform these functions from anywhere using their laptops.

This rosy picture is not without its thorns. People are not able to perform these routine functions without facing a host of problems. Indeed, the need to wait for a long time for the computer to boot up, even in dire emergencies, has been caricatured in Hollywood films. The need to memorize usernames and the associated passwords and PINs is a familiar headache, with each service provider imposing its own set of rules on the user. Is there a way a user can be helped to learn to choose good passwords and memorize them? Should the technique of password-based authentication be the same for desktops and handheld devices? Is there a way to train users to learn the process of selecting new passwords when the old ones expire? Is there some way users can manage the plethora of passwords that they are required to memorize? Would graphical passwords solve the problem? Are graphical passwords immune to dictionary attacks?

In addition to these, there are many other problems. For example, there is a need to know the procedures of handling files with a host of extensions. Another particularly vexing problem that is grabbing headlines is the issue of coping with virus and worm attacks.

1.2 Cyber-Security

We, as a society, are paying a price for these developments. A program called Elk Cloner, written for Apple II systems in 1982, is credited with being the first computer virus to appear "in the wild" — that is, outside the single computer or lab where it was created. On November 2, 1988, a Cornell University graduate student named Robert Morris purportedly launched one of the first computer worms that gained significant mainstream media attention. Around 6,000 major UNIX machines were infected by the Morris worm. The General Accounting Office of the United States

Table 1.1 Computer Economics' Estimate of Damages Caused by Viruses and Worms

Virus/Worm	Year	Cost (Billions)
Melissa	1999	$1.10
LoveBug	2000	$8.75
CodeRed	2001	$2.75
Slammer	2003	$1.25
SoBig.F	2003	$1.10

put the cost of the damage at $10 to $100 million. Robert Morris was tried and convicted of violating the 1986 Computer Fraud and Abuse Act (Title 18). After appeals, he was sentenced to three years' probation, 400 hr of community service, and a fine of $10,000. During 2003–2004, virulent attacks by viruses and worms, such as CodeRed, Slammer, and MyDoom, have taken a toll on organizations and individuals that rely on computers. The sad realization is that the computer community is still vulnerable to attacks — after two decades of research and in the face of threats of prosecution.

Table 1.1 is one estimate of the damage (in U.S. dollars) caused by viruses and worms alone. These costs include services and hardware needed to remove viruses from networks, shore up defenses, and repair damage.

The years 2003 and 2004 seemed to be especially harsh on computer security professionals. In the immediate aftermath of the MyDoom attack in early 2003, a *New York Times* article, "Geeks Put the Unsavvy on Alert: Learn or Log Off," dated February 5, 2004, quotes the president of the World Wide Web Artists Consortium as lamenting, "It takes affirmative action on the part of the clueless user to become infected ... How to beat this into these people's heads?" A similar know-all geekish attitude exhibited by U.S. automobile manufacturers in the 1960s paved the way for the high-quality Japanese imports we are enjoying today. "The tension over the MyDoom virus underscores a growing friction between technophiles and what they see as a breed of technophobes who want to enjoy the benefits of digital technology without making the effort to use it responsibly," concludes the *New York Times*.

One hears more about viruses and worms because they impact everyone, and the media also gives these events high coverage because every user can identify with them. However, the damage caused by these nuisance makers — high as it is — pales in the face of the damage caused by someone stealing confidential information from high-profile organizations (e.g., a bank) — which is rarely disclosed in public or even within closed groups. This is done to protect the interests of the organization. One exception to this trend can be cited. On February 10, 2004, the Associated Press reported the discovery of a major vulnerability in the Windows operating system, although researchers at eEye had discovered the problem more than six months earlier: "Microsoft Corporation warned customers ... about unusually serious security problems with its Windows software that could let hackers quietly break into their computers to steal files, delete data, or eavesdrop on sensitive information." As some of Microsoft's built-in security features — such as its Kerberos cryptography system — rely on the flawed software, the breadth of systems affected is probably the largest ever. Computer systems that control critically important infrastructures, such as power and water utilities, are now vulnerable. Intrusion detection systems, therefore, play a supporting role in identifying virus and worm spreads and a key role in protecting organizations with confidential data.

Indeed, products are available to block viruses and worms at the gateway to an organization, at the desktop level, at the server level, and at the application level (e.g., messaging servers). Once such technology is in place, there should be strong processes to monitor and track viruses and worms. What is needed is teamwork between management personnel who are aware and will provide focus, system administrators who are trained in countering these threats, and end users who are aware. (Don't open unknown attachments from strangers!) Virus and worm control is a classic example of the requirement for technology, processes, and people to secure an environment. It is these interrelationships that make security complex.

The computer community's effort to develop patches each time a new virus is detected is somewhat analogous to the medical community's effort to look for known pathogens in a community's blood supply before a transfusion is attempted. In the early days of the AIDS epidemic, many innocent people were inadvertently infected via blood transfusions because the doctors at that time had no idea about what causes AIDS. There is no reason to believe that the current blood supply is completely safe because we still have no idea what other hitherto unidentified viruses are lurking out there. What is potentially more useful than screening for known pathogens is something analogous to pasteurization — a process by which all pathogens are eliminated. In the case of milk, one simply heats the milk. In the case of blood, we have no analog to pasteurization. The computer security community also needs a process analogous to the pasteurization process. Any hope of finding such an analogy is not dependent on luck; it can only come from a deeper understanding of the current crop of intrusion detection methods. Many subtle issues are making it difficult to exploit this pasteurization metaphor in the context of computer security.

With the popularity of wireless and mobile networks, attacks have taken a different flavor. Attacks need not be concentrated over a particular direction or link and are hence difficult to detect. Every bit of the data is transmitted through an open medium and, thus, intruders have free access to it. In such a scenario, security becomes even more challenging. Lack of resources available at the mobile device for processing and encoding of messages makes these challenges much harder to overcome than in conventional networks.

1.3 Cyber-Trust

Associated with security, but not synonymous with it, are other issues such as privacy and trust. Privacy, from a business point of view, is influenced by how personal information is collected and stored. Almost all businesses collect some information about their customers. They must find a way to manage this information in a responsible manner. How an organization manages confidential information with which it is entrusted speaks a lot about that organization's respect for its customers. Major companies such as JetBlue, Mrs. Fields Cookies, and Victoria's Secret have learned their lessons at great cost. Some hospitals also learned the hard way when they outsourced their transcription work to untrustworthy offshore companies.

Trust is a critical element in Web-based communities, E-commerce, and in influencing the attitudes of laypeople toward Web-based information systems. Trustworthiness is a concept that is intertwined with dependability and security. The attributes of dependability are reliability, availability, integrity, and safety, whereas the attributes of security are confidentiality, availability, and integrity. It is easier to recognize an untrustworthy system when you see one than to define it. For example, the National Science Foundation made an attempt to define their vision of cyber-trust by seeking answers to questions such as:

- Can people justifiably rely on computer-based systems to perform critical functions securely?
- Can people justifiably rely on computer-based systems to process, store, and communicate sensitive information securely?
- Can people justifiably rely on a well-trained and diverse workforce to develop, configure, modify, and operate essential computer-based systems?

Today, one of the most common situations happening when anyone uses a computer is the trail of records, such as HTTP logs and cookies, left behind. Records of user activity are invaluable tools for research, but every hidden history file is a potential threat to security and individual privacy. Because of this conflict and other proprietary considerations, it is becoming almost impossible for academic researchers to work with realistic data.

Consider a simple user transaction. From a naive user's point of view, trust comes from flexibility of the operation sequence and transparency to what is happening. The solution to the twin problems of security and trust is not to remove all records of activity or make records hard to access but to provide feedback to users so they know what is being recorded about their transaction and give the user some control and access to what is being recorded about the transaction. This means that we must first understand how people view different types of records of their activity. A user may not mind leaving behind aggregated access patterns so that some search engine can be built based on page ranks derived from these patterns.

Trustworthiness of, say, Web sites can be improved by process-oriented, design-oriented, or security-oriented features. Different domains inspire trust in different ways. Branding is a popular business strategy. Customers flock to a familiar (not necessarily a better) brand. Brand recognition and reputation go hand in hand. To earn that reputation, companies should publish reliable reports of their performance (say, on-time arrival statistics), or they may seek certification from a third party (say, VeriSign certification for secure data transfer), and so on. A popular mechanism for building reputation is by tracking the past behavior of earlier participants. Under its Feedback Forum initiative, eBay seeks feedback from users and makes it available to all. Amazon.com allows users to submit their own book reviews. Such peer-rating schemes have their own drawbacks.

In view of these considerations, designers of cyber-trust are facing three basic challenges.

1.3.1 Challenge 1: The Distribution of Expertise

This refers to the distribution of knowledge or expertise about computing systems throughout society. The relationships between different categories of users can be visualized as a pyramid built of several layers. The base level is by far the biggest because it consists of ordinary people who possess relatively little technical expertise, whose interest is based on the capacity of computers to facilitate communication for transactions, and who often lack access to the expert consultants that users with technical expertise take for granted. The next level is one containing fewer people, who routinely use a digital infrastructure to complete work tasks. Doing so requires them to be savvy and sophisticated (e.g., many business and industry users), although they often have access to technical assistance through formal and informal pathways at work. The third level is that of individuals with technical expertise in information technology and engineering. Our pyramid is capped by a still-smaller number of computing professionals who design and build systems (hardware and software) and whose technical competence provides deeper knowledge of how a computer functions. They typically take for granted operational knowledge that is utterly incomprehensible to most other users.

1.3.2 Challenge 2: Proliferating Devices and Functionality

The second challenge is the proliferation of computing systems, the variety of digital devices, and their increasing functionality. Examples abound:

■ Cars are becoming laden with digital devices that increase functionality: navigation systems, sensors that alert drivers when they drift from the center of a lane, remote unlocking from a central place, tracking the position of cars, plug-and-play diagnostics of vehicles, etc.
■ Toys are getting smarter.
■ Products from companies such as Nokia are concealing the technology, emphasizing usability by careful study of everyday users, and simplifying design and functionality.

Such digital devices are characterized by, among other things:

■ Shrinking sizes (e.g., laptop versus desktop)
■ Greater mobility (e.g., PDAs)
■ The specialization of device functionality (and, paradoxically, increasingly diverse functionality of individual devices; e.g., "smart" cellular phones/cameras)
■ A variety of operating systems
■ The embedding of digital devices in various products (e.g., automobiles with GPS capability)
■ Incorporating them into larger, geographically distributed systems (e.g., cellular phone that allows the user to point and click at a vending machine that then automatically charges the soft drink to the user's bank account)

1.3.3 Challenge 3: Burgeoning Purposes

Accompanying the proliferation of digital devices and their incorporation into society is an expansion of the purposes to which they are put. It was not so long ago that experts contemplated how ordinary households would ever use personal computers (and be convinced to buy one), which seemed destined to remain in the realms of work and education. The implication here is that concerns about trustworthy computing systems may have as much to do with the nature of information sent, stored, and received as it does with the devices *per se*. Ordinary users may be relatively less concerned about these issues, for example, the trustworthiness of digital devices and the systems of which they are part, than they are about the use and misuse of particular categories of information. These include:

- Health and medical records, such as test results
- Personal and family finance, investment, and banking data
- Specific purchases and larger patterns of consumption
- Recreational activities, hobbies, and networks of friends and family
- Physical location and movements between locations
- Political affiliations
- Educational and training certifications and transcripts

1.4 What the Future Holds

No one predicted the Internet and WWW as we are experiencing them today, although there are people who claim that they "invented" the Internet. No one predicted viruses, worms, spam, phishing, identity theft, and the host of other ills that we are putting up with. Hence, it would be foolhardy to make predictions in a textbook such as this. However, there is one prediction we can safely make: Usage of computers, in some form or another, will continue to increase. We will continue to face challenges to our security and privacy. Even if the underlying technologies change, there is commonality in the challenges brought forth by these technologies.

The rest of this book introduces some of the techniques and methods that are likely to survive and find their way into the cyber-world to help us combat the attendant ills.

Chapter 2

Network Firewalls

Kenneth Ingham and Stephanie Forrest

Abstract

Firewalls are network devices that help enforce an organization's security policy. Since their development, various methods have been used to implement firewalls. These methods filter network traffic at one or more of the seven layers of the ISO network model, most commonly at the application, transport, network, and data-link levels. Newer methods, which have not yet been widely adopted, include protocol normalization and distributed firewalls.

Firewalls involve more than the technology required to implement them. Specifying a set of filtering rules, known as a *policy,* is typically complicated and error prone. High-level languages have been developed to simplify the task of correctly defining a firewall's policy. Once a policy has been specified, testing is required to determine if the firewall correctly implements it.

Because some data must be able to pass in and out of a firewall for the protected network to be useful, not all attacks can be stopped by firewalls. Some emerging technologies, such as virtual private networks (VPNs) and peer-to-peer networking, pose new challenges to existing firewall technology.

2.1 Introduction

The idea of a wall to keep out intruders dates back thousands of years. Over 2000 years ago, the Chinese built the Great Wall for protection from neighboring northern tribes. European kings built castles with high walls and moats to protect themselves and their subjects, both from invading armies and from marauding bands intent on pillaging and looting. The term "firewall" was in use as early as 1764 to describe walls that separated the parts of a building most likely to have a fire (e.g., a kitchen) from the rest of a structure [40]. These physical barriers prevented or slowed a fire's spread throughout a building, saving both lives and property. A related use of the term is described by Schneier [60]:

> Coal-powered trains had a large furnace in the engine room, along with a pile of coal. The engineer would shovel coal into the engine. This process created coal dust, which was highly flammable. Occasionally the coal dust would catch fire, causing an engine fire that sometimes spread into the passenger cars. Since dead passengers reduced revenue, train engines were built with iron walls right behind the engine compartment. This stopped fires from spreading into the passenger cars, but didn't protect the engineer between the coal pile and the furnace.

This chapter is concerned with firewalls in a more modern setting — computer networks. The predecessors to firewalls for network security were the routers used in the late 1980s to separate networks from one another. A network misconfiguration that caused problems on one side of the router was largely isolated from the network on the other side. In a similar vein, the so-called "chatty" protocols on one network (which used broadcasts for much of their configuration) would not affect the other network's bandwidth [2]. These historical examples illustrate how the term firewall came to describe a device or collection of devices that separates its occupants from potentially dangerous external environments (e.g., the Internet). A firewall is designed to prevent or slow the spread of dangerous events.

Firewalls have existed since about 1987, and several surveys and histories have been written [11,34,42,52]. In this chapter, we present an updated and more comprehensive survey of firewall technology. Several books have been written that describe how to build a firewall [15,71]. These books are excellent for people either wanting to evaluate a commercial firewall or implementing their own firewall. However, neither

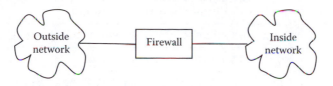

Figure 2.1 A firewall at the perimeter of an organization's network. The inside network may be as simple as a few machines or may consist of several divisions located in geographically distant locations connected by telecommunication lines.

spends much time on firewall history, nor do they provide references to peer-reviewed literature.

For the purposes of this chapter, we define a *firewall* as a machine or collection of machines between two networks, meeting the following criteria:

- The firewall is at the boundary between the two networks.
- All traffic between the two networks must pass through the firewall.
- The firewall has a mechanism to allow some traffic to pass while blocking other traffic (often called filtering). The rules describing what traffic is allowed make up the firewall's policy.

Additional desirable criteria include:

- Resistance to security compromise.
- Auditing and accounting capabilities.
- Resource monitoring.
- No user accounts or direct user access.
- Strong authentication for proxies (e.g., smart cards rather than simple passwords).
- Fail-safety: If it fails, the protected system is still secure because no traffic is allowed to pass through the firewall.

The fact that a firewall is at the boundary between two networks has also led to them being called "perimeter security" — see, for example, Figure 2.1.

Firewalls function by filtering traffic at one or more (today, normally multiple) layers in the network protocol stack. These layers are described using the ISO seven-layer model for networking [36]:

ISO Layer	Internet Example
Application	File Transfer Protocol (FTP) and Telnet
Presentation	Common Object Request Broker Architecture (CORBA)
Session	No directly corresponding protocol
Transport	Transmission Control Protocol (TCP) and User Datagram Protocol (UDP)
Network	Internet Protocol (IP)
Data link	Ethernet or Asynchronous Transfer Mode (ATM)
Physical	Twisted pair or fiber-optic cable

The protocols used on the Internet for these layers, as well as all other Internet standards, are specified by documents known as Requests for Comments (RFCs) [67].

This chapter is divided into several sections. Section 2.2 describes the history and rationale for organizations adopting firewalls. Security professionals build firewalls using many different architectures, depending on the security needs of the organization, and Section 2.3 describes several of these choices. Section 2.4 reviews the ISO protocol layers, describing firewall technology at each relevant layer. Section 2.5 considers alternative approaches to firewall construction; these approaches are typically more experimental, but they represent technology that could appear in common firewalls in the near future. Once a firewall is constructed, it must be tested to show that it actually enforces the organization's security policy; testing is the subject of Section 2.6. Although firewalls are an important tool for securing an organization's network, they have limitations, which are discussed in Section 2.7. Section 2.8 discusses some projected challenges for firewalls in the face of technological change, and Section 2.9 concludes the chapter.

2.2 The Need for Firewalls

In the early years, the Internet supported a small community of users who valued openness for sharing and collaboration. This view was challenged by the Morris worm [22]. However, even without the Morris worm, the end of the open, trusting community would have come soon through growth and diversification. Examples of successful or attempted intrusions around the same time include Clifford Stoll's discovery of German spies tampering with his system [63] and Bill Cheswick's "Evening with Berferd"

[13], in which he set up a simple electronic "jail" for an attacker. In this jail, the attacker was unable to affect the real system but was left with the impression that he or she had successfully broken in. Cheswick was able to observe everything the attacker did, learning from these actions and alerting system administrators of the networks from which the attacks were originating. Such incidents clearly signaled the end of an open and benign Internet. In 1992, Steve Bellovin described a collection of attacks that he had noticed while monitoring the AT&T firewall and the networks around it [7]. The result was clear — there were many untrustworthy and even malicious users on the Internet.

When networks are connected together, different levels of trust often exist on the different sides of the connection. "Trust" in this sense means that an organization believes that both the software and the users on its computers are not malicious. Firewalls enforce trust boundaries, which are imposed for several reasons:

Security problems in operating systems: Operating systems have a history of insecure configurations. For example, Windows 95 and Windows 98 were widely distributed with file sharing enabled by default; many viruses exploited this vulnerability (for example, see Reference 16 and Reference 17). A second example is Red Hat Linux version 6.2 and version 7.0, which were vulnerable to three remote exploits when the operating system was installed using default options [18]. It is an ongoing and expensive process to secure every user's machine, and many organizations consciously decide not to secure the machines inside their firewall. If a machine on the inside is ever compromised, the remaining machines also are likely vulnerable [53], a situation that has been described as "a sort of crunchy shell around a soft, chewy center" [14].

Preventing access to information: National firewalls attempt to limit the activities of their users on the Internet, for example, China [49]. A similar idea in the United States is the Children's Internet Protection Act (CHIPA), which mandates that certain information be filtered. This law requires that schools and libraries that receive federal funding block certain classes of Web content.

Preventing information leaks: Because all traffic leaving a network must pass through the firewall, it can be used to reduce information leaks [55]:

> The key criterion for success for the digital corporate gateways is preventing an unauthorized or unnoticed leak of data to the outside.

Enforcing policy: Firewalls are one part of an overall security policy; they enforce the rules about which network traffic is allowed to enter or leave a network. These policies control the use of certain applications, restrict which remote machines may be contacted, or limit the bandwidth.

Auditing: If a security breach (which does not include the firewall) occurs, audit trails can be used to help determine what happened. Audit trails have also been used to monitor employees, e.g., for using office network resources for nonwork purposes.

Using a personal firewall, individuals can protect a single machine connected to the Internet. Rather than trying to secure the underlying operating system, these firewalls simply prevent some types of communication. Such firewalls are often used in homes and on laptops when they are outside their normal firewall. In this case, the trust boundary is the network interface of the machine.

Organizations often use firewalls to prevent a compromised machine inside from attacking machines outside. In this case, the firewall protects the organization from possible liability because of propagating an attack.

2.3 Firewall Architectures

Firewalls range from simple machines designed to be purchased off-the-shelf and installed by a person unskilled in network security (e.g., as shown in Figure 2.1) to complex, multiple-machine, custom installations used in large organizations. Regardless of their complexity, all firewalls have the concept of "inside" for the protected network and "outside" for the untrusted network. These terms are used even when a firewall protects the outside world from potentially compromised machines inside.

Another common feature of firewalls is the existence of a DMZ (named after the demilitarized zone separating North Korea and South Korea) or "screened network." Examples of how a DMZ may be constructed are illustrated in Figure 2.2 and Figure 2.3. Machines such as e-mail and Web servers are often placed in the DMZ. These machines are not allowed to make connections to machines inside the firewall, but machines on the inside are allowed to make connections to the DMZ machines. Thus, if a server in the DMZ is compromised, the attacker cannot directly attack machines on the inside. Servers are particularly vulnerable because they must be accessed to be useful, and current firewalls are largely ineffective against attacks through these services (see Section 2.4). Examples of attacks on servers include the CodeRed and Nimda worms that attacked Microsoft

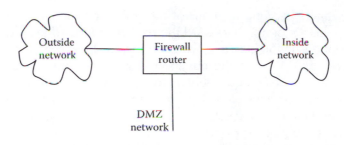

Figure 2.2   A firewall with a DMZ on a third network attached to the firewall router. Some commercial products are configured this way, as are custom firewalls.

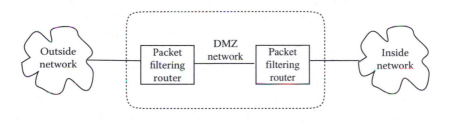

Figure 2.3   A screened network as a DMZ. The firewall is enclosed by the dashed line.

Windows machines running Microsoft's Web server, IIS, and in the case of Nimda, several additional routes.

Firewall architectures are constrained by the type of filtering (described in the following text) and the presence or absence of a DMZ.

2.3.1 Packet Filtering

Packet filtering is the process of analyzing the headers in network packets and deciding whether or not to allow the packets, based on the policy enforced by the firewall. Packet filtering for network security began with Mogul's paper describing *screend* in 1989 [50]. Most of the early work on packet filtering for security emphasized performance [4]; later papers continued this trend [43,66]. In addition to its efficiency, packet filtering is appealing because, unlike proxies, it does not require the cooperation of users, nor does it require any special action on their part (see Subsection 2.3.2).

Packet filters use one or more of the following pieces of information to decide whether or not to forward the packet: source address, destination address, options in the network header, transport-level protocols (i.e., TCP, UDP, ICMP, etc.), flags in the transport header, options in the transport header, source port or equivalent if the protocol has such a construct, destination port or equivalent if the protocol has such a construct, the interface on which the packet was received or will be sent, and whether the packet is inbound or outbound.

Although packet filtering is fast, it has some drawbacks, the most important of which is the difficulty in writing correct filters. For example, Chapman compares packet filter languages to assembly language [12]. In 1995, Molitor proposed an improved commercial filter language [51].

A second drawback is that packet filtering cannot identify which user is causing what network traffic. It can inspect the IP address of the host from which the traffic originates, but a host is not identical to a user. If an organization with a packet-filtering firewall is trying to limit the services some users can access, it must either implement an additional, separate protocol for authentication (see Subsection 2.3.2 for an example of how this might be done) or use the IP address of the user's primary machine as a weak replacement for true user authentication.

Also, because IP addresses can be spoofed, using them for authentication can lead to other problems. If the router is running a properly configured filter, remote attackers should not be able to spoof local addresses, but they could spoof other remote addresses. Local machines can spoof other local machines easily. In spite of these problems, many organizations still use IP addresses or DNS names for access control.

With packet filters, the local machine directly initiates the connection to the remote machine. A result is that the entire internal network is potentially reachable from external connections; otherwise, reply packets from the remote host would not be delivered properly. As a consequence, hostile remote computers can potentially exploit weaknesses in the protocol implementation of the local computer [61].

Protocols such as FTP are difficult for packet filters. FTP uses a control channel opened from the client to the server for commands. However, when getting a file, one method of using FTP (active FTP) has the server open a connection back to the client, contrary to the communication patterns in other client/server protocols. FTP's lack of encryption protecting user authentication data has led to reduced usage, and eventually it may no longer be used.

2.3.1.1 Packet Filtering with State

Originally, packet filters ignored the state of a connection. This means that a remote host could send in packets that appeared to be part of an established TCP connection (with the TCP ACK flag set), but which in reality were not. Attacks against bugs in the TCP/IP protocol stack [61] can pass through the packet-filtering firewalls that do not keep state by claiming to be part of an established TCP session. Some network-mapping software [24] can map the inside network as if the firewall did not even exist.

The solution to this problem is to record the state of a connection, a property referred to variously as *stateful firewalls*, *adaptive firewalling*, and *packet inspection*. In other words, the packet filter records both the network-level and the transport-level data. For example, a router can monitor the initial TCP packets with the SYN flag set and allow the return packets only until the FIN packet is sent and acknowledged. A similar pseudostate can be kept for most UDP (e.g., DNS and NTP) and some ICMP communication (e.g., ping) — a request sent out opens a hole for the reply, but only for a short time. In 1992, Chapman was one of the first to point out the problem of the stateless packet-filtering firewalls [12]. The first peer-reviewed paper to describe adding state to packet filters was by Julkunen and Chow in 1998, which describes a dynamic packet filter for Linux [37]. Today, all major packet-filtering firewalls are capable of using connection state.

2.3.1.2 Improving Packet Filter Specification

Firewalls were originally built and configured by experts. However, firewalls are now commodity products that are sold with the intent that nearly anyone can be responsible for their network's security. Typically, a graphical user interface (GUI) is used to configure packet-filtering rules. Unfortunately, this GUI requires the user to understand the complexities of packet filters, complexities originally pointed out by Chapman in 1992 [12]. In many cases, the only advance since then is the GUI. The prevalence of transparent proxies only increases the complexity of the administrator's task because he or she must understand the advantages and drawbacks of using proxies compared to packet filtering.

Some researchers have therefore developed higher-level languages for specifying packet filters. Specific examples include using binary decision diagrams (BDDs) to specify the policy, a compiler for a higher-level language that produces packet-filtering rules, a LISP-like language describing policy, and the Common Open Policy Service (COPS) protocol standard.

In 2000, Hazelhurst proposed BDDs for visualizing router rule sets [31]. Because BDDs represent Boolean expressions, they are ideal for representing the block or pass rules that occur in packet filters. BDDs also make automated analyses of packet filter rules easier, in addition to providing better performance than the table lookups used in many routers.

The filter language compiler, flc [58], allows the use of the C preprocessor, specification of a default block or pass policy for various directions of traffic flow, and provides a simple if-then-else facility. flc also generates rules for several different packet filters (IPF, ipfw, ipfwadm, ipfirewall, Cisco-extended access lists, and screend).

Guttman described a LISP-like language for expressing access control policies for networks in which more than one firewall router is used to enforce the policy [28]. The language is then used to compute a set of packet filters that will properly implement the policy. He also describes an algorithm for comparing existing filters to the policy to identify any policy breaches. However, the automatically generated filters are not expressed in the language of any router; the network administrator must build them manually from the LISP-like output.

The Internet standards RFC2748, RFC3060, and RFC3084 describe the COPS protocol. This protocol is used between a policy server (policy decision point or PDP) and its clients (policy enforcement points or PEPs). The basic idea is that the policy is specified at a different location from the firewall (a PEP), and the policy server ensures that the various policy enforcers have and use the correct policy. The policy may relate to quality of service (QoS), to security, or to some other part of network policy (e.g., IPSec); the COPS protocol is extensible. The network is modeled as a finite state machine, and a policy is modeled as a collection of policy rules. These rules have a logical expression of conditions and a set of actions. If the logical expression is true, then the actions are executed. These actions may cause a state change in the network finite state machine. The policy rules can be prioritized, allowing conflict resolution when two or more rules match but specify conflicting actions. As these proposed standards are adopted, they will likely have a significant impact on how firewalls are constructed.

Stone et al. survey policy languages through 2000 and describe a new approach to policy specification [64]. In addition to security concerns, their approach also takes into account QoS. In specifying policies, they note that some policies are static, e.g., for security reasons, all access to certain network addresses are prohibited. Other policies are dynamic, e.g., if the available bandwidth is too low, streaming video is no longer allowed. Finally, different users may receive different levels of service (e.g., customers in the company Web store have priority over employees browsing the Web). Their policy language is called the path-based policy language (PPL), and it corrects some of the deficiencies in the other policy languages.

Damianou et al. describe a policy language called Ponder [19]. Ponder is a declarative, object-oriented language, which uses its structures to represent policies. Constraints on a policy can also be represented in Ponder. Although Ponder appears to be a rich and expressive language for expressing policies, there is not yet an automated policy implementation path.

Bartal et al. describe firmato [5], which has an underlying entity-relationship model that specifies the global security policy, a language in which to represent the model, a compiler that translates the model into firewall rules, and a tool that displays a graphical view of the result to help the user visualize the model. A module for use with firmato is the firewall analysis engine, Fang (Firewall ANalysis enGine) by Mayer et al. [48]. Fang reads the firewall configurations and discovers what policy is described. The network administrator can then verify whether the actual policy on various routers matches the desired policy. For example, the network administrator can ask questions such as "From which machines can our DMZ be reached, and with which services?" Fang builds a representation of the policy; it is not an active testing program. This difference allows Fang to test both the case in which authorized packets succeed and the one in which unauthorized packets are blocked. It also allows testing before the firewall is deployed; by contrast, active test tools require the firewall to be up and running to test it. Also, active testing cannot test the network's vulnerability to spoofing attacks, whereas Fang can. Fang provides a GUI to collect queries and to display the results.

A recent example of this family of firewall test and analysis tools is the Lumeta Firewall Analyzer (LFA) [70]. LFA is a commercial product that extends Fang to synthesize its own "interesting" queries based only on the firewall configuration. The result is a system that hides the complexities of the underlying router configurations, providing a much more comprehensible picture of the resulting policy.

Other tools for analyzing packet filter rules and highlighting problems (in some cases, with proposed solutions) include those by Hari et al. [30] and Al-Shaer and Hamed [1].

2.3.2 Proxies

A proxy is a program that receives traffic destined for another computer. Proxies sometimes require user authentication; they can verify that the user is allowed to connect to the destination and then connect to the destination service on behalf of the user. One example of a firewall architecture that makes use of a proxy server is shown in Figure 2.4.

When a proxy is used, the connection to the remote machine comes from the machine running the proxy instead of the original machine making the request. Because the proxy generates the connection to the remote machine, it has no problems determining which connections are real and which are spoofed; this is in contrast to stateless packet-filtering firewalls (described in Subsection 2.3.1).

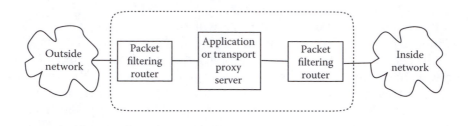

Figure 2.4   A network using a proxy server. Some commercial products combine all the machines shown in the dashed lines into one to reduce the cost.

Proxies appear in firewalls primarily at the transport and application layers of the ISO network model. On the Internet, the transport level consists of only two protocols, TCP and UDP. This small number of protocols makes writing a proxy easy — one proxy suffices for all protocols that use TCP. Contrast this with the application-level proxies (covered in the following text), in which a separate proxy is required for each service, e.g., Telnet, FTP, HTTP, SMTP, etc.

Transport-level proxies have the advantage that a machine outside the firewall cannot send packets through the firewall that claim to be a part of an established connection (some of the packet filters described in Subsection 2.3.1 have this problem). Because the state of the TCP connection is known by the firewall, only packets that are a legitimate part of a communication are allowed inside the firewall.

Proxies at the application level provide the benefits of transport-level proxies, and additionally, they can enforce the proper application-level protocol and prevent the abuse of the protocol by either client or server. The result is excellent security and auditing. Unfortunately, application proxies are not without their drawbacks:

- The proxy must be designed for a specific protocol. New protocols are developed frequently, requiring new proxies; if there is no proxy, there is no access.
- To use an application proxy, the client program must be changed to accommodate the proxy. The client needs to understand the proxy's authentication method, and it must communicate the actual packet destination to the proxy. Because source code is not publicly available for some applications, the required changes in these cases can be made only by the application's vendor, a significant bottleneck.

■ Each packet requires two trips through the complete network protocol stack, which adversely affects performance. This is in contrast to packet filtering, which handles packets at the network layer.

One of the most common proxies is SOCKS, by Kolbas and Kolbas [2]. SOCKS simplifies the changes needed to the source code of the client application; a SOCKS call replaces a normal socket call, which results in all outbound traffic using the proxy. This approach is a clean solution, and it works well if one has the source code for the relevant operating system utilities. Some commercial applications (e.g., Netscape) were written to accommodate SOCKS. A system using SOCKS and TCP connections is transparent to the user (assuming the proxy allows access to the destination host). In 2000, Fung and Chang described an enhancement to SOCKS for UDP streams, such as that used by RealNetworks' RealPlayer [23].

Ranum and Avolio developed the Trusted Information Systems (TIS) Firewall Toolkit (FWTK), a collection of proxies for building firewalls [3,57]. This freely available toolkit provided SMTP, the Network News Transport Protocol (NNTP), FTP, and Telnet application proxies, as well as a generic circuit-level proxy. To improve security, the proxies used the UNIX system called *chroot* to limit how much of the system is exposed; this way, if a proxy were compromised, the rest of the firewall would more likely remain trustworthy. The TIS FWTK had no proxies for UDP services; instead, the firewall machine ran DNS and the Network Time Protocol (NTP). The internal machines used the firewall for those services. When TIS and Network Associates, Inc. (NAI), merged in February 1998, the TIS firewall became NAI's Gauntlet Internet Firewall.

A limitation of proxies is that client software must be modified or the user must work differently when using the proxy. Transparent proxies address this limitation. With a transparent proxy, the client sends packets to the destination as usual. When the packets reach the firewall, access control checks and logging are performed as in a classical proxy system. The "magic" is implemented by the firewall, which notes the destination address and port, opens up a connection to it, and then replies to the client, as if the proxy were the remote machine. This relaying can take place at either the transport level or the application level. RFC1919 compares classical proxies with transparent proxies.

Transparent proxies are demanding because the firewall must operate both at the network and application levels, affecting performance. One solution proposed by Spatscheck et al. [62] and Maltz and Bhagwat [45] is that of "splicing." In splicing, after the proxy verifies that communication is allowed to proceed, the firewall converts to a network-level packet-filtering firewall for that communication. Splicing provides the extra control of proxies but maintains performance closer to that of packet filters.

2.4 Firewalls at Various ISO Network Layers

2.4.1 Physical Layer

The physical layer of the network is usually covered by an organization's physical security — conventional locks, keys, and other forms of physical access control. Untrusted persons must not have access to the physical cables and other network hardware that make up the network.

Wireless communication, especially radio, introduces new complications. For example, radio waves travel through most walls easily. This feature necessitates the use of encryption. Wired Equivalent Privacy (WEP) was the first attempt at providing security on wireless links. However, Borisov et al. [10] discovered a weakness in key management, with the result that after an attacker had received a sufficient number of packets, he or she could see all traffic and inject fake packets. The new standard is Wi-Fi Protected Access (WPA), which, at the time of this writing, has no known flaws.

2.4.2 Data-Link Layer

At the data-link layer, two types of firewall technologies are used. Filtering based on the media access control (MAC)-layer address (in most cases, the MAC address is the 48-bit Ethernet address) determines which machines are allowed to communicate with which. Bridging firewalls are more traditional firewalls, but with the advantage that they can be placed anywhere in a network.

2.4.2.1 Filtering on MAC Address

The MAC address of a machine uniquely identifies it on the local network. Some switches and firewalls are able to use this address to decide what communication to allow. This form of filtering has three limitations:

1. The MAC address is not routed; therefore, any filtering must occur at or before the first router.
2. Some Ethernet cards can have a MAC address programmed into them via software running on the machine. Therefore, the MAC address must be verified at the connection to the network for it to provide security.

3. A machine is not a person; determining who is actually operating the machine is not possible with the MAC address.

2.4.2.2 Bridging Firewalls

A bridge is a network device that works at the ISO data-link layer. Operating at this level, it does not need access to routing information. A bridging firewall uses the information listed in Subsection 2.3.1 to decide whether or not to block a packet. As a result, a bridging firewall can examine data in several other levels of the IP suite, including the network and transport layers. Because a filtering bridge is still a filter, the disadvantages of packet filtering still apply to it.

What makes a bridging firewall different from a packet-filtering router is that it can be placed anywhere — it is transparent at the network level. It can be used to protect a single machine or a small collection of machines that would not normally warrant the separate network required when using a router. As it does not need its own IP address, the bridge itself can be immune to any attack that makes use of IP (or any of the protocols on top of IP). Also, no configuration changes are needed in the protected hosts when the firewall is installed. Installation times can be minimum (for example, Limoncelli claims 3-s installation times [41]), so users are minimally disrupted when the bridge is installed.

2.4.3 Network

At the network level, addresses indicate routing information, and hosts can be grouped together into networks. These differences from the data-link layer provide important filtering options. An additional firewall feature at this level is network address translation (NAT), in which an address on one side of the router is changed to a different one on the other side. In addition, multicast protocols — sending packets to a collection of hosts — operate at this level. Multicast presents a new set of problems: the sender does not necessarily know the identities of all the participants in the session. This is also true for the recipients, who do not know in advance all the possible people who might be sending to them.

2.4.3.1 Network- and Host-Based Filtering

Sometimes, all machines attached to a network can be assigned a similar trust level; for example, consider a DMZ network as in Figure 2.2 or Figure 2.3. In this case, packet-filtering rules can be developed that enforce the trust (or lack thereof). Two problems must be addressed:

1. IP version 4 (IPv4) does not contain authentication (unless IPSec is in use, which is rare for non-VPN communication), and it is not required in IP version 6 (IPv6). Many programs exist that can spoof another host — they put packets on the network claiming to have originated from the spoofed host. Any IP-based authentication faces the problem of not knowing that the correct host generated these packets. Blocking spoofed packets generated on a remote network is easy with packet filters: add a rule that says any packet with a source address cannot arrive on a network interface attached to any other network. However, preventing one machine on the local network from impersonating another is more difficult; a firewall that is not on the offending machine cannot help.

2. IP has a feature known as source routing, in which the source indicates the routing the packet should take (instead of allowing the routing algorithms on the intervening routers to determine the route). Return packets take the reverse route to return. The specified source route may be bogus, or it may be valid and allow a spoofed IP address to communicate with a remote machine. The result is that most firewalls block all source-routed packets.

2.4.3.2 Multicast

On the Internet, multicast is often used for various forms of multimedia. In contrast to traditional unicast communication, the sender in a multicast communication does not necessarily know the identities of the recipients, and recipients do not know in advance who might be sending data to them. This difference makes proxies such as SOCKS difficult to implement unless they change the multicast into a collection of unicasts, a change that defeats the benefits of multicast. With multicast, once a client inside the firewall has joined a group, others may join without needing to authenticate. Additionally, the Multicast Routing Protocol, the Internet Group Management Protocol (IGMP), specifies only multicast groups and not UDP ports; in a default configuration, a multicast source has access to the complete set of UDP ports on client machines. If a source has access to all UDP ports, then it could potentially attack other services (e.g., Microsoft networking) that are unrelated to the service it is providing.

A classic paper on multicast and firewalls was published by Djahandari and Sterne [20]. In this paper, they describe an application proxy for the TIS Firewall Toolkit. The proxy has the following features: it allows authentication and auditing, it prevents multicast traffic from reaching hosts that did not request it, and it allows the multicast traffic to be sent only to safe ports. The proxy converts multicast traffic into unicast traffic.

Unfortunately, this approach also means that it does not scale well, as a collection of N users, all receiving the same multicast stream, increases the traffic inside the firewall by a factor of N over what it would have been if multicast had been retained. On the other hand, they do solve all of the security problems mentioned in the previous paragraph and later in this subsection.

RFC2588 suggests several possible solutions to the problem of multicast and firewalls. For example, communication between external and internal machines could be tunneled through the firewall using the UDP Multicast Tunneling Protocol (UMTP). This protocol was designed to connect clients to the Multicast Backbone (the MBone), but would work for tunneling through multicast-unaware firewalls.

RFC2588 also mentions the possibility of dynamic firewall rules, and Oria describes in further detail how they can be implemented [54]. A program runs on the router, which monitors multicast session announcements. The program reads the announcements, and if the specified group and UDP port are allowed by the policy, it generates the necessary rules permitting the data to pass through the firewall. When a client informs the router that it wishes to join a multicast group, it sends an IGMP join message to the router. The dynamically generated rules permit or deny this access. This approach to multicast on the firewall assumes that session announcements can be trusted. Unfortunately, this is not a valid assumption because they can be spoofed.

2.4.3.3 NAT

Because the Internet is short of IPv4 addresses, many people use NAT to gain more mileage out of a single IP address. When a router uses NAT, it changes the source address of outbound packets to its own address (or one from a pool of addresses that it controls). It chooses a local, unused port for the upper-layer protocol (TCP or UDP) and stores in a table the association between the new address and port and the real sender's address and port. When the reply arrives, it looks up the real destination in this table, rewrites the packet, and passes it to the client. When the connection is finished (or after the timeout period for UDP packets), the entry is removed from the table.

NAT provides a form of protection similar to that of proxies. In NAT, all connections originate from the router performing the address translation. As a result, someone outside the local network cannot gain access to the protected local machines unless the proper entry exists in the table on the router. The network administrator can manually install such an entry, causing all traffic destined for a specific port to be forwarded to a server for that service (in effect, providing an Internet-accessible service on an inside machine*).

RFC2663 notes some limitations of NAT. For example, NAT may prevent IPSec from working correctly. One feature of IPSec is the ability to ensure that a packet is not modified in transit. However, one of the purposes of NAT is to modify packets; the source address and possibly the source port must be modified for NAT to work. DNS problems can also occur. A machine behind a router using NAT has a name and an IP address. However, most networks using NAT also use RFC1918 private IP addresses, which are not globally unique. Therefore, DNS inside the network is not meaningful outside.

2.4.4 Transport

When they can be used, transport-level proxies (from Subsection 2.3.2) work well. Because a transport-level proxy initiates the connection, it cannot be spoofed by a packet claiming to be part of an established communication. A problem analogous to the authentication problem of the data-link and network layers exists here: one cannot guarantee that the expected application is running on its "well-known" port. The solution to this problem lies in using an application-level proxy.

Note that packet filtering is faster than using proxies, so performance considerations may dictate which to use.

2.4.5 Presentation

Little exists on the Internet at the presentation layer, and even less exists in terms of firewalls. The CORBA allows applications written in one language to make requests of objects possibly written in different languages or running on a different machine. CORBAgate by Dotti and Rees [21] is a presentation-level proxy. When a request is made to an object that is on the other side of the firewall, the proxy transparently changes the references. The result is that objects on either side of the firewall end up referring to an object on the firewall.

2.4.6 Application

If the performance needs can be met, application-level proxies offer the best security. They can:

---

* Setting up such an entry is usually a bad idea from a security standpoint. Maintaining a server inside a firewall is risky because, if it is compromised, the attacker then has access inside the network, which, as noted in Section 2.2, is likely to be insecure.

- Avoid being deceived into accepting spoofed packets
- Ensure that both sides follow the expected application-level protocol
- Limit the communication to an approved subset of the application-level protocol
- Authenticate users and limit their communication according to their authorization
- Monitor traffic for known problems, such as worms in e-mail or hostile Web server attacks against vulnerable clients

With the advent of transparent proxies, network administrators can achieve most of these benefits without the awareness or cooperation of the users. The primary drawbacks were described in Subsection 2.3.2: performance concerns, each protocol requiring a separate proxy, and the development of proxies lagging behind the development of new protocols.

2.5 Other Approaches

Although filtering and proxies are the most common approaches to firewalls, they are not the only ones. Researchers have experimented with dynamic or distributed firewalls. Because attackers abuse protocol specifications, protocol normalization can also be beneficial. As some communication is known to be hazardous, signature-based firewalls might help improve security against already-known attacks. Transient addressing provides the security benefits of NAT to a single machine. This section will discuss all of these approaches in more depth.

2.5.1 Distributed Firewalls

There are several limitations to the firewall technology that we have presented so far. One common assumption is that all the hosts inside a firewall are trustworthy. This assumption is not always valid — for example, see Subsection 2.8.1. A related problem is that firewalls are unaware of internal traffic that violates the security policy. Because firewalls are typically centralized in one location, they can become performance bottlenecks and provide a single point of failure. A further limitation of conventional firewalls is that, in some cases, the local machines know context that is not available to the firewall. For example, a file transfer may be allowed or denied based on what file is being transferred and by whom. The firewall does not have this local, contextual knowledge.

One solution to these problems, proposed by Bellovin [8], is a distributed firewall. This was implemented by Ioannidis et al. in 2000 [35] and by Markham and Payne in 2001 [46]. In this firewall, the network administrator has a single policy specification, loaded onto all machines. Each host runs its own local firewall implementing the policy. Machines are identified by cryptographic certificates, a stronger form of authentication than IP addresses. With a distributed firewall, the common concept of a DMZ or screened network, in which servers accessible to the outside world are located, is no longer necessary (for examples of a DMZ or screened network, see Figure 2.2 or Figure 2.3).

Gangadharan and Hwang [25,33] propose using firewalls on all devices attached to the protected network, in which the firewalls can be combined with an intrusion detection system (IDS). When the IDS detects an anomalous event, it modifies the firewall to react to the threat. Lower overhead can be achieved with this approach than that reported for the distributed firewall developed by Ioannidis [35].

Distributed firewalls have a different set of problems from centralized ones. The most significant is that a distributed firewall relies on its users (who have physical access to the machine) not to override or replace the policy. Additionally, if the firewall is running as a part of the operating system, then the operating system must protect the firewall software. However, the local firewall is protecting the operating system, creating a circular set of dependencies. Markham and Payne propose implementing the distributed firewall on a programmable network interface card (NIC) to reduce reliance on the operating system for protection [46].

Around the same time that Bellovin proposed the distributed firewall, Ganger and Nagle also proposed a distributed approach to security [26] in which each device is responsible for its part of the security policy. Ganger and Nagle argue that if each device were more secure, then an attacker who succeeds in passing the outer defenses (the firewall) would not find vulnerable targets inside. They propose installing security devices on many parts of a network, including NICs, storage devices, display devices, routers, and switches. The idea is that the devices would dynamically adjust their approach to security based on the overall network defense level. As with Bellovin's proposal, programmable NICs are an important part of the overall strategy.

2.5.2 Dynamic Firewalls

Dynamic firewalls change their rules depending on the traffic passing through them. The simplest approach is to just block traffic deemed as bad. However, this approach leaves one open to attacks in which an attacker spoofs an attack from an important site (e.g., Google), causing the important site to get blocked. Better systems do more than just block, e.g., throttle network traffic [32]. Others that can be dynamic include OpenBSD's pf, Linux iptables, and some commercial products.

2.5.3 Normalization

Attackers often abuse protocol specifications, e.g., by sending overlapping IP fragments or out-of-order TCP byte sequences. Handley et al. stressed that a firewall is a good location for enforcing tight interpretation of a protocol [29]. Besides protecting the computers behind the firewall from attacks based on protocol abuses, this so-called "normalization" also makes signature-based intrusion detection systems more reliable because they see a consistent data stream. Handley et al. provide a list of possible normalizations, ranging from those guaranteed to be safe to others that are potentially too strict in their interpretation of the standard. They were not the first to suggest normalization, however. Malan et al. describe "transport scrubbing" [44], and more recently the idea is elaborated by Watson et al. [69]. At about the same time, Strother [65] proposed a similar idea. Her solution involved different rings of trust, in which a network packet must pass through one ring before proceeding to the next. Many of her rings achieve the same effect as normalization.

2.5.4 Signature-Based Firewalls

Malan et al. discuss "application scrubbing" [44]. In this approach, a user-level program is established as a transparent proxy (see Subsection 2.3.2) that monitors the data stream for strings known to be hazardous (and presumably to prevent these strings from reaching the client). Watson et al. refer to the same concept as a "fingerprint scrubber" [69].

Snort [59] is a common intrusion detection system. Hogwash [39] is a firewall that blocks packets matching the Snort rules. It runs on a bridging firewall (Subsection 2.4.2.2), and the authors claim that it can handle network speeds of up to 100 Mbps on hardware that is not state-of-the-art.

Commercial products such as Web and e-mail anti-virus and anti-spam software often make use of signatures. The advantage is high accuracy on known attacks. The disadvantage is that they do not prevent attacks that are not in their database of signatures.

2.5.5 Transient Addressing

Many protocols, such as FTP, RealAudio, and H.323 (a protocol used for programs such as Microsoft's NetMeeting), open secondary channels for additional communication. These additional channels are a problem for firewalls unless the firewall makes use of a stateful proxy. Gleitz and Bellovin propose a solution to this problem by taking advantage of IPv6, which has 128 bits of address space [27]. This is large enough for each host to have multiple addresses. A client initiating a connection to an FTP server uses an address that includes the process group ID of the FTP client process. The firewall sees a connection from a specific IPv6 address going to an FTP server at a remote site, and then allows all communication from the server back to the client's address. On the client side, this address is only used for the FTP process; connections from the FTP server to other ports on the client will not be accepted, because only the FTP client is using that specific address.

2.6 Firewall Testing

As communications needs and patterns of no two organizations are identical, few, if any, will have identical firewalls. This leads to the problem of determining whether or not the firewall is correctly enforcing the policy. Firewall testing was originally an ad hoc exercise, with the thoroughness being determined by the skill of the person running the tests. A second phase of testing methodology included security scanners such as the Security Administrator Tool for Analyzing Networks (SATAN) and the Internet Security Systems (ISS) Internet scanner. These scanners provided the basis for the National Computer Security Association (NCSA) certification [68] for a period of time. Vigna extended this approach by defining a formal model of a network's topology [68]. His model can also represent the TCP/IP protocol stack up through the transport level. Using this model, he was able to generate logical statements describing the requirements for the firewall. Given these requirements, he then generated a series of locations for probes and packets to attempt to send when testing the real firewall. From a formal standpoint, this work is promising, but it fails to address the common problem of how to develop a correct formal description. Producing complete formal descriptions for realistic networks represents a significant amount of work and is difficult to perform correctly. Additionally, the test generator must have a complete list of vulnerabilities for which to generate tests.

Marcus Ranum took a different approach to firewall testing in [56]; he notes that firewalls are (or at least should be) different for different organizations. After a firewall is deployed, an expert can study the policy specification for the firewall and decide which tests will verify that the firewall properly implements the policy, using a top-down approach. He emphasizes the importance of testing both the security of the firewall itself (that the firewall is secure from attack) and the correctness of the policy implementation. Unfortunately, such testing is both expensive and time consuming.

Some of the tools for firewall policy specification (Subsection 2.3.1.2) also provide testing or guidance for testing.

2.7 What Firewalls Do Not Protect Against

No firewall provides perfect security. Several problems exist that are not addressed by the current generation of firewalls. In the event that a firewall does try to provide protection for the problems discussed in this section, either it is not in widespread use or there are problems with the protection it provides.

2.7.1 Data That Passes through the Firewall

A firewall is probably best thought of as a permeable membrane. That is, it is only useful if it allows some traffic to pass through it (if not, then the network could be isolated from the outside world and the firewall would not be needed). Unfortunately, any traffic passing though the firewall is a potential avenue of attack. For example, most firewalls have some provision for e-mail, but e-mail is a common method of attack; a few of the many e-mail attacks include the "I Love You" letter, the "Sobig" worm, VBS/OnTheFly (Anna Kournikova) worm, etc. The serious problem of e-mail-based attacks has resulted in demand for some part of the firewall to check e-mail for hostile code. Open-source products such as AMaViS and commercial e-mail virus scanners are responses to this challenge. However, they are only as good as the signatures for which they scan; novel attacks pass through without a problem. Additionally, spam is turning into a denial-of-service attack because of the volume, causing anti-spam products to be merged into anti-virus e-mail-checking systems.

If Web traffic is allowed through the firewall, then network administrators must cope with the possibility of malicious Web sites. With scripting languages such as Java, JavaScript, and ActiveX controls, malicious Web administrators can read arbitrary files on client machines (e.g., when a bug in Netscape allows Java applets to read protected resources) and execute arbitrary code on the client (e.g., when an ActiveX control allows local files to be executed or when a weakness in the Java bytecode verifier allows applets to do whatever they want). ActiveX controls are of particular concern, because they do not run in any form of "sandbox" the way Java applets do [6]. ActiveX controls can be digitally signed, and if properly used, can be used to authenticate the author, if not the author's intentions.

In 1997, Martin et al. described some attacks written in Java [47]. They advocate the draconian solution of blocking all applets, on the grounds that it cannot be determined which Java applets are dangerous. They suggest the following methods of blocking Java applets at the firewall:

1. Using a proxy to rewrite <applet> tags. This requires that the proxy be smart enough to rewrite only the tags in HTML files and not if

they appear in other file types, such as image files. This requires that the proxy parse the HTML documents in the same manner as the browser.

2. Java class files always begin with a four-byte hex signature CAFE BABE. A firewall could block all files that begin with this sequence. A possibility of false-positives exists with this scheme, but Martin et al. believe that this problem is less likely to occur than the <applet> tag appearing in non-HTML files.

3. Block all files whose names end in .class. This solution is weak because Java classes can come in files with other extensions, for example, packing class files in a Zip file is common.

Their suggestion is to implement all three of these, and they wrote a proxy that does everything except look inside Zip files.

2.7.2 Servers on the DMZ

Because the networks inside a firewall are often not secure, servers that must be accessible from the Internet (e.g., Web and mail servers) are often placed on a screened network, called the DMZ (for a picture of one way a DMZ may be constructed, see Figure 2.2 or Figure 2.3). Machines in the DMZ are not allowed to make connections to machines inside the firewall, but machines on the inside are allowed to make connections to the DMZ machines. The reason for this architecture is that if a server on the DMZ is compromised, the attacker cannot directly attack the other machines inside the firewall. Because a server must be accessible to be of use, current firewalls other than signature-based ones (Subsection 2.5.4) can do little against attacks through the services offered. Examples of attacks on servers include worms such as CodeRed and Nimda.

2.7.3 Insider Attacks

In spite of the fact that early firewalls such as the DEC SEAL were initially set up to prevent information leaks, they cannot protect against insiders intent on getting information out of an organization. Consider a hostile employee with access to a DVD burner. The resulting DVD will not be traveling through the firewall, so the firewall cannot prevent this data loss. Muffett also points out that inside a firewall, security tends to decrease over time unless the internal machines are frequently updated [53]. There-fore, a hostile insider can generally penetrate other internal machines, and because these attacks do not go through the firewall, it cannot stop them. To reduce this threat, some organizations have set up internal firewalls.

2.8 Future Challenges for Firewalls

All the topics discussed in the previous section pose serious challenges to firewalls. In addition, two emerging technologies will further complicate the job of a firewall: VPNs and peer-to-peer networking.

2.8.1 VPNs

Because firewalls are deployed at the network perimeter, if the network perimeter is expanded, the firewall must somehow protect this expanded territory. VPNs provide an example of how this can happen. A laptop being used by a traveling employee in an Internet cafe or a home machine that is connected to an ISP via a DSL line or cable modem must be inside the firewall. However, if the laptop's or home machine's security is breached, the entire internal network becomes available to the attackers.

Remote-access problems are mentioned by Avolio and Ranum [3]. Because of the fact that VPNs had not yet been invented then, it is easy to understand why they failed to discuss the problem of a remote perimeter that includes hosts always connected to the Internet (via DSL or cable modems) and which are also allowed inside through a VPN tunnel.

2.8.2 Peer-to-Peer Networking

The music-sharing system Napster is the most famous example of peer-to-peer networking. However, several other peer-to-peer systems exist as well, including Gnutella and AIMster (file sharing over AOL Instant Messenger). When not used for music sharing, peer-to-peer file sharing is used to support collaboration between distant colleagues. However, as Bellovin points out [9], these systems raise serious security concerns. These include the possibility of using Gnutella for attacks, buggy servants (server + client programs), and the problems of Web and e-mail-based content in yet another form. Current firewalls are unable to provide any protection against these types of attacks beyond simply blocking the peer-to-peer networking.

2.8.3 HTTP as a "Universal Transport Protocol"

The development of firewalls and the filtering that usually occurs at an organization's perimeter has affected the design of new protocols. Many new protocols are developed on top of HTTP because it is often allowed through firewalls. In some cases, this piggybacking is a reasonable use of HTTP. In other cases, such as the Simple Object Access Protocol (SOAP), HTTP is used as a remote procedure call protocol. A good proxy is required to determine what HTTP is allowed with whom.

2.9 Conclusion

The need for firewalls has led to their ubiquity. Nearly every organization connected to the Internet has installed some sort of firewall. The result of this is that most organizations have some level of protection against threats from the outside. Attackers still probe for vulnerabilities that are likely to only apply to machines inside the firewall. They also target servers, especially Web servers. However, these attackers are also now targeting home users (especially those with full-time Internet connections), who are less likely to be well protected. The purpose of these attacks is twofold: (1) to take advantage of the lower security awareness of the home user and (2) to get through a VPN connection to the inside of an organization.

Because machines inside a firewall are often vulnerable to both attackers who breach the firewall as well as hostile insiders, we will likely see increased use of the distributed firewall architecture. The beginnings of a simple form of distributed firewalls are already here, with personal firewalls being installed on individual machines. However, many organizations will require that these individual firewalls respond to configuration directives from a central policy server. This architecture will simply serve as the next level in an arms race, as the central server and the protocols it uses become special targets for attackers.

Firewalls and the restrictions they commonly impose have affected how application-level protocols have evolved. Because traffic initiated by an internal machine is often not as tightly controlled, newer protocols typically begin with the client contacting the server, not the reverse as active FTP did. The restrictions imposed by firewalls have also affected the attacks that are developed. The rise of e-mail-based attacks is one example of this change.

An even more interesting development is the expansion of HTTP and port 80 for new services. File sharing and remote procedure calls can now be accomplished using HTTP. This overloading of HTTP results in new security concerns, and as a result, more organizations are beginning to use a (possibly transparent) Web proxy so they can control the remote services used by the protected machines. The future is likely to see more of this coevolution between protocol developers and firewall designers until the protocol designers consider security when the protocol is first developed. Even then, firewalls will still be needed to cope with bugs in the implementations of these protocols.

References

1. E.S. Al-Shaer and H.H. Hamed. Firewall policy advisor for anomaly discovery and rule editing. *8th International Symposium on Integrated Network Management*, pp. 17–30, 2003.

2. Frederic Avolio. Firewalls and Internet security, the second hundred (Internet) years. *The Internet Protocol Journal*, 2(2): 24–32, June 1999. http://www.cisco.com/warp/public/759/ipj_2-2/ipj_2-2_fis1.html. Accessed February 20, 2002.

3. Frederick M. Avolio and Marcus J. Ranum. A network perimeter with secure external access. In *Internet Society Symposium on Network and Distributed Systems Security*, February 3–4, 1994, San Diego, CA, USA, pp. 109–119, Reston, VA, USA. Internet Society. http://www.ja.net/CERT/Avolio_and_Ranum/isoc94.ps. Accessed February 20, 2002.

4. Mary L. Bailey, Burra Gopal, Michael A. Pagels, Larry L. Peterson, and Prasenjit Sarkar. Pathfinder: a pattern-based packet classifier. In *1st Symposium on Operating Systems Design and Implementation*, November 14–17, 1994, Monterey, CA, USA, pp. 115–123, Berkeley, CA. USENIX Association.

5. Yair Bartal, Alain J. Mayer, Kobbi Nissim, and Avishai Wool. Firmato: A novel firewall management toolkit. In *1999 IEEE Symposium on Security and Privacy*, May 9–12, 1999, Oakland, CA, USA, pp. 17–31, Los Alamitos, CA, USA. IEEE. http://www.wisdom.weizmann.ac.il/~kobbi/papers/firmato.ps. Accessed February 20, 2002.

6. S.M. Bellovin, C. Cohen, J. Havrilla, S. Herman, B. King, J. Lanza, L. Pesante, R. Pethia, S. McAllister, G. Henault, R.T. Goodden, A. P. Peterson, S. Finnegan, K. Katano, R.M. Smith, and R.A. Lowenthal. Results of the Security in ActiveX Workshop Pittsburgh, PA, USA, August 22–23, 2000. Technical report, CERT Coordination Center, Software Engineering Institute, Carnegie Mellon University, Pittsburg, PA 15213, USA, December 2000. http://www.cert.org/reports/activeX_report.pdf. Accessed February 20, 2002.

7. Steven M. Bellovin. There be dragons. In *UNIX Security Symposium III Proceedings*, September 14–16, 1992, Baltimore, MD, USA, pp. 1–16, Berkeley, CA. USENIX Association. http://www.research.att.com/~smb/papers/dragon.pdf. Accessed February 20, 2002.

8. Steven M. Bellovin. Distributed firewalls. *Login*, 24(Security), November 1999. http://www.usenix.org/publications/login/1999-11/features/firewalls.html. Accessed February 20, 2002.

9. Steven M. Bellovin. Security aspects of Napster and Gnutella, June 2000. Invited talk at the USENIX 2001 Annual Technical Conference, June 25–30, 2001. http://www.research.att.com/~smb/talks/NapsterGnutella/index.htm. Accessed February 20, 2002.

10. Nikita Borisov, Ian Goldberg, and David Wagner. Intercepting mobile communications: The insecurity of 802.11. In *Proceedings of the 7th International Conference on Mobile Computing and Networking*, July 16–21, 2001, Rome, Italy.

11. R. Braden, D. Clark, S. Crocker, and C. Huitema. Report of IAB workshop on security in the Internet architecture, February 8–10, 1994, RFC 1636 June 1994. ftp://ftp.isi.edu/in-notes/rfc1636.txt. Accessed February 20, 2002.

12. D. Brent Chapman. Network (in)security through IP packet filtering. In *UNIX Security Symposium III Proceedings,* September 14–16, 1992, Baltimore, MD, USA, pp. 63–76, Berkeley, CA. USENIX Association. http://www.greatcircle.com/pkt_filtering.html. Accessed February 20, 2002.

13. B. Cheswick. An evening with Berferd in which a cracker is lured, endured, and studied. In *Winter 1992 USENIX Conference,* January 20–24, 1992, San Francisco, CA, USA, pp. 163–173, Berkeley, CA. USENIX Association. http://www.cheswick.com/ches/papers/berferd.ps. Accessed February 20, 2002.

14. William R. Cheswick. The design of a secure Internet gateway. In *USENIX 1990 Summer Conference*, Berkeley, CA, June 1990. USENIX Association. http://www.cheswick.com/ches/papers/gateway.ps. Accessed February 20, 2002.

15. William R. Cheswick, Steven M. Bellovin, and Ariel D. Rubin. *Firewalls and Internet Security: Repelling the Wily Hacker, Second Edition*. Addison-Wesley, Reading, MA, 2003.

16. Computer Emergency Response Team (CERT). CERT incident note IN-2000-02: Exploitation of unprotected windows networking shares, April 2000. http://www.cert.org/incident_notes/IN-2000-02.html.

17. Computer Emergency Response Team (CERT). CERT incident note IN-2000-03: 911 worm, April 2000. http://www.cert.org/incident_notes/IN-2000-03.html.

18. Computer Emergency Response Team (CERT). CERT incident note IN-2001-01: Widespread compromises via "ramen" toolkit, January 2001. http://www.cert.org/incident_notes/IN-2001-01.html.

19. N. Damianou, N. Dulay, E. Lapu, and M. Sloman. The ponder policy specification language. In *Policies for Distributed Systems and Networks. International Workshop, Policy 2001. Proceedings,* January 29–31, 2001, Bristol, UK, Springer-Verlag, Berlin, Germany. http://www.doc.ic.ac.uk/˜mss/Papers/Ponder-Policy01V5.pdf. Accessed February 20, 2002.

20. K. Djahandari and D. Sterne. An MBone proxy for an application gateway firewall. In *Proceedings of the 1997 Conference on Security and Privacy (S&P-97)*, pp. 72–81, Los Alamitos, CA, USA, May 4–7, 1997. IEEE Press.

21. Paola Dotti and Owen Rees. Protecting the Hosted Application Server. Technical Report HPL-1999-54 990413, Hewlett-Packard Labs, Bristol, UK, 1999. http://www.hpl.hp.com/techreports/1999/HPL-1999-54.pdf. Accessed February 20, 2002.

22. Mark W. Eichin and Jon A. Rochlis. With microscope and tweezers: An analysis of the Internet virus of November 1988. In *1989 IEEE Computer Society Symposium on Security and Privacy*, pp. 326–343, Los Alamitos, CA, USA, May 1989. IEEE Computer Society.

23. King P. Fung and Rocky K.C. Chang. A transport-level proxy for secure multimedia streams. *IEEE Internet Computing*, 4(6): 57–67, November–December 2000.

24. Fyodor. Nmap — free security scanner for network exploration and security audits, May 2004. http://www.insecure.org/nmap/. Accessed June 8, 2004.

25. Muralidaran Gangadharan and Kai Hwang. Intranet security with micro-firewalls and mobile agents for proactive intrusion response. In *Proceedings of the International Conference on Computer Networks and Mobile Computing, 2001*, pp. 325–332, Los Alamitos, CA, USA, 2001. IEEE Computer Society.

26. Gregory R. Ganger and David F. Nagle. Enabling Dynamic Security Management of Networked Systems via Device-Embedded Security. Technical Report CMU-CS-00-174, School of Computer Science, Carnegie Mellon University, Pittsburgh, PA, 15213-3890, USA, December 2000. http://reports-archive. adm.cs.cmu.edu/anon/2000/CMU-CS-00-174.pdf. Accessed February 20, 2002.

27. Peter M. Gleitz and Steven M. Bellovin. Transient addressing for related processes: Improved firewalling by using IPV6 and multiple addresses per host. In *Proceedings of the 10th USENIX Security Symposium*, pp. 99–113, Berkeley, CA, USA, August 2001. USENIX Association. http://www.usenix. org/publications/library/proceedings/sec01/full_papers/gleitz/gleitz.pdf. Accessed February 20, 2002.

28. Joshua D. Guttman. Filtering postures: Local enforcement for global policies. In 1997 *IEEE Symposium on Security and Privacy*, May 4–7, 1997, Oakland, CA, USA, pp. 120–129, Los Alamitos, CA, USA, 1997. IEEE Computer Society Press. http://www.mitre.org/support/papers/filtering_postures/filtering_postures.pdf. Accessed February 20, 2002.

29. Mark Handley, Vern Paxson, and Christian Kreibich. Network intrusion detection: Evasion, traffic normalization, and end-to-end protocol semantics. In *Conference Proceedings: 10th USENIX Security Symposium*, pp. 115–131, Berkeley, CA, USA, August 2001. USENIX Association. http:// www.aciri.org/vern/papers/norm-usenix-sec-01.pdf. Accessed February 20, 2002.

30. Hari Adiseshu Hari, Subhash Suri, and Guru M. Parulkar. Detecting and resolving packet filter conflicts. In *Proceedings IEEE INFOCOM 2000. Conference on Computer Communications. Nineteenth Annual Joint Conference of the IEEE Computer and Communications Societies*, pp. 1203–1212, 2000.

31. Scott Hazelhurst, Adi Attar, and Raymond Sinnappan. Algorithms for improving the dependability of firewall and filter rule lists. In *Proceedings of the International Conference on Dependable Systems and Networks (DSN 2000)*, pp. 576–585, Los Alamitos, CA, USA, June 2000. IEEE Computer Society.

32. R. Hunt and T. Verwoerd. Reactive firewalls — a new technique. *Computer Communications*, 26(12):1302–17, July 21, 2003.

33. Kai Hwang and Muralidaran Gangadharan. Micro-firewalls for dynamic network security with distributed intrusion detection. In *IEEE International Symposium on Network Computing and Applications, NCA 2001*, pp. 68–79, Los Alamitos, CA, USA, 2001. IEEE Computer Society.

34. Kenneth Ingham and Stephanie Forrest. A History and Survey of Network Firewalls. Technical Report 2002-37, University of New Mexico Computer Science Department, 2002. http://www.cs.unm.edu/colloq-bin/tech_reports.cgi?ID=TR-CS-2002-37. Accessed December 29, 2002. May be accepted for publication in the International Journal of Information Security.

35. Sotiris Ioannidis, Angelos D. Keromytis, Steven M. Bellovin, and Jonathan M. Smith. Implementing a distributed firewall. In *ACM Conference on Computer and Communications Security*, pp. 190–199, One Astor Plaza, 1515 Broadway, New York, NY 10036-5701, USA, 2000. Association for Computing Machinery. http://www.cis.upenn.edu/~angelos/Papers/df. ps.gz. Accessed February 20, 2002.

36. ISO/TC97/SC16. Reference Model of Open Systems Interconnection. Technical Report N. 227, International Organization for Standardization, June 1979.

37. H. Julkunen and C.E. Chow. Enhance network security with dynamic packet filter. In K. Makki, I. Chalamrac, and N. Pissinou, Eds., *7th International Conference on Computer Communications and Networks,* October 12–15, 1998, Lafayette, LA, USA, pp. 268–275, Piscataway, NJ, USA, 1998. IEEE.

38. Davis Koblas and Michelle R. Koblas. Socks. In *UNIX Security Symposium III Proceedings,* September 14–16, 1992, Baltimore, MD, USA, pp. 77–83, Berkeley, CA, USA. USENIX Association.

39. Jason Larsen. HogWash, November 2001. http://hogwash.sourceforge.net/. Accessed February 20, 2002.

40. T. Lightoler. *The gentleman and farmer's architect. A new work. Containing a great variety of ... designs. Being correct plans and elevations of parsonage and farm houses, lodges for parks, pinery, peach, hot and green houses, with the fire-wall, tan-pit, &c particularly described ...* R. Sayer, London, UK, 1764.

41. Tom Limoncelli. Tricks you can do if your firewall is a bridge. In *1st Conference on Network Administration,* April 7–10, 1999, Santa Clara, CA, USA, pp. 47–55, Berkeley, CA, USA, April 1999. USENIX Association. http://www.bell-labs.com/user/tal/papers/. Accessed February 20, 2002.

42. Steven W. Lodin and Christoph L. Schuba. Firewalls fend off invasions from the net. *IEEE Spectrum*, 35(2): 26–34, February 1998.

43. Michael R. Lyu and Lorrien K.Y. Lau. Firewall security: Policies, testing and performance evaluation. In *Proceedings of the 24th Annual International Computer Software and Applications Conference*, Los Alamitos, CA, USA, October 2000. IEEE Computer Society.

44. G. Robert Malan, David Watson, Farnam Jahanian, and Paul Howell. Transport and application protocol scrubbing. In *IEEE INFOCOM 2000. Conference on Computer Communications. 19th Annual Joint Conference of the IEEE Computer and Communications Societies,* March 26–30, 2000, Tel Aviv, Israel, pp. 1381–1390, Piscataway, NJ, USA, March 2000. IEEE Computer Society; IEEE Communications Society.

45. D. Maltz and P. Bhagwat. TCP Splicing for Application Layer Proxy Performance. Technical Report RC 21139, IBM, March 1998. http://domino.watson.ibm.com/library/cyberdig.nsf/a3807c5b4823c53f85256561006324be/88d1e552b09ffa65852565e6006616f1?. Open Document Accessed February 20, 2002.

46. T. Markham and C. Payne. Security at the network edge: A distributed firewall architecture. In *DARPA Information Survivability Conference and Exposition II. DISCEX'01*, June 12–14, 2001, Anaheim, CA, USA, pp. 279–286, Los Alamitos, CA, USA. IEEE Computer Society.

47. Martin, D.M., Jr., S. Rajagopalan, and A.D. Rubin. Blocking Java applets at the firewall. In *SNDSS '97: Internet Society 1997 Symposium on Network and Distributed System Security*, February 10–11, 1997, San Diego, CA, USA, pp. 16–26, Los Alamitos, CA, USA. IEEE Computer Society.

48. Alain Mayer, Avishai Wool, and Elisha Ziskind. Fang: A firewall analysis engine. In *Proceedings of the 2000 IEEE Symposium on Security and Privacy (S&P 2000)*, pp. 177–187, Los Alamitos, CA, USA, May 2000. IEEE Computer Society.

49. Niall McKay. China: The great firewall, December 1998. Web publication: http://www.wired.com/news/politics/0,1283,16545,00.html. Accessed February 20, 2002.

50. Jeffrey C. Mogul. Simple and flexible datagram access controls for Unix-based gateways. In *Proceedings of the USENIX Summer 1989 Conference*, pp. 203–222, Berkeley, CA, 1989. USENIX Association. ftp://ftp.digital.com/pub/Digital/WRL/research-reports/WRL-TR-89.4.ps.gz. Accessed February 20, 2002.

51. Andrew Molitor. An architecture for advanced packet filtering. In *Proceedings of the Fifth USENIX UNIX Security Symposium*, pp. 117–126, Berkeley, CA, USA, June 1995. USENIX Association. http://www.usenix.org/publications/library/proceedings/security95/full_papers/molitor.ps. Accessed February 20, 2002.

52. Alec Muffett. Proper care and feeding of firewalls. In *Proceedings of the UKERNA Computer Security Workshop*, Atlas Centre, Chilton, Didcot, Oxfordshire, OX11 0QS UK, November 1994. United Kingdom Education and Research Networking Association. ftp://coast.cs.purdue.edu/pub/doc/firewalls/Muffett_Alec_feeding_firewalls.ps. Accessed February 20, 2002.

53. Alec Muffett. Wan-hacking with *AutoHack* — auditing security *behind* the firewall. In *The Fifth USENIX UNIX Security Symposium*, pp. 21–34, Berkeley, CA, USA, June 1995. USENIX Association.

54. Loic Oria. Approaches to multicast over firewalls: An analysis. Technical Report HPL-IRI-1999-004 990827, Hewlett-Packard Laboratories, August 1999. http://www.hpl.hp.com/techreports/1999/HPL-IRI-1999-004.html. Accessed February 20, 2002.

55. Marcus J. Ranum. A network firewall. In *Proceedings of the First World Conference on System Administration and Security*, 5401 Westbard Ave. Suite 1501, Bethesda, MD 20816, USA, 1992. SANS Institute.

56. Marcus J. Ranum. On the topic of firewall testing, 1995. http://web.ranum.com/pubs/fwtest/index.htm. Accessed February 20, 2002.

57. Marcus J. Ranum and Frederick M. Avolio. A toolkit and methods for Internet firewalls. In *Conference Proceedings: USENIX Summer 1994 Technical Conference*, pp. 37–44, Berkeley, CA, USA, 1994. USENIX Association.

58. Darren Reed. Filter language compiler, Undated Web page. http://coombs.anu.edu.au/ipfilter/flc.html. Accessed February 20, 2002.

59. Martin Roesch. Snort — lightweight intrusion detection for networks. In *13th Systems Administration Conference — LISA '99*, pp. 229–238, 1999. http://www.usenix.org/events/lisa99/roesch.html. Accessed June 30, 2002.

60. Bruce Schneier. *Secrets and Lies: Digital Security in a Networked World*, pp. 188–193. John Wiley & Sons, New York, 2000.

61. Securityfocus.com. Multiple vendor "out of band" data (winnuke.c) DoS vulnerability, May 1997. Vulnerability database. http://www.securityfocus.com/bid/2010. Accessed February 20, 2002.

62. Oliver Spatscheck, Jorgen S. Hansen, John H. Hartman, and Larry L. Peterson. Optimizing TCP forwarder performance. *IEEE/ACM Transactions on Networking*, 8(2): 146–157, 2000. http://www.cs.arizona.edu/scout/Papers/TR98-01.ps. Accessed February 20, 2002.

63. Cliff Stoll. Stalking the wily hacker. *Communications of the ACM*, 31(5): 484–497, May, 1988.

64. Gary B. Stone, Bert Lundy, and Geoffrey G. Xie. Network policy languages: A survey and a new approach. *IEEE Network*, 15(1): 10–21, January–February 2001.

65. Elizabeth Strother. Denial of service protection: The nozzle. In *Annual Computer Security Applications Conference,* December 11–15, 2000, New Orleans, LA, USA, pp. 32–41, Los Alamitos, CA, USA, December 2000. IEEE Computer Society. http://www.acsac.org/2000/papers/41.pdf. Accessed February 20, 2002.

66. Subhash Suri and George Varghese. Packet filtering in high speed networks. In *Tenth Annual ACM-SIAM Symposium on Discrete Algorithms (SODA'99)*, pp. 969–970, 3600 University City Science Center, Philadelphia, PA 19104-2688, USA, 1999. SIAM. http://siesta.cs.wustl.edu/~suri/psdir/soda_filter.ps. Accessed February 20, 2002.

67. The RFC Editor. Request for comments (RFC), frequently asked questions, April 2001. http://www.rfc-editor.org/rfcfaq.html. Accessed February 20, 2002.

68. Giovanni Vigna. A Formal Model for Firewall Testing. Unpublished paper. 1997. http://citeseer.nj.nec.com/279361.html. Accessed February 20, 2002.

69. D. Watson, M. Smart, G.R. Malan, and F. Jahanian. Protocol scrubbing: Network security through transparent flow modification. In *DARPA Information Survivability Conference and Exposition II, 2001. DISCEX '01. Proceedings*, Vol. 2, pp. 108–118, Los Alamitos, CA, USA, 2001. IEEE Computer Society.

70. Avishai Wool. Architecting the Lumeta firewall analyzer. In *Conference Proceedings: 10th USENIX Security Symposium*, pp. 85–97, Berkeley, CA, USA, August 2001. USENIX Association. http://www.usenix.org/events/sec01/full_papers/wool/wool.pdf. Accessed February 20, 2002.

71. Elizabeth D. Zwicky, Simon Cooper, and D. Brent Chapman. *Building Internet Firewalls,* 2nd ed. O'Reilly and Associates, 101 Morris St., Sebastopol, CA 95472, USA, 2000.

Chapter 3

Web Application Security: The Next Battleground

Abhishek Kumar, Roshen Chandran, and
Vinod Vasudevan

Web technologies have evolved over the last five years. This evolution
has led to enterprises developing Web-enabled applications and to browsers becoming the user interface of choice for most applications. This trend
has been significant in industries such as banking, insurance, manufac-
turing, and telecom. Business imperatives have required companies to
expose core applications to customers, partners, and vendors over public
networks via Web interfaces. Thus, Web applications — applications
accessible via a browser — are now used for business-critical functions
and to handle transactions of high value. This makes Web applications
attractive targets for attackers who rely on the anonymity of the Web and
hope to reap rich gains by compromising these systems.

Weaknesses in operating systems and insecure network devices were
the traditional focal points of attackers. With better awareness, stronger
operating systems, and improved security defenses, the underlying systems
are not easy to exploit anymore. From what we have seen recently, the
attacker's battlefield has shifted from the network layer to the application
layer. Thus, it is essential that developers and security practitioners understand the security of Web applications better.

This chapter presents the risks that Web applications face today, the
origin of these risks, the types of vulnerabilities that result in these risks,

and the techniques used by attackers to exploit these vulnerabilities. Drawing on our work of assessing the security of Web applications such as online banking applications, financial trading applications, sales force automation software, and others, we take the reader from the big picture about the risks to specific vulnerabilities and exploit mechanisms used by attackers. In the process, we also study a few of the more common exploit techniques in greater detail to understand how easy these attacks are. Finally, we present steps for integrating security into the development lifecycle of Web applications.

3.1 Threats to Web Applications

Web applications are vulnerable to a number of threats. A Web application uses the HTTP protocol and is accessed over the Internet using a Web browser such as Internet Explorer. Unlike client/server applications that relied on a proprietary client connecting through private links to the server, Web applications can be accessed from anywhere on the Internet with a Web browser. This significantly increases the population of users who can access the application and abuse it. Attackers can hide behind the relative anonymity of the Internet to attack Web applications. Anonymous attackers who want to abuse the system, industrial espionage agents who steal corporate secrets, and disgruntled employees who want to harm the company can use Web applications to inflict damage.

To understand the threats a Web application faces, let us take the example of an Internet banking application. What are the typical threats to a typical online banking application? Here are five things that an attacker could do to harm the bank or its clients:

- Impersonate a customer or a bank employee and execute fraudulent transactions
- Illegally transfer funds from another customer's account
- Steal financial and personal information about the bank's customers
- Open fake accounts for money laundering
- Deny access to the application to the bank's clients

Clearly, these have a high impact on the safe functioning of the bank. A vulnerable Web application can lead to these threats being realized, so let us take a look at the origin of vulnerabilities in Web applications.

3.1.1 Origin of the Risks

Web applications, similar to all other applications, frequently have bugs in their code that could be used by an attacker to compromise the system.

These range from simple errors of omission to more complex flaws in logic. However, the consequences of these are usually much greater in Web applications. Why are Web applications more at risk in the first place? What is it that makes them insecure? We have seen three reasons why many Web applications are insecure:

- *Lack of awareness of the threats:* Developers and application designers are frequently unaware of the threats that a Web application faces. Developers are often trained in a new language or technology; however, they are seldom taught the security issues underlying the technology or the language. They develop blind spots about security issues, and this leads to insecurely developed applications. Developers, at times, wrongly assume that security should be built in at the infrastructure level with firewalls and encryption. Although firewalls and encryption might indeed be required, they are only a part of the security strategy. They cannot protect against an insecurely developed application.
- *Testing methods have not matured:* Whereas the functional testing techniques that have evolved over the last 30 years have been adapted to Web application testing, a similar model does not exist for testing security. Security testing, especially for Web applications, is an evolving discipline and will take time to mature. The absence of strong tools to perform automated testing, the relative obscurity of some of these tests, and the shortage of skilled professionals to perform these tests have resulted in applications going into production inadequately tested for security. The race to meet deadlines also results in security testing's being missed out in many softwares.
- *Ease of reverse engineering:* Web applications use the HTTP protocol, a plaintext protocol, to transport application-layer requests and responses. The commands and variables used by Web applications are easy to reverse engineer, and an attacker can predict vulnerabilities in a Web application by studying the flow of requests and responses.

3.2 Vulnerabilities in Web Applications

In this section, we discuss common vulnerabilities affecting Web applications. It is these weaknesses that let attackers abuse a Web application and inflict harm.

- *Inadequate input validation:* If the application accepts user input without validating the content, it might inadvertently accept overly long inputs and special characters where they should not be allowed and cause unforeseen side effects, some of which might be harmful. The most damaging of these attacks have their origins in developers missing out strong validation for specific inputs. In the next section, we discuss the SQL injection technique that exploits inadequate validation of user inputs.

■ *Undue faith on client-supplied information:* Web application developers tend to implicitly trust the data in query-string variables, cookies, and hidden variables, as the data in these variables were originally set by the application. However, when the data comes back from the client, it is possible that the data may have been modified (even if it is inside a hidden variable); hence, the application must verify that the data from the client is authentic. If the application trusts the data supplied by the client without checking again, an attacker could manipulate select variables and inflict damage.

■ *Insecure use of cryptography:* At times, developers choose the wrong set of cryptographic schemes for solving a problem. Encryption of the highest grade may not be the right solution for every problem. Improper understanding of the merits and demerits of a cryptographic solution leads to wrong and unsafe implementations. For instance, we have seen instances of a strong one-way hash algorithm being used during the log-in process to transmit the password from the client to the server. This algorithm is indeed a good solution for storing passwords; but it is insecure for transmitting passwords, as it is vulnerable to replay attacks.[1]

■ *Improper use of page caching:* The lifetime of HTML pages in the client's browser cache is controlled by cache control tags set by the application while serving the page to the client.[2] If sensitive pages are cached on the browser, unauthorized users might get access to them after a valid user has used the application. Developers sometimes mistakenly use the wrong cache control directives, and this leads to pages being visible in the cache after the safe duration.

■ *Wrong choice of HTTP actions and variable types:* The HTTP requests made by the client may be either a GET or a POST request.[3] Developers sometimes use the two actions interchangeably, as the server-side programming language understands both the requests equally well. However, a GET request is unsafe if sensitive information is being sent, as the request is subsequently visible in the history of the browser and in the Web server's access log. When sensitive data is to be sent to the server, the query string is also an unsafe location to place them for the same reason; instead, it is safer to use hidden variables that are POST-ed to the server in such situations.

■ *Inadequate sanitization of output:* When HTML is served to the browser, Web applications sometimes do not check the data that is being inserted into the HTML template. Developers assume that the data must be safe because it is coming from a database or a trusted system. However, it is quite possible that the database contains data that was received from a malicious user. Thus, a contact's e-mail address might contain an embedded JavaScript that executes on a victim's machine when rendered on the browser. In the next section, we also discuss cross-site scripting attacks, a technique used to exploit this weakness to steal sensitive information from an innocent user.

■ *Insecure configuration of application on the Web server:* The application is at times deployed insecurely after devoting a lot of care to developing it safely. This usually happens because adequate care has not been given for documenting the safe deployment environment for the application. For instance, a Web application that requires a file system folder to give "write" access to users might wrongly be assigned "execute" permissions additionally, making the entire system unsafe. Thus, improper configurations make Web applications vulnerable.

■ *Insecurely designed authentication mechanisms:* Weaknesses are very common in the log-in sections of Web applications. Log-in systems are sometimes poorly designed, and this results in high-risk vulnerabilities. For instance, consider the authentication system that locks out a user for 24 hr after three failed log-in attempts. An attacker could exploit this feature to continuously lock out all users by using a script to make three log-in attempts for every user. Similarly, log-in best practices require that the application redirect the browser to a new location after authentication and then proceed. However, many applications skip the redirection and serve pages directly. This could let an attacker steal the previous user's password from a logged-out browser window.

■ *Weak "forgot-password" schemes:* Another common vulnerability is poorly designed forgot-password schemes. From applications that use hint questions whose range of answers is limited (your favorite color would be any one of 12 popular guessable colors) to those that e-mail a new password in plaintext to the user, the forgot-password scheme is frequently used by attackers in tandem with social-engineering techniques to steal valid accounts.

■ *Browser vulnerabilities:* Frequently, limitations of the browser result in vulnerabilities for the application. For instance, some popular browsers store all the variables posted in a session in plaintext in their memory. This could let an attacker extract passwords from the memory of the browser. If the application has not taken precaution against this browser vulnerability and designed its log-in mechanism accordingly, it could let an attacker steal passwords.

■ *Insecure server hosting the application:* The Web server that hosts the Web application is another source of vulnerabilities. If the Web server is compromised, it could give an attacker very high privileges on the application and the database. The default configurations of popular Web servers have become safer recently; however, these Web servers need to be patched regularly to fix new holes that are discovered. If the server is not patched, it is a source of high risk to the application.

3.3 Attack Techniques

Now that we have seen the general class of vulnerabilities, let us dive deeper into specific exploit techniques for these vulnerabilities. These exploits could allow a person to bypass authentication or get unauthorized access to sensitive data from vulnerable applications.

3.3.1 SQL Injection

One popular and very damaging attack on Web applications is SQL injection.[4] *SQL injection* is an exploit technique in which dynamically generated SQL queries are manipulated by specially crafted inputs to achieve the goal of the attacker.

Most Web applications work on data stored in a database. This data is very important for the organization. SQL injection becomes the weapon of attack for retrieving sensitive data through vulnerable Web applications. In this technique, the attacker sends malicious input that modifies the SQL queries the application creates to interact with the database. The execution of these modified SQL queries can cause damage. The risk can be understood by looking at a few consequences of a successful SQL injection attack:

1. SQL injection gives the attacker the ability to bypass the authentication system. It can be used to avoid the authentication process and let a user log in to the application without a valid username and password.

2. SQL injection can result in the unauthorized retrieval of data. It can be used to access data that does not belong to the user who has logged in. Thus, a malicious user could view sensitive data belonging to other users.

3. SQL injection can be used to modify or delete sensitive data in the database. This can lead to permanent loss of data.

How does SQL injection work? Let us understand this by looking at a few fundamental concepts. We shall then drill into the details with some examples.

Most SQL queries either read data from or write to a database. The data retrieved is based on the selection criteria given in the SQL query. The criteria are given in the "where" clause of a "Select" query. For example, the following SQL query will retrieve records for a user named "SAM" from the User_Details table:

```
Select * from User_Details where User_Name = 'SAM';
```

The selection criterion in this query is the value of the User_Name field of the User_Details table. It dictates which records should be retrieved from the database. Now, a malicious user could try to retrieve or modify some other data by supplying an input that effectively modifies the actual SQL query. The query can be modified by supplying an input that changes the selection criterion in the where clause. Another method could involve supplying an input that appends a different query to a valid query.

A point worth noting here is that the exact input for SQL injection depends on the type of database being used. Although all databases can be exploited, the input may need modification to suit the database in use.

3.3.1.1 SQL Injection — Bypass Authentication

Authentication is usually the first hurdle in compromising an application. Let us look at an example of how SQL injection can be used to bypass authentication and log in to an application. For purposes of illustration, let us assume a banking application www.SampleBankApplication.com. The user logs in to the banking application by supplying the username and password in the log-in page. A user table called User_Login_Details stores the details of the user in the database as shown in Table 3.1.

When a user submits the credentials, a program in the application server performs the authentication. This code, in most cases, would use an SQL query to retrieve user details and compare against the user-supplied input. Here is what the SQL query would look like:

```
"Select User_Id, User_Password from User_Login_Details where
User_Id = ' " & strUserId & " ' and User_Password = ' "
& strUserPassword & "';"
```

Table 3.1   User Log-In Details

User_Id	User_Password	User_Age	User_Sex	User_Role
Anderson	Qaz123	21	M	Admin
Trinity	Wsx098	25	F	User
Morpheus	Edc456	36	M	User
Smith	Rfv765	40	M	User

(Here, strUserId and strUserPassword are the variables that store the username and password supplied by the user in the log-in page.)

The SQL query would be used to check whether the combination of username and password supplied by the user exists in the User_Login_Details table. If the query retrieves at least one row, the authentication is considered a success; but if no rows are returned, the authentication fails. For example, if a user supplies the following information, the query would retrieve the record set for Anderson from the User_Login_Details table, and the authentication process would succeed:

```
strUserName = Anderson
strUserPassword = Qaz123
```

But an attacker does not know a valid username or password. The attacker can still log in by using the right combination of some special characters that modify the SQL query — this is termed SQL injection. For instance, let us assume that the user supplies the following information in the log-in page:

```
strUserName = ' or 1=1--
strUserPassword = <blank>
```

(The value of the password field may be left blank or any random value could be given; we shall see that it is immaterial.)

Let us replace the user-supplied information in the SQL query as shown in Figure 3.1.

After replacement, the original query would be framed as given in the following text:

```
Select User_Name, User_Password from User_Login_Details
where User_Name = ' ' or 1=1-- ' and User_Password = ' ';
```

The -- is used to comment statements in an SQL query. Any text after -- is regarded as a comment and is ignored while executing the query.

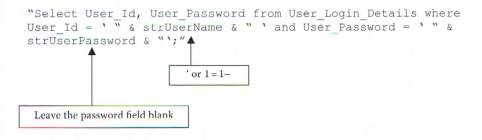

Figure 3.1   SQL injection query.

Thus, the final modified query will be executed effectively as given in the following text:

```
Select User_Name, User_Password from User_Login_Details
where User_Name = ' ' or 1=1
```

If we look closely at the where clause [User_Name=" or 1=1], we find that though the username field is blank, the query will execute successfully and return all rows from the User_Login_Details table. This happens because the second condition in the where clause [or 1=1] always holds true. Because the query returns one or more rows, the authentication is considered a success. Hence, the user can log in to the application. We also notice that the exact value of the password field really does not matter, as it becomes part of the comment fragment that is ignored.

But whose account would the attacker be logged into? Although this usually depends on the application, it is a fair guess that the user would log in to that user's account whose record is first in the record set returned by the query.

3.3.1.2 SQL Injection — Bypass Authentication, a Variation

Now let us look at a variation of the previous exploit. What if a malicious user wants to log in to the account of a particular user, i.e., a targeted attack? It is possible to log in to the account of a particular user only if the user ID of that user is known when the application is vulnerable to SQL injection. Now, let us assume that the malicious user supplies the following information in the log-in page:

```
strUserId = Trinity'--
strUserPassword = <blank>
```

Let us replace the user-supplied information in the SQL query as shown in Figure 3.2.

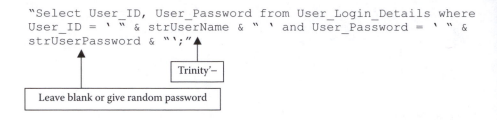

```
"Select User_ID, User_Password from User_Login_Details where
User_ID = ' " & strUserName & " ' and User_Password = ' " &
strUserPassword & "';"
```

Trinity'–

Leave blank or give random password

Figure 3.2   SQL injection query.

After replacement, the original query would be framed as:

```
Select User_Id, User_Password from User_Login_Details where
User_Id = 'Trinity'--' and User_Password = ' ';
```

The -- would comment out everything after it. Thus, the final modified query would be executed as:

```
Select User_Name, User_Password from User_Login_Details
where User_Name = 'Trinity'
```

The execution of this query would allow a user to log in to the account of Trinity even though a valid password has not been given. Now, if the username of an administrator is known, then the attacker can log in to that account and have administrative privileges. We hope you have understood how attackers use SQL injection to bypass authentication.

3.3.1.3 SQL Injection — Get Unauthorized Access to Data

Most banking applications will provide the user with a facility to view account details by submitting the account number. The banking application has tables that hold the account details of users. Consider the sample table Account_Details shown in Table 3.2.

Table 3.2   User Account Details

Account_No	Acc_Balance	Account_Type	User_Name
10006789	4656	Current	Anderson
10006245	57676	Current	Trinity
10002459	19873	Current	Morpheus
10001456	236990	Current	Smith

The application uses an SQL query to extract account information from the Account_Details table based on a user-supplied account number. The SQL query might look like this:

```
Select * from Account_Details where Account_Number = ' "
& accNumber & " ' ;
```

(accNumber is the variable that stores the account number supplied by a user.)

For example, if a user named Anderson logs in to the application and makes a query for account details by providing the account number 10006789, the following query will be executed:

```
Select * from Account_Details where Account_Number =
'10006789';
```

Now, a malicious user may try to access account details of some other user by providing account numbers at random. This could be difficult considering the fact that the account numbers will often be a long string of random numbers. Moreover, the chances of a malicious user finding account details of a particular user by giving account numbers at random is very remote.

But SQL injection can be used to find details of not just a particular user but many more users all at one time. Assume the attacker supplies the following information while making a query for account details:

```
Account Number = ' or 1=1--
```

Let us replace the user-supplied information in the SQL query as shown in Figure 3.3.

After replacement, the original query would be framed as:

```
Select * from Account_Details where Account_Number = ' '
or 1=1--';
```

```
"Select * from Account_Details where Account_Number = ' " &
accNumber & " ' ;"
```

```
' or 1=1–
```

Figure 3.3 SQL injection query.

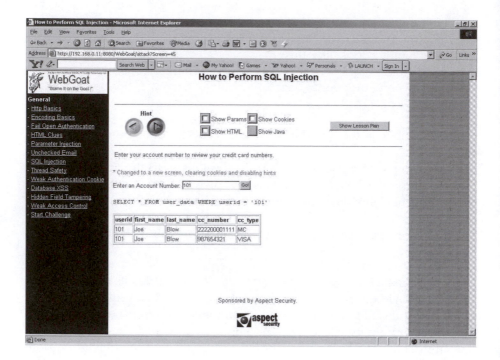

Figure 3.4   WebGoat — SQL injection attack.

The modified query would return account details of all the users in the Account_Details table. This is possible because the where clause of the query always evaluates to "true," thanks to the subclause 'or 1=1'.

We shall now illustrate this SQL injection attack with a real Web application. We use WebGoat, which is a test application developed by the OWASP foundation to illustrate common Web application vulnerabilities. This application is freeware and can be downloaded from www.owasp.org. Displayed in Figure 3.4 is a page in which a user can see the credit card details by using the account number. The SQL statement used is:

```
Select * from user_data where userid = '101'
```

Figure 3.5 displays the SQL injection used in the account number field. This SQL injection modifies the original SQL query to the one given below:

```
Select *from user_data where userid = '101' or 1=1'
```

The execution of the modified SQL query returns all the records from the user_data table. The retrieved records are displayed in Figure 3.6.

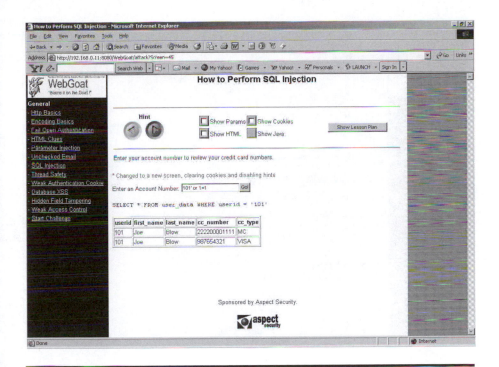

Figure 3.5   WebGoat — SQL injection attack.

3.3.1.4 SQL Injection — Get Unauthorized Access to Data by Using the "Union" Operator

An operator that is sometimes used in an SQL query is "union." The union operator combines the results of two or more SQL queries into a single set. This operator can also be used to craft an SQL injection attack. Using a union operator, a malicious user can extract data from a table other than the original table intended by the query.

Once again, consider our banking application. The application provides the user with the facility to view and change user details. The SQL query given in the following text is used to select and display user details based on the user ID supplied by user:

```
Select * from User_Login_Details where User_Id = ' " &
strUserId & "';
```

To craft an SQL injection, a user could input the following value instead of a valid user ID:

```
' union select username, password from DBA_USERS where '1'='1
```

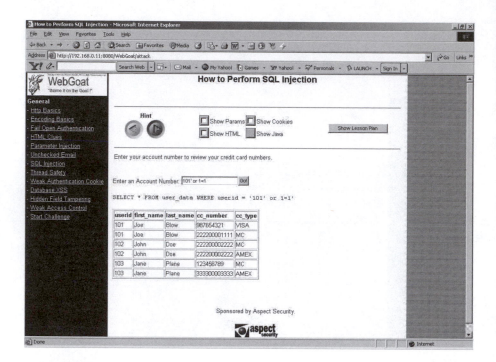

Figure 3.6 WebGoat — SQL injection attack.

```
"Select * from User_Login_Details where User_Id = ' " &
strUserId & "';"
```

┌───┐
│ 'Union select username, password from   │
│   DBA USERS where '1' = '1   │
└───┘

Figure 3.7 SQL injection query.

(DBA_USERS table contains the username, password, and other details for users created in the database.)

Assume that an attacker replaces the user-supplied information in the SQL query as shown in Figure 3.7.

After replacement, the query would be framed as:

```
Select * from User_Login_Details where User_Id = ' ' union
select username, password from DBA_USERS where '1' = '1';
```

This query would not select any rows from the User_Login_Details table as the User_Id field is blank, but it would select the username and password records from the DBA_USERS table. Some databases may not accept a blank value in an SQL query. In such cases, any random value can be sent for the User_Id field, as shown in the SQL injection:

```
Xv1yd56' union select username, password from DBA_USERS
where '1'='1
```

One prerequisite to using the union operator is that the number and type of columns returned from the first table should be the same as those returned from the second table. A blank or random value is sent for the User_Id field to ensure that no record is selected from the User_Login_Details table. Otherwise the number and type of columns returned from User_Login_Details table may be different from those returned by the DBA_USERS table, and the SQL injection would not work.

Now, instead of DBA_USERS, a malicious user could supply any known table name. At times, the error messages returned from the Web application reveal a lot of information about database structure, including table name or column name. Sometimes the error messages contain parts of SQL queries used by the application. All this information can help a malicious user in crafting an exact input for SQL injection and obtaining sensitive information from the database.

3.3.2 Cross-Site Scripting

A unique and interesting way to exploit a Web application is through cross-site scripting attacks.[5] In cross-site scripting, the attack is not directly targeted at the Web application but at a different user accessing the application. As the name suggests, cross-site scripting uses scripts to achieve its purpose. *Scripts* are pieces of code written for specific actions. These scripts can be written using common scripting languages such as VBScript or JavaScript. Most Web browsers know how to interpret and execute these scripts. Modern scripting languages are very powerful, and a script can be written for malicious activities as well. The impact of a cross-site scripting attack would depend on the way a script has been written. For example, a script could be written to steal the valid session ID or the username and password of a user. For all these attacks, the attacker must first execute the script on the victim's browser. So, an attacker must find a way to send the script to the victim's browser, and a vulnerable application can help send such a script. There are different methods by which an attacker can deliver a malicious script to the victim's browser. Some of these techniques are:[6]

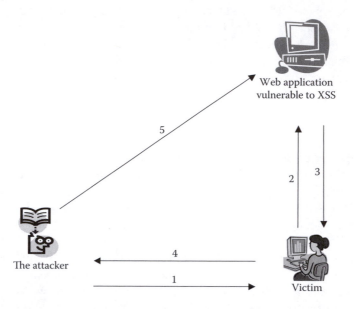

Figure 3.8   Cross-site scripting attack.

■ Many Web applications deliver dynamic content to a user in response to some request. Often, the information sent by a user in a request is returned by the server and displayed in the user's browser. It is possible for an attacker to send a link to another user, possibly in an e-mail message with some embedded malicious script. The unsuspecting user would click on the link to make a request to a Web application, sending along the script content. The server would reflect the response along with the script that has been input. This script gets executed on the user's browser when the response from the server is rendered. This concept is illustrated in Figure 3.8 with the following sequence of actions:

1. An attacker crafts an e-mail with an embedded script and sends it to the targeted user.
2. The victim clicks on a link in the e-mail and sends the script to a vulnerable Web application.
3. The web application reflects the user-supplied script, and the script is rendered in the user's browser.
4. The script, on execution, transfers the cookie that may contain a session ID of the targeted user to the attacker.
5. The attacker utilizes the session ID to log in to the account of the targeted user in the vulnerable application.

Figure 3.9   Popup message box.

■ A Web-based application may also provide the user with the facility to upload information that is stored in the database. This information may later be viewed by another user, say a Help Desk Admin responding to a query. An attacker could use such a facility to upload a script to the server instead of genuine content. The script gets executed in the victim's browser when the user views the uploaded content.

It is important to understand that in both these examples, the application is used to transfer the malicious script to an unsuspecting user. But before executing a cross-site scripting attack, the attacker needs to find out whether the application can actually act as a channel or not. An application is vulnerable and can serve as a channel if it does not clean user input of scripts and instead sends the script to the client's browser. This can be checked using a simple script as given in the following text. The script is written in between the two HTML tags <script> and </script>.

```
<script>alert(Vulnerable To XSS);</script>
```

When this script is displayed in the browser, it gets executed and displays a popup message box as shown in Figure 3.9.

The attacker can use it as a test script to check whether the application is vulnerable. The script can either be sent appended to some URL parameter or through some form field. In the URL given in the following text, the script is sent appended to a parameter. If the value of this parameter is sent back to the user for display, it will get executed in the browser instead of being displayed:

```
http://SampleBankApplication.com/servlets/AccountView?
Product=Current&SubProduct=</script>alert
(Vulnerable);</script>
```

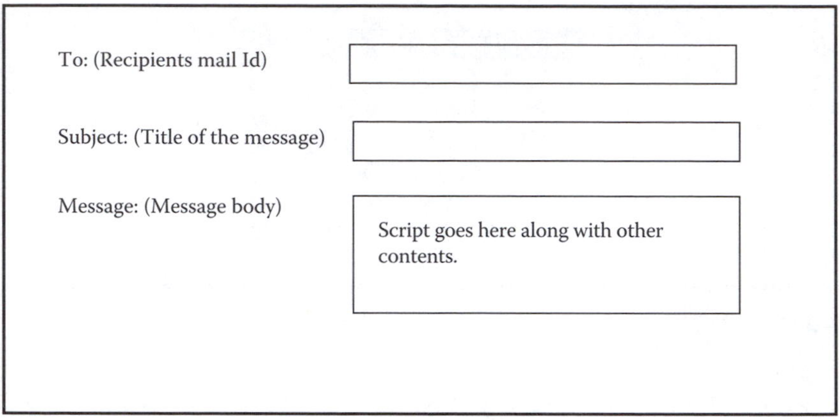

To: (Recipients mail Id)

Subject: (Title of the message)

Message: (Message body)

Script goes here along with other contents.

Figure 3.10 Mail message with script.

Once the execution of the script is confirmed, it is up to the attacker how it is exploited. Let us take a simple example to understand the cross-site scripting attack.

3.3.2.1 Cross-Site Scripting to Steal a Session Cookie

Many Web applications provide an e-mail facility that is used by the organization to communicate with its customers who have an account in the application. We will again take the example of our banking application, which provides a Web-based e-mail feature. The mail can be used by various employees of the bank in different departments to send information to the customers as well as to allow customers to send messages back to employees. Figure 3.10 shows the input fields of a mail page.

If an application is not validating user input, then an attacker can send the script through the mail message body. To check mail, a user logs in to the application and gets a valid session ID. When the targeted user views mail messages, the malicious mail is rendered in the browser, and the script gets executed. This script can be written in such a way that on execution it reads the user's session ID and sends it to the attacker. The attacker would then be able to access the user's account with the valid session ID.

We now illustrate this attack using the WebGoat Web application. Figure 3.11 displays a page in which a user can send a mail message to another user. The message body contains a test JavaScript that, on execution, would display an Alert message box.

Figure 3.12 displays a link to the message sent earlier. On clicking the link, the mail message is displayed in the user's browser.

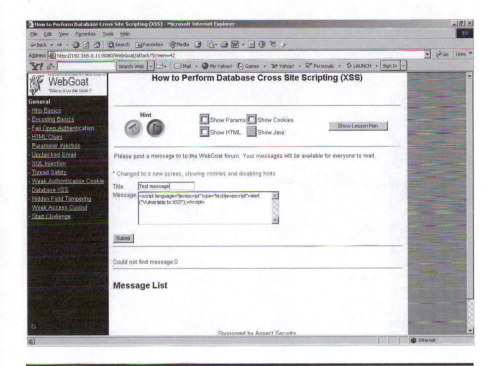

Figure 3.11   WebGoat — cross-site scripting attack.

Figure 3.13 confirms the execution of the script in the user's browser by displaying an Alert message box. This script could instead have been written to achieve tasks such as stealing a session ID.

3.3.2.2   Cross-Site Scripting to Steal Credit Card Information

Web-based applications sometimes use persistent cookies to remember returning users and track their session. The persistent cookies are stored on the user's permanent storage. Sometimes these cookies contain some sensitive information such as credit card numbers, etc. An attacker may not have direct access to the user's computer but could still use a vulnerable application to steal the cookie containing sensitive information.

Consider a fictitious Web application called www.eshopping-Demo.com. This application allows the users to shop online using credit cards. Once the user has performed a transaction, the user's credit card number is stored in a persistent cookie. This is done so that the next time the same user visits the site, the credit card number field can be automatically filled in by reading the cookie.

Typically, an attacker would start by locating a page within the application that reflects inputs supplied by the user in the URL. Once such a

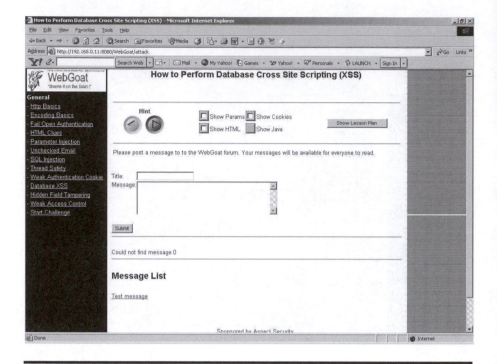

Figure 3.12   WebGoat — cross-site scripting attack.

page has been identified, the attacker could craft a link to that page with an embedded script. The link is sent to a user in an e-mail message that lures the user into clicking the link.

Now consider the following URL. A request to this URL is sent when a user confirms the purchase.

```
www.eshoppingDemo.com/goods/electronics?ItemCode=12001&
Action=Yes&Delivery=Local
```

In the server response, the ItemCode number is sent back to the user and displayed in the browser. Now, the attacker crafts a link with the script embedded in the ItemCode parameter as shown:

```
www.eshoppingDemo.com/goods/electronics?ItemCode=<script>
alert(ScriptContentGoesHere);</script>&Action=Yes&
Delivery=Local
```

When the victim clicks on this link, the script is sent to the server in the ItemCode field. The server would send back the response with some error information and the script, which then gets executed on the user's

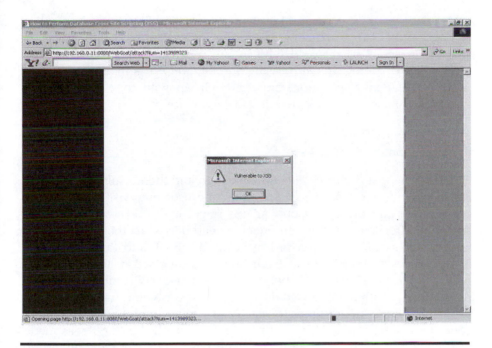

Figure 3.13   WebGoat — cross-site scripting attack.

browser. The script, on execution, can send the cookie to the malicious user.

3.3.3 Stealing Passwords with Browser Refresh

Two common ways of making a request to the Web server are GET and POST. If some information is sent to the Web application in a GET request, then it can be seen by viewing the history of the browser. But the links associated with the POST request are not cached in the browser's history. Hence, sensitive information such as username and password should be sent to the Web application only as a POST request. But the information associated with a POST request can also be retrieved by exploiting some of the features of the browser.[7]

The browser keeps track of the pages recently browsed by a user and the variables sent in a POST request. Please note that this is not to be confused with the storing of links in the history of the browser, which happens with GET but not with POST. We shall show that an attacker can utilize the "Back" and "Refresh" features of the browser to retrieve critical information such as username and password that had been POST-ed by a previous user if the application has been designed incorrectly.

Let us take an example to understand the vulnerability. Consider the log-in page of the sample banking application, www.SampleBankApplication.com/Login.jsp. A user would type in the username and password and press "Submit" to log in. On pressing Submit, a POST is made to the page www.SampleBankApplication.com/afterLogin.jsp with the following two variables containing the username and password:

```
userInput = "Morpheus"
passwordInput = "Edc456"
```

This page first performs the authentication and then displays its content if the authentication succeeds. After this, the user may visit a number of other pages and finally log out. At this stage, if the browser window is left open after log-out, then an attacker with access to the machine can find the username and password by using the Back and Refresh buttons of the browser cleverly. (The Back button allows a user to navigate to previous pages. The Refresh button allows a user to resubmit the Web request along with the POST-ed data.) The attacker would start by pressing the Back button several times to reach the www.SampleBankApplication.com/afterLogin.jsp page. This is the page for which the POST was made in the log-in page with the username and password. The page would be shown to be expired as in Figure 3.14.

Now, if the Refresh button is pressed, the browser would prompt the user with a Retry message, as shown in Figure 3.15.

If the attacker presses Retry, the browser would repost the username and password of the last logged-in user. Now, how do we view the information that is reposted? This is possible through the use of a Web proxy tool such as Achilles. (A Web proxy can be used to intercept, view, and modify the requests made by the browser and also the response sent by the server.) On reaching the www.SampleBankApplication.com/afterLogin.jsp page, the attacker can configure the browser to use a Web proxy and then press the Refresh button. The POST request made by the browser can then be intercepted and seen in the proxy as shown in Figure 3.16.

This vulnerability affects any information that is sent to the application in a POST request. Thus, another vulnerable page from which a password can be found is the "change password" page. It should be kept in mind that this vulnerability is applicable only if the user does not close the browser after logging out. Because information about POST requests are kept in memory, it is lost once the browser window is closed.

This vulnerability can be prevented by introducing an intermediate page (say, www.SampleBankApplication.com/IntermediateLogin.jsp) that does the authentication but is not sent to the user. Instead, once the

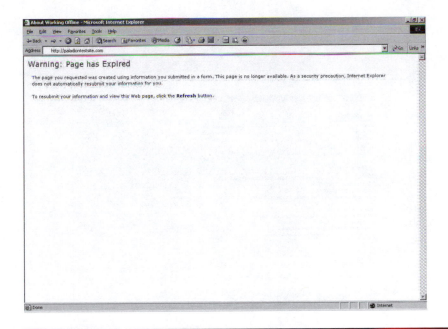

Figure 3.14   Expired Web page.

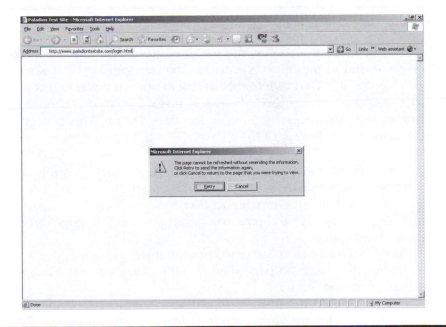

Figure 3.15   Resubmission of information.

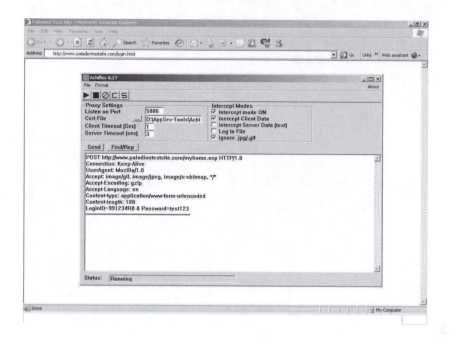

Figure 3.16   Intercepting information using Achilles.

authentication process succeeds, the intermediate page can send a redirection command to the browser to reach the next page. The username
and password is POST-ed to IntermediateLogin.jsp, but because this page
is never displayed in the user's browser, there is no possibility of an
attacker reaching that page by pressing the Back button. This concept is
explained further in Figure 3.17.

1. User makes a request for the log-in page of Web application
   (www.SampleBankApplication.com/Login.jsp)
2. Server sends the log-in page to user
3. User posts user ID and password to an intermediate page through
   the log-in page
   (www.SampleBankApplication.com/IntermediateLogin.jsp)
4. IntermediateLogin.jsp page sends a redirect to user after successful
   authentication
   (www.SampleBankApplication.com/AfterIntermediateLogin.jsp)
5. User makes a request for AfterIntermediateLogin.jsp page
6. Server sends the AfterIntermediateLogin.jsp page to user

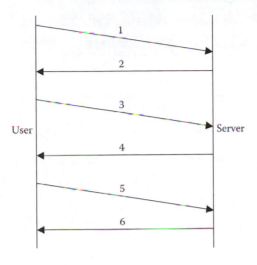

Figure 3.17   Stealing password with browser refresh.

3.3.4 Variable Manipulation Attacks

Let us now look at a different vulnerability, which is easier to exploit and can have a huge impact. Often, Web applications use hidden form fields to transfer sensitive information to the server. Consider our banking application, www.SampleBankApplication.com. This application gives an option to users to view their account details. The server retrieves account details based on the account number that is sent to the server in a hidden form field. An attacker could modify the account number assigned in the hidden form field. This is possible by using a Web proxy tool such as Achilles. The browser used to access the application can be configured to use a Web proxy tool. All Web requests and responses can then be seen and modified in the Web proxy. Using a Web proxy, an attacker can intercept requests for account details and change the account number before it reaches the server. Retrieval of records would now depend on whether the changed account number is present in the database or not.

To illustrate this attack, let us again take the help of the WebGoat application. The screen in Figure 3.18 asks a user to confirm the purchase of a television. The price of the television is sent to the server in a form field variable named "Price."

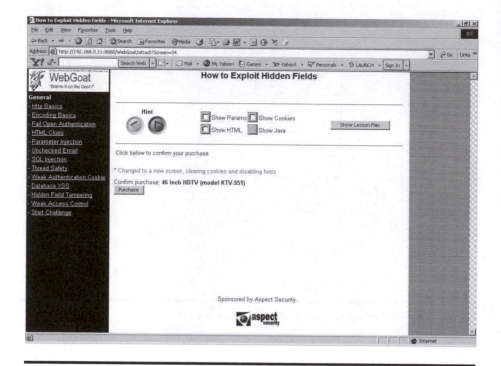

Figure 3.18   WebGoat — variable manipulation attack.

A normal user would not be aware of the Price field and go ahead to purchase the television, which is priced at $4999.99 as shown in Figure 3.19.

An attacker, however, could intercept the request sent from the browser by using a Web proxy tool, change the value assigned in Price variable, and resend it to the server. These steps are shown in Figure 3.20 and Figure 3.21.

Finally, a malicious user can reduce the price of a television before buying it, as shown in Figure 3.22.

This example portrays the dangers of form field modification. An application may use form field values such as user ID, account number, etc., for a number of tasks. Real implications of such modification would depend on the purpose of the form field value. Variable manipulation attacks could be performed on any variable and not just form fields. We have even come across applications that are vulnerable to their cookie variables being manipulated.

3.4 Preventing Vulnerabilities in Web Applications

The adage that prevention is better than cure applies to Web application security vulnerabilities, too. Because most application vulnerabilities have

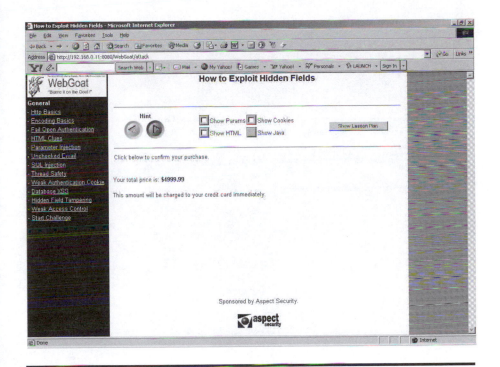

Figure 3.19 WebGoat — variable manipulation attack.

their origin during the software development lifecycle, prevention of vulnerabilities also starts there. An application designed and developed with knowledge of potential security vulnerabilities will be safer than one that is not. In this section, we discuss best practices that you could adopt to prevent security vulnerabilities from entering your Web application at each stage of the software development lifecycle.

Traditional software development lifecycles use four stages — requirements, design, development, and testing — before an application is ready for deployment. From our experience, each of these stages contributes to the overall security of the system; hence, it is important that enough time be invested in addressing security issues at each stage.

3.4.1 Requirements

The requirements phase focuses on capturing the functional requirements of the application; the specifications from this phase help the designers design the system. Thus, if security-related information is captured in this phase, it helps the designers conceptualize a more secure system.

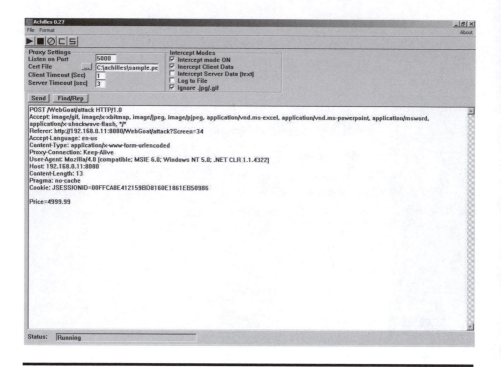

Figure 3.20   Intercepting information using Achilles.

1. Explicitly define the security requirements of the application, in addition to the functional requirements.
2. Specify the threats to the business and the risks it exposes the business to as it helps the designer understand the threat environment better and choose the appropriate technologies.
3. Specify the relevant regulatory systems that the application must comply with. These help the designers understand minimum security and privacy requirements of the application.

3.4.2 Design

The design phase conceptualizes the overall architecture of the system, the composition of each component, and the interactions between these components. This is where technology and protocol decisions are made. In our experience, this is the most critical stage for preventing security weaknesses in the system. Errors made at this level are frequently difficult to fix once coding has begun, and are very costly to fix during testing. A few guidelines for designing secure software are presented in the following text:

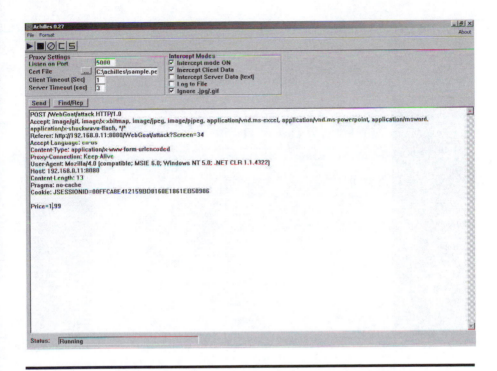

Figure 3.21 Changing information using Achilles.

- Design for a fail-safe system, i.e., if the system fails, design it to fail to a safe state. For instance, if a bank account has inconsistent transactions that the system cannot resolve, lock the account and not just the transaction.
- Factor the presence of firewalls into the deployment architecture while designing the protocols. Application-layer protocols that initiate reverse connections or carry transport-layer information frequently break while traversing a firewall. If the firewall is removed to accommodate the application, your entire system becomes less secure.
- For each input, specify what the valid inputs are in as much detail as possible. This will let the developers write code to reject any input that does not meet the specifications. For instance, specify that a specific input is for a name field and should allow only up to ten English letters and numerals.
- Choose the appropriate cryptographic solution for the problem. Choosing the strongest level of encryption might not always be the best solution; message digests, salted hashes, or signed messages may be a more appropriate solution for your requirement.

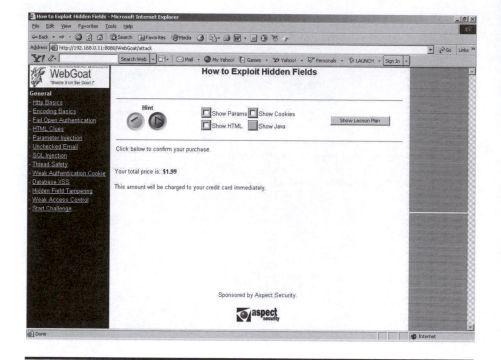

Figure 3.22   WebGoat — variable manipulation attack.

Study your requirement closely before deciding on the crypto-graphic system.

■ Specify the abuse-test cases that the testing team should derive to test the system.

■ Specify the deployment conditions that affect the security of the system, so that the documentation for the application includes these for the engineers who deploy the application. For instance, if the file upload directory should have only write permissions for Internet users, then specify this during the design stage.

3.4.3 Development

Good designs followed through with safe coding practices go a long way in ensuring a safe application.[8] Here are a few guidelines that Web application developers should follow to ensure security:

■ Do not trust the data coming from the client; use the session token from the client and rely on data stored in internal session variables as far as possible. Use inputs supplied by the user only when it is absolutely required. For instance, the user's account number need not be received from the client each time, but can be populated in the session object directly from the database. Not all data can, however, be taken from the database. The amount of money that the user wants transferred is an example of when the user's input is absolutely required.

■ Validate each input before accepting it. It is quite likely that attackers are using invalid input to try fraudulent activity. If the design has specified the content type or format that is acceptable for an input field (and they should, wherever possible), then verify that the data received meets those criteria. Exploits like SQL injection can be thwarted by ensuring that all inputs are valid.

■ Check the output that is to be rendered before dispatching it. Please ensure that the HTML your application generates contains scripts that you intended and none injected by an attacker. Sanitize the output of all scripts that were not explicitly placed by the application. Cross-site scripting attacks can be prevented by cleansing the output of such scripts.

■ Do not place comments in the HTML to be rendered. Although it is generally a good practice to add comments in the code, please ensure that these comments are not placed in HTML pages that are to be rendered. Whenever required, place comments in the code processed by the server-side engine. This lets developers who read the application code understand the logic, while ensuring that the comments are not sent out in the generated HTML.

3.4.4 Testing

Introducing security testing during the regular testing phase improves the overall security of the software.

■ Develop abuse-test cases that mimic an attacker's behavior. Although routine functional testing focuses on use cases and the boundaries for them, it is important to recognize that an attacker might rely on fundamentally different inputs to cause harm. Foreseeing those and including them in the test plan goes a long way in detecting security weaknesses at the testing stage.

■ Use fault injection techniques to check if the application is safe even when faults are deliberately introduced.

■ Train the testing team on the attacks that are popular on Web applications. Their ability to conceptualize security test cases will improve when they are familiar with the techniques used by attackers.

■ If security is critical, do an independent third-party assessment of the application. Although your testers might be very competent, their job might not let them become experts in security testing. Professional security-testing teams usually have wide experience across multiple applications; they track new security issues constantly and could complement your regular testing team.

3.5 Conclusion

Web application security is still an emerging field that deserves to get more attention in the developer community. The large number of new attack techniques that are getting published and the lack of awareness about these issues do not bode well for the security of Web applications. Web applications can be secured by a combination of better awareness and employing security principles correctly in the various stages of the software development lifecycle.

Notes

1. Pakala, Sangita. Paladion Networks, OWASP Application Security FAQ. www.owasp.org/documentation/appsecfaq.
2. Nottingham, Mark. Caching Tutorial for Web Authors and Webmasters. http://www.mnot.net/cache_docs/.
3. World Wide Web Consortium. HTTP RFC. www.w3.org/Protocols/rfc2616/rfc2616-sec14.html#sec14.9.1.
4. Integrigy. Introduction to SQL Injection. www.integrigy.com/info/IntegrigyIntrotoSQLInjectionAttacks.pdf.
5. Olmann, Gunter. Cross Site Scripting. www.technicalinfo.net/papers/CSS.html.
6. CGI Security. The Cross Site Scripting FAQ. www.cgisecurity.net/articles/xss-faq.shtml.
7. Kohli, Karmendra. Stealing passwords via browser refresh, Paladion Networks. www.paladion.net/papers/Stealing_passwords_via_browser_refresh. pdf.
8. Howard, Michael and LeBlanc, David. Writing Secure Code. www.microsoft.com/mspress/books/toc/5612.asp.

References

1. CGI Security. The Cross Site Scripting FAQ. www.cgisecurity.net/articles/xss-faq.shtml.
2. Grossman, Jeremiah. Cross Site Tracing. www.cgisecurity.com/whitehat-mirror/WhitePaper_screen.pdf.

3. Howard, Michael and LeBlanc, David. Writing Secure Code. www.microsoft. com/mspress/books/toc/5612.asp.

4. Integrigy. Introduction to SQL Injection. www.integrigy.com/info/ IntegrigyIntrotoSQLInjectionAttacks.pdf.

5. Kohli, Karmendra. Stealing passwords via browser refresh, Paladion Networks. www.paladion.net/papers/Stealing_passwords_via_browser_refresh. pdf.

6. Kumar, Abhishek. Discovering passwords in memory, Paladion Networks. www.paladion.net/papers/Discovering_Passwords_In_Memory.pdf.

7. Microsoft. HTTP Only cookies. http://msdn.microsoft.com/library/default. asp?url=/workshop/author/dhtml/HTTPonly_cookies.asp.

8. Nottingham, Mark. Caching Tutorial for Web Authors and Webmasters. http://www.mnot.net/cache_docs/.

9. Olmann, Gunter. Cross Site Scripting. www.technicalinfo.net/papers/CSS.html.

10. OWASP. The OWASP Guide to Building Secure Web Application and Web Services. www.owasp.org/documentation/guide.

11. Pakala, Sangita. Paladion Networks, OWASP Application Security FAQ. www.owasp.org/documentation/appsecfaq.

12. RSA Security. Secure Sockets Layer FAQ. www.rsasecurity.com/standards/ ssl/basics.html.

13. Securiteam. SQL Injection. www.securiteam.com/securityreviews/ 5DP0N1P76E.html.

14. Shah, Saumil. HTTP Fingerprinting. http://net-square.com/HTTPrint/ HTTPrint_paper.html.

15. Spett, Kevin. Cross Site Scripting: Are your web applications vulnerable? www.spidynamics.com/whitepapers/SPIcross-sitescripting.pdf.

16. Ummer, Firosh. Insecurities in non-exclusive socket binding, Paladion Networks. www.paladion.net/papers/SocketBinding.pdf.

17. W3C. HTTP RFC. www.w3.org/Protocols/rfc2616/rfc2616-sec14.html#sec 14.9.1.

18. Wheeler, David. Secure Programming for Linux and Unix HOWTO. www. dwheeler.com/secure-programs.

Chapter 4

Relevance of Machine Learning

V Rao Vemuri

4.1 Introduction

This book is about enhancing computer security through smart technology. The previous three chapters examined various facets of the security problem. Chapter 5 to Chapter 9 will discuss various methods of introducing the "smarts" into the security domain. This chapter provides some rationale for the need for smart technology and, in a brisk manner, covers some of the relevant ideas from artificial intelligence (AI) and machine learning.

Today's computer systems comprise a broad range of processors, communication networks, and information depositories. These systems are increasingly ubiquitous and, consequently, they are increasingly subject to attack, misuse, and abuse. The complexity of these systems makes it exceedingly difficult to reason about their behavior. It is difficult to design security policies that are simple to understand and flexible to tolerate. Power and bandwidth limitations constrain security features in lightweight wireless devices. Cost considerations limit the usage of high-assurance implementation methods. Software-bundling policies make the software unwieldy; many vulnerable functions present in these bundles are rarely used by many users. System engineering tradeoffs are rarely based on technology issues alone; social, organizational, economic, regulatory, and legal factors play a major role. Unfortunately, at today's state-of-the-art, we do not have adequate understanding to develop an integrated solution to these challenging problems. The best we can do in the rest of the book is to present those technology issues we do understand and hope to lay the foundation so as to develop an ability to address the broader issues at a future time.

An examination of security issues reveals that security threats and vulnerabilities have been evolving very rapidly. Indeed, over the past 25 years, the knowledge and expertise levels required to make a successful attack have been decreasing, and the quality levels of tools available to attackers have been increasing. This changing environment obsoletes many security measures. For example, the current methods of malware (short for "malicious software," i.e., software designed specifically to damage or disrupt a system, such as a virus or a Trojan horse) detection do not work with polymorphic malware (i.e., malware that uses encryption as a defense mechanism to change itself to avoid detection, typically by encrypting itself with an encryption routine, and then providing a different decryption key for each mutation). Even if detection methods are successful in some cases, it often gives precious little time to react and respond. Serendipitous seeding of malware makes the attacks hard to detect until the damage is done. The key to defending against this type of threat is to recognize that the attack mechanisms (viruses, worms, DDOS, etc.) are evolving and mutating. New connectivity options are opening doors for new types of attacks. The old model of "perimeter protection" is not keeping pace with these threats and vulnerabilities. This realization opens the doors for intelligent and adaptive methods for developing protection strategies.

According to current conventional wisdom, one promising way of protecting a computer system is based on an approach called *defense-in-depth,* which advocates multiple layers of protection to guard against failure of a single security component; hardware devices can fail, software can have flaws and bugs, and system administrators can make configuration errors. To overcome these potential vulnerabilities, defense-in-depth advocates a layered approach. The first step of this approach is the separation of systems into several "network sections" in one of the defense layers. Placement of a firewall to control the flow of traffic between section boundaries is another step. Another defense mechanism would be a "border router," placed between the Internet service provider (ISP) and the firewall, to filter traffic entering and leaving a network. Another layer of defense could be the placement of switches (a combination of a hub and a bridge) on individual sections of a network to make sniffing less effective. Yet another layer of defense is to use encryption. In spite of this battery of defensive weapons, intrusions still occur. The final layer of defense includes network-based intrusion detection systems (NIDSs) and host-based intrusion detection systems (HIDSs). Much of the AI and machine learning work, to date, has been targeted at this layer.

The defense-in-depth strategy is a general concept. Instead of looking at the system as a collection of physical layers, one can look at the logical or functional layers for defense. For example, in the so-called enclave/policy-tuned approach, the normal mode of operation has security policies that allow free flow of information between clients and servers. An event, such as Internet propagation of a new worm, could trigger a degraded mode of operation, tightening security policies to allow communication between essential users and servers, but excluding or at least severely limiting access by nonessential entities. Nonessential clients can be quarantined either through brute-force network methods (turn off router port) or through implementation of autonomics/circuit breakers on hosts themselves. Essential IT services can include directory services, DNS, messaging, and e-mail. Priority-mode policy changes can include rate-limiting connections, throttling system connectivity to the network to minimum levels, and elevated intrusion detection and prevention.

4.2 Place of Intrusion Detection in the Security Landscape

Information security is best achieved in three stages: prevention, detection, and response. The earlier one intervenes, the more cost effective the solution will be. Although prevention gives the biggest bang for the buck, to rely solely on prevention would be a bad tactic; one may end up paying a heavy price if an attack eventually manages to get through.

Preventing subversion by building completely secure systems from the requirements stage upward is considered by many to be a very difficult task. The vast installed base of systems worldwide is a virtual guarantee that any transition to a fully secure design would take a long time. Secure systems, designed and built from the requirements stage up, are nevertheless vulnerable to insider attacks. Enforcing levels of access control mechanisms is believed to lower efficiency and user-friendliness. Thus, there is a need for intrusion detection systems (IDSs).

Detecting intrusions to take remedial actions is a more reachable goal than preventing them altogether. The term *intrusion detection* refers to the broad range of techniques used to protect computer systems from malicious attacks. An intruder can be someone from within an organization (insider) or an outsider. An efficient detection system and a well-articulated incident-response procedure should be an integral part of any defensive strategy.

Network-based IDSs are necessary because most of the attacks come from the Internet. Although most of these attacks can be stopped by a properly configured firewall, one needs to be concerned about attacks that succeed in penetrating this outside perimeter. The final defensive layer is the HIDS. In this case, the defensive software is installed on every protected host computer. This requires an expenditure of system resources as well as administrative resources to monitor each and every system. Furthermore, this may demand a customized detection policy to reduce false-alarm rate. In spite of these drawbacks, HIDS does have a place because NIDS has limitations imposed by high-speed, switched, and encrypted networks.

Many IDSs are based on detecting signatures of previously seen attacks. Schemes that identify attacks based on anomalies (i.e., behaviors deviating from normal activity) exhibit unacceptably high false-alarm rates and relatively poor coverage of the attack space. Whichever method is used, these methods often use data gathered from sensors that were originally designed for audit purposes — not for detecting attacks. These audit trails are records of activities that are logged to a file in chronological order and are of the order of 100 MB/day. These records can be inspected, and attributes that are believed to shed some light on the intrusive behavior of a user are extracted: machine-oriented attributes (host attributes) such as user ID, host ID, time of log-in, duration of a session, as well as items such as instructions used, speed of keyboard entry, CPU and memory resources consumed, number of processes created, system calls generated, and so on. Instead of analyzing a host machine's audit trails, one can also look at network-related attributes such as TCP/IP packet data, TCP/IP connection data, and so on. Instead of building one centralized IDS passively defending a system, one can conceivably have a team of cooperating autonomous agents actively defending and maintaining the integrity and trustworthiness of a system.

Although much emphasis, in the subsequent chapters, is placed on the detection problem, the issue of responding to an intrusion is no less important. A majority of intrusion response systems (IRSs) react to intrusions by generating reports and alarms. Research indicates that the greater the time gap between detection and response, the greater the probability of success of the attack. For rapid response, manual methods are not quite adequate. Most of the automated response methods depend on using stateless methods (say, a decision table) in which a particular response is associated with a particular attack; the same response is used for the same type of attack — always. More work is necessary in automating the response mechanism. Perhaps intelligent software agents and cooperating agents can play a role here. Some of the ideas discussed in Section 4.6 of this chapter will come in handy while developing a single-policy decision based on inputs from multiple agents, each having its own world view and each monitoring the system and making recommendations to a "head agent" [Vemuri, 2000].

Although there is no shortage of ideas in detection *per se*, there is, however, very little understanding — at a theoretical level — of how attacks manifest. Indeed, there is inadequate understanding of how to characterize an attack. On the flip side, there is no adequate definition of what constitutes normal behavior either. In the absence of this knowledge, it is not easy to detect wide excursions from the norm. One possibility is to design systems that are capable of learning, over time, their own normal behavior. With this capability, a system would be better capable of analyzing itself, tune its operation on the fly, and exhibit better robustness in performance.

As the rest of the book is devoted to an examination of the issues related to intrusion detection from the point of view of machine learning, this chapter provides a brief overview of machine learning formulations and identifies considerations that might lead to a better insight into the intrusion detection problem.

4.3 Machine Learning beyond Intrusion Detection

Clearly, there is a role for machine learning in computer security research that transcends intrusion detection. A typical university course in computer security covers such topics as authentication and identification, policies and models, architectures, malicious software, cryptographic algorithms and protocols, access control, network security, database security, social engineering and awareness, intrusion detection and response, and cyber forensics. Machine learning has a potential role to play in many of these areas.

For example, one can consider the design of self-adaptive systems that can survive an attack. There is certainly a need to understand multistage attack processes in which cascading failures can occur because the compromise of one resource may lead to the compromise of a more valuable resource. Modeling these processes can lead to a better design of self-adaptive systems that can survive attacks.

Learning for the diagnosis of a system state as a classification problem is another way machine learning can be harnessed for computer security. In this case, the current system state can be assigned to normal or abnormal state.

4.4 Machine Learning and Computational Learning Theory

Unlike in the natural sciences — in which one proposes a hypothesis, tests it using well-defined metrics, and validates it to build a theoretical foundation — much of the current research in intrusion detection is ad hoc. The use of empirical observations to augment knowledge derived from first principles to develop a scientific model (or hypothesis) is called *learning*. In many learning scenarios, it has become popular to use the computer to learn the correct model based on examples of observed behavior. When computers are used to implement these learning algorithms, the discipline is termed *machine learning*.

Besides artistic creativity, ethical behavior, and social responsibility, the most difficult intellectual skill to computerize is learning. A possible reason for this difficulty is that learning is the result of the confluence of several intellectual capabilities. At the current state-of-the-art, four different types of activities appear to fall under the machine learning rubric: symbol-based, connectionist-based, behavior-based, and immune-system–based learning.

Symbol-based learning has its roots in classical AI. It draws its strength from the symbol system hypothesis, which states that all knowledge can be represented in symbols, and the ability to manipulate these symbols to produce new symbols — and therefore new knowledge — is the essence of intelligence. Classical AI methods such as search and decision tree induction belong to this category.

Connectionist-based learning, inspired by the biology of the brains, deemphasizes the explicit representation of knowledge using symbols. Neural-network–based methods are exemplars of connectionist systems. Symbol-based systems are implemented as computer programs and draw their conclusions from logical inference procedures. Connectionist systems are also implemented, quite often, as computer programs, but they are "trained" and draw their conclusions by recognizing patterns. Supervised classification methods such as perceptrons, support vector machines, kernel machines, and a whole host of unsupervised classification (called clustering) methods belong to this category.

Behavior-based learning is inspired by Darwinian evolution. Here, one assumes that a population of candidate solutions is always available, and the challenge is to search this pool to find one that fits the problem at hand. These methods can be characterized by the phrase, "solutions in search of problems." Genetic and evolutionary algorithms fall in this category.

Immune-system–based learning draws its strength from the observation that the human body (or, for that matter, any biological system) is very adept at recognizing foreign objects entering the body. This ability to discriminate "self" from "nonself" can be exploited to develop powerful pattern recognition and classification algorithms.

Which of these four approaches is considered superior? The spate of experimental evidence from the 1990s suggests that none of these is markedly superior to the others. However, there is reason to believe that factors such as feature selection and the encoding methods used for their representation may have some beneficial impact.

In contrast to the representational view, the learning task can also be viewed by considering the utilitarian objective of the learning system: learning for classification, learning for planning, learning for acting, learning for understanding, and so on.

The theoretical underpinning of machine learning is called computational learning theory (COLT). Machine learning, then, is the science of building predictors from data randomly sampled from an assumed probability distribution while accounting for the computational complexity of the learning algorithm and the predictor's performance on future data. Much of the work in machine learning is empirical. In such research, the performance of learning algorithms heavily depends upon the type of training experience from which the learning machine will learn. The learning algorithms themselves are typically judged by their performance on sample sets of data. Stated differently, in machine learning, training data is used to search (or build or learn) for a model (or a hypothesis) in a space of possible models (hypotheses). Given some training data, machine learning is tantamount to searching the hypothesis space (or model space) for the best possible hypothesis that describes the observed training data. Evidently, a well-defined learning problem requires a well-posed problem, a performance metric, and a source of training experience.

Although ad hoc approaches do provide some insight, it is difficult to compare two learning algorithms carefully and rigorously, or to understand situations in which a given learning algorithm performs well. Therefore, the following issues become central to machine learning:

- Given sufficient training data, what algorithms exist so as to guarantee convergence to a hypothesis?
- How much training data is sufficient? Is there a particular sequence in which training data is to be presented for optimum learning experience? Does more training data give more confidence in what the machine learned?

- How does one go about getting the training data? If a sufficient amount of real data is not available or is hard to get, can one create training datasets via simulation experiments conducted in a laboratory setup? In such a case, how much confidence can one place on a machine's predictions while it is operating in a real operational condition?
- Can prior knowledge about potential hypotheses help guide the learning process? If learning is not a memorization of what the machine saw during training but an ability to generalize from examples, how can prior knowledge help if it is only approximately correct?

COLT provides a framework under which a rigorous analysis of both the predictive power and computational efficiency of learning algorithms can be carried out. COLT can shed light on some important questions: What kinds of guarantees can one provide about learning algorithms? What are good algorithms for achieving certain types of goals? Can one devise models that are both amenable to mathematical analysis and make sense empirically? What can be said about the inherent ease or difficulty of learning problems? Addressing these questions will require pulling in notions and ideas from AI, probability and statistics, computational complexity theory, cognitive psychology, game theory, and empirical machine learning research.

4.5 Some Popular Machine Learning Methods

Among the more popular methods implementing the classification step are neural nets, clustering methods, decision trees, Bayesian nets, and a whole host of hybrid methods. Within the broad category of neural nets fall perceptrons, support vector machines, multilayer nets with gradient-type training, radial basis function networks, and self-organizing nets.

4.5.1 Multilayer Networks with Back Propagation

This is a multilayer (typically input, hidden, and output layers), feed-forward neural network that relies on the classical gradient-descent method for error minimization. During the forward pass, a feature vector is presented at the input layer, which propagates toward the output layer and produces an output. This output is compared with the expected output, assumed to be known, and the resulting error is propagated backward through a system of interconnected weights between the neural layers. These weights are adjusted until an error measure (typically the sum of the squares of errors) is minimized. This process is called *training*. The algorithm is a well-established procedure and is described in many textbooks. The challenge really is at the preprocessing stage: selecting the features in the feature vector, the feature vectors to use during training and testing, deciding when to stop training, and so on. This method has been applied by many for intrusion detection [Dao and Vemuri, 2002].

4.5.2 Support Vector Machines

These are really sophisticated versions of perceptrons. Whereas a perceptron allows many, theoretically infinite, possible separating hyperplanes between classes, an SVM produces a unique, optimum hyperplane. If a pattern is not linearly separable in the original feature space, an SVM permits linear separability in a higher-dimensional space. SVMs have been successfully applied to the intrusion detection problem [Hu et al., 2003].

4.5.3 Probabilistic Models

It appears that many probabilistic models such as Markov chains, hidden Markov models as well as non-Markovian models such as Gaussian classifiers, naive Bayes [Valdes and Skinner, 2000], Fuzzy neural systems (ARTMAPs, neurofuzzy ART [Liao et al., 2004; Hoffmann et al., 2003]), and statistical models (decision trees, Markov models, etc.) can be effectively used for intrusion detection with comparable results. For example, the generalized Markov chain may improve the accuracy of detecting statistical anomalies. However, these are complex and time consuming to construct.

4.5.4 Clustering

The k-nearest neighbor method [Liao and Vemuri, 2002; Rawat et al., 2004] and one-class classification for masquerade detection [Pasos, 2004] also gave promising results. Some research is also going on in behavior-based security via user profiling [Dao and Vemuri, 2000; Stolfo et al., 2003]. Profiling users, characterizing user intent, and capturing profile drift are problems that are waiting for a satisfactory solution.

4.5.5 Decision Trees

Although decision trees are easy to learn and implement, they do not seem to enjoy as much popularity as, say, neural nets in the context of intrusion detection. A possible reason for this is that the problem of finding the smallest decision tree that is consistent with a set of training examples is known to be NP-hard.

4.5.6 Bayesian Networks

Bayes networks are powerful tools for decision and reasoning under uncertainty. A very simple form of Bayes networks is called naive Bayes, which is particularly efficient for inference tasks. However, naive Bayes is based on a very strong independence assumption. Surprisingly, the naïve Bayes still gives good results even if the independence assumption is violated, triggering further research in this area.

The exemplar for using any of the methods to develop IDSs is based on implementing the following four canonical steps: (a) data collection, (b) feature extraction, (c) creation of training and test datasets, and (d) pattern recognition and classification. This recipe has been followed by a number of investigators. Implementation methods may differ, but the general recipe has been the same. Insofar as intrusion detection applications are concerned, much of the published work seems to follow this sequence of steps: selecting a feature set to characterize a user, selecting a metric to measure similarity (or distance) between users, using a training dataset (the most widely used being the DARPA dataset) [Lippmann et al., 2000] to train and test their models, and representing the results in terms of detection rates, false-alarm rates, ROC curves, and so on.

4.6 Making Machine Learning More Useful

In a canonical *supervised* learning problem, a learner (or a learning program) is given a set of training examples in the form $\{(\mathbf{x_1}, y_1), (\mathbf{x_2}, y_2), \ldots, (\mathbf{x_m}, y_m)\}$, and the learner is asked to learn some unknown function $y = f(\mathbf{x})$ from this data. Here, the values $\mathbf{x_i}$ are typically vectors of the form $< x_{i1}, x_{i2}, \ldots, x_{in} >$ where the components x_{ij} are typically discrete or real values such as height, weight, color, and age and are termed *features* (or attributes) of the vector $\mathbf{x_i}$ — the feature vector. The notation x_{ij} refers to the *j*th feature of the feature vector $\mathbf{x_i}$. The subscript *j* is usually dropped if the context makes the meaning obvious. The *y* values are drawn from a discrete set of classes $\{1, 2, \ldots, K\}$ if the problem is a classification problem, and the real line if it is a regression problem. It is generally assumed that the training examples might be corrupted with noise. It is generally convenient to assume that the training examples are indeed a sample drawn from a known probability distribution (say, the normal distribution) whose parameters may or may not be known.

Given a sample set S of training examples, a learning algorithm outputs a *classifier.* The classifier is a hypothesis of the unknown function *f.* Just as a number of regression lines can be drawn for a given dataset, one can develop a family of classifiers (or hypotheses) from a given set of training examples. Given a new **x,** each of these hypotheses h_1, h_2, ..., h_L can be used to make a prediction.

The classification step can be implemented by a variety of supervised methods such as neural nets (e.g., back propagation, radial basis functions, and support vector machines), probabilistic methods (e.g., decision trees, Gaussian, Bayesian, and Markov models), as well as by unsupervised methods such as clustering (e.g., k-nearest neighbor, k-means). Some of these methods will be discussed later in this chapter as well as in the next two chapters.

Most of the methods listed in the preceding paragraph share some common drawbacks. For example, no rationale seems to exist in selecting the features (number of features and the features themselves) defining a feature vector. A similar comment can be made about the selection of distance metrics (see Chapter 5). Finally, little progress appears to have been made in defining fundamental concepts such as normal behavior and intrusive behavior. Is there an abstract way to characterize an intrusion? Can one build a model that can generate intrusive sequences with specified characteristics? Is there a way to explain the behavior of the current crop of intrusion detection models? Are there any limits to the learning methods in terms of their performance (say, in terms of false-positives)?

There are several ways of overcoming these drawbacks. The bulk material in the rest of this section is summarized from a 1997 survey paper by Dietterich.

4.6.1 Ensemble of Classifiers

One method of improving the classification accuracy is to combine the outputs of different classifiers (hypotheses) in some suitable fashion by some sort of voting. If all the classifiers agree, the question of voting becomes mute. If the classifiers disagree and if the errors committed by the classifiers are uncorrelated, then a majority vote would produce a good answer [Dietterich, 1997]. However, if the error rates of individual classifiers exceed 0.5, then the error rate of the voted ensemble increases as a result of voting. The key to the success of this method is to make the individual classifiers as good as possible to start with.

4.6.2 Constructing an Ensemble by Manipulating Training Data

A fairly general method of constructing an ensemble of classifiers is by manipulating the training examples. Instead of using up all of the training data for one swoop, it is divided into subsets, and different classifiers are trained with each subset. This strategy works well when the hypothesis generated is fairly sensitive to small changes in training data. This is indeed the case with neural nets and decision trees.

4.6.2.1 Cross Validation

A popular method of manipulating training data is to subdivide the training data into m disjoint subsets and to reconstruct training sets by leaving out some of the subsets, in turn, from the training process. For example, if the training data is divided randomly into ten disjoint subsets, ten overlapping training sets can be constructed by dropping out one of the subsets, in turn, to get the *leave-one-out method of cross validation*. This process can be generalized to get *leave-k-out cross validation*.

4.6.2.2 Bagging

A second method of manipulating the training data is to pick a subset of m training examples as a random sample "with replacement." Such a sample is called *bootstrap replicate* of the original training data. Each of these bootstrap datasets is used to train a different *component classifier*. It is customary to select the same type of learning machine for all component classifiers — say, all neural nets, all hidden Markov models, all decision trees, and so on. The final classification decision is based on a voting procedure. For this reason, the method is also called *bootstrap aggregation*, from which the name *bagging* is derived [Breiman, 1996]. It can be shown that each bootstrap aggregate contains, on the average, 63.2 percent of the original training set. In general, bagging improves the classification accuracy of those classifiers whose classification accuracy is sensitive to small changes in training data. Decision trees and neural nets, which are deemed sensitive, are therefore called *unstable*.

4.6.2.3 Boosting

A third method of manipulating training data — similar to bagging — is boosting, which is a general method of converting a rough rule of thumb (or a weak hypothesis) into a highly accurate prediction rule.

4.6.2.4 Adaboost

Adaboost, a variation of boosting, picks — at iteration l — a subset of m training examples "with replacement," according to a probability distribution $p_l(\mathbf{x})$. The hypothesis generated with this training data is labeled h_l. The error rate ε_l of this classifier is computed and used to adjust $p_l(\mathbf{x})$. This procedure puts more weight on instances that were misclassified. A final classifier is then constructed by a weighted average of the individual classifiers [Freund and Schapire, 1996].

4.6.3 Constructing an Ensemble by Manipulating Input Features

Another general method of constructing an ensemble of classifiers is by manipulating the input features. Selecting what and how many features to be included in the feature vector is an early design decision. Quite often, this decision is made for expediency by looking at features that are already there in the available training data. For example, in intrusion detection, NIDES uses up to 30 attributes such as CPU and I/O usage, commands used, local network activity, and so on, to define a feature vector. Values of these attributes are typically logged routinely. Is it really necessary to use all these? Would a subset suffice? If so, what subset? How does one select that subset? As the size of the feature vector influences the size of the classifier, and therefore the effort in building it, there is some merit in trying to work with feature vectors of small dimension.

How does one select the subsets from the training data? There are no standard rules. Typically, they are selected manually by using some ad hoc criterion, not necessarily justified by any problem-driven considerations. For example, 100 contiguous samples of a signal (in the time domain or in the frequency domain) can be grouped into several contiguous nonoverlapping segments, or into several overlapping segments by sliding a window, or every tenth sample is placed in a bin to create ten bins, and so on. Or, in a preprocessing stage, the input data is first clustered into groups and training datasets created by using some systematic selection from the clusters. In any event, this process of manipulating input features seems to work if the features are highly redundant.

4.6.4 Constructing an Ensemble by Injecting Randomness

This is probably the most commonly used method in neural networks. In backpropagation training, for example, a recommended method is to start with a randomly selected initial weight set, train the network, and then restart with a different random set of initial weights, and repeat the experiment several times. Each such trial results in a different classifier. This approach is fairly widespread and has been successfully applied to decision trees and rule-based expert systems.

4.6.5 Constructing an Ensemble Using Different Learning Algorithms

Finally, it is possible to build an ensemble of classifiers, each using a different learning algorithm. Learning algorithms using radically different principles probably will produce very different classifiers, but there is no guarantee that they will produce the necessary diversity.

Indeed, there are many more ways of creating ensembles of classifiers.

4.6.6 Combining the Results from an Ensemble of Classifiers

Once results from a family of classifiers are available, there are many ways of combining them. Indeed, there are as many ways as there are voting procedures. Three prominent methods are: unweighted voting, weighted voting, and gating.

4.6.6.1 Majority Vote

The simplest of these is to take a simple majority vote. This idea can be extended if each classifier can produce not just a classification decision but also a class probability estimate. The class probability estimate for data point $\mathbf{x}$ is the probability that the true class is k, $k = 1, 2, ..., K$, given the hypothesis h_l. Then the class probability of the ensemble is given by

$$P(f(x) = k) = \frac{1}{L} \sum_{l=1}^{L} P(f(x) = k \mid h_l)$$

The class with the highest probability (analogue to majority vote) becomes the predicted class.

4.6.6.2 Gating

Here, the idea is to learn a gating function that takes $\mathbf{x}$ as input and produces as output the weights w_l to be associated with classifier h_l. That is, one seeks to simultaneously learn the gating function while learning the classifier.

4.6.6.3 Stacking

This starts with the assumption that there are L different training algorithms $A_1, A_2, ..., A_L$. Each of these algorithms takes the training data as input and produces L different hypotheses $h_1, h_2, ..., h_L$. In stacking, the goal is to find a classifier h^* such that the final classification will be computed by $h^* (h_1(x), h_2(x), ..., h_L(x))$. In other words, one has to learn h^* in some fashion.

4.6.7 Why the Ensemble Idea Works

The ensemble idea works because uncorrelated errors made by individual classifiers can be removed by voting. Do individual classifiers commit uncorrelated errors? Is it possible to find a single classifier that works as well as a voting ensemble?

Answers to these questions can be found by looking at some of the theoretical foundations of machine learning and COLT. Learning in machine learning is tantamount to a search in the hypothesis space, H. The search is carried out until one finds a hypothesis h that best approximates the unknown function f. The success of this search depends upon two important factors: size of the hypothesis space and the fact that such a search indeed ends in finding a good hypothesis that meets the criterion for "best."

If the hypothesis space is large, then a large training set is required to progressively constrain the search until a good approximation is found. Indeed, each training example can be used to rule out all the hypotheses that misclassify it. In a two-class classification problem — the most common scenario in intrusion detection — it is theoretically possible to use each training example to rule out one of the hypotheses in H. This suggests that O (log $|H|$) training examples would suffice to select a classifier.

Finding the weights for the smallest possible neural net consistent with the training data is NP-hard. Therefore, people use local search methods, such as the gradient method, to find locally optimum weights. Because of these reasons, it is quite possible that one may never succeed in finding the best hypothesis even after factoring in prior knowledge to assist the search process.

In spite of these positive attributes of the ensemble methods, very few attempts seem to have been made to apply this method to intrusion detection.

4.7 Summary

The complexity of many learning problems of today goes well beyond the capabilities of current machine learning methods. Specifically, in the computer security area, the machine learning technology that has been used until now is not adequate to allow the calculation of acceptable solutions while simultaneously assessing their accuracy. This inadequacy is responsible, in part, for the poor performance (high false-positive rates, for instance) of the current crop of machine learning methods. Although COLT, which has revolutionized the solution of classification, prediction, and regression problems, has established itself as the framework of choice in machine learning, its full potential has not yet been brought to bear in addressing computer security problems.

In the intrusion detection problem domain, the available first principle knowledge is generally not adequate to characterize an intruder. The available empirical knowledge (in the form of labeled examples for training and testing) is inadequate because of small sample sizes. Much of the available data has been collected under artificial conditions, and even that data does not contain an adequate number of intrusion scenarios to learn from [McHugh, 2000].

To apply COLT to real-life problems, such as computer security in general and intrusion detection in particular, the following methodological steps are suggested:

1. Precisely define the problem, preserving key features while maintaining simplicity.
2. Select the appropriate formal learning model.
3. Design a learning algorithm.
4. Analyze the performance of the algorithm using the formal model.

While selecting the formal learning model in step 2 in the preceding list, there are a number of issues to consider:

■ What is being learned?
■ How does the learner interact with the environment? (Is there a helpful teacher, a critic, or an adversary?)
■ What is the prior knowledge of the learner?
■ How is the learner's hypothesis represented?
■ What are the criteria for successful learning?
■ How efficient is the learner in time, space, and data?

In the computer security area, it seems reasonable to restrict the type of problems to the so-called concept-learning problems, in which there are a set of *instances* (training data) and a single *target concept* that classifies each instance. The goal of the learner is to devise a hypothesis (say, a neural net) that correctly classifies each instance as a positive (intruder) or negative instance (nonintruder). The hypotheses in the hypothesis space must make a binary prediction every time an instance of data is presented; it is not acceptable for the learning machine to return an "I do not know" for some instances.

References

1. Breiman, L. Bagging predictors, *Machine Learning,* 24: 2, pp. 123–140, 1996.
2. Dao, Vu and V Rao Vemuri. Profiling users in the UNIX OS environment, *International ICSC Conference on Intelligent Systems and Applications,* University of Wollongong, Australia, December 11–15, 2000.
3. Dao, Vu and V Rao Vemuri. Computer network intrusion detection: A comparison of neural networks methods, *Differential Equations and Dynamical Systems,* 10:1/2, pp. 201–214, 2002.
4. Dietterich, T.D. Machine Learning Research: Four Current Directions, *AI Magazine,* AAAI, Winter 1997.
5. Dietterich, T.D. and P. Langley. Machine Learning for Cognitive Networks: Technology Assessment and Research Challenges. http://web.engr. oregonstate.edu/~tgd/kp/dl-report.pdf, May 11, 2003.
6. Freund, Y. and Schapire, R.E. Experiments with a new boosting algorithm, *Proc. 13th Intl. Conf. Machine Learning,* Ed. L. Sattina, pp. 148–156, Morgan Kaufmann, San Francisco, 1996.
7. Hoffmann, A. and B. Sick. Evolutionary optimization of radial basis function networks for intrusion detection, *Joint International Conference ICANN/ICONIP 2003,* Istanbul, Turkey, June 2003.
8. Hu, Wenjie, Yihua Liao, and V Rao Vemuri. Robust support vector machines for anomaly detection in computer security, *International Conference on Machine Learning and Applications,* Los Angeles, CA, July 2003.
9. Liao, Yihua and V Rao Vemuri. Using text categorization techniques for intrusion detection, *Proc. Usenix San Francisco,* August 2002.
10. Liao, Yihua, V Rao Vemuri, and A. Pasos. A general framework for adaptive anomaly detection with evolving connectionist systems. *SIAM Inter. Conference on Data Mining,* Lake Buena Vista, FL, April 22–24, 2004.
11. Lippmann, R.P., R.K. Cunningham, D.J. Fried, S.L. Garfinkel, A.S. Gorton, I. Graf, K.R. Kendall, D.J. McClung, D.J. Weber, S.E. Webster, D. Wyschogrod, and M.A. Zissman. MIT Lincoln Laboratory offline component of DARPA 1998 Intrusion detection Evaluation, 2000. http://www.ll.mit.edu/IST/ideval/docs/docs_index.html.
12. McHugh, John. Testing intrusion detection systems: A critique of the 1998 and 1999 DARPA intrusion detection system evaluations as performed by Lincoln laboratories, *ACM Trans. on Information and Systems Security,* 3:4, pp. 262–294, November 2000.

13. Pasos, Alejandro. *Machine Learning Techniques in Masquerader Detection.* Masters thesis, University of California, Davis, 2004.

14. Rawat, Sanjay, A.K. Pujari, V.P. Gulati, and V Rao Vemuri. Intrusion detection using text processing techniques with a binary-weighted cosine metric, *International Journal of Information Security*, Springer-Verlag, Submitted 2004. http://www.cs.ucdavis.edu/~vemuri/publications.

15. Stolfo, S.J., S. Hershkop, K. Wang, O. Nimerkern, and C-W. Hu. A behavior-based approach to securing e-mail systems, *Proc. Mathematical Methods, Models and Architectures for Computer Networks Security,* Springer-Verlag, September 2003.

16. Valdes, A. and K. Skinner. Adaptive, model-based monitoring for cyber attack detection, *Lecture Notes in Computer Science*, Number 1907, Springer-Verlag, Toulouse, France. October, 2000. In H. Debar, L. Me, and F. Wu, Eds., *Recent Advances in Intrusion Detection (RAID 2000)*.

17. Vemuri, Rao V. Agent assist for computer games, *International ICSC Conference on Intelligent Systems and Applications*, University of Wollongong, Australia, December 11–15, 2000.

Chapter 5

Machine Learning in Intrusion Detection

Yihua Liao and V Rao Vemuri

5.1 Introduction

In this chapter, we examine various aspects of machine learning–based anomaly detection in computer security. Indeed, detection of anomalies in data is one of the fundamental machine learning tasks. Anomaly detection (also known as novelty detection, outlier detection, change detection, or activity monitoring) provides the core technology for a broad spectrum of security-centric applications including detection (credit cards, cell phones, etc.), crisis (e.g., epidemic or bioterrorism) monitoring, news story monitoring, hardware fault detection, and network performance monitoring [1]. Although these applications may differ greatly in representation, they share significant characteristics that differentiate them from other machine learning tasks. The goal of anomaly detection is to identify anomalous activities (i.e., rare, unusual events) in a data stream accurately and in a timely fashion. In applications such as computer security, it is also desirable to be able to explain the reason for the anomaly and propose the appropriate response actions. Because of the lack of first-principle models to describe the complex behavior of the monitored systems, learning from the audit data is necessary. Standard machine learning techniques such as classification, regression, and time series analysis are useful as solution components, but they do not completely address the goal of anomaly detection, which has its own idiosyncrasies (e.g., the asymmetry of class distributions and error costs).

We begin by briskly reviewing the major problem formulations and associated learning methods that have been studied for anomaly detection. Then we examine some fundamental issues involved in anomaly detection and discuss the open questions and future directions. Finally, we present an adaptive anomaly detection example with evolving connectionist systems.

5.2 Intrusion Detection

Intrusion detection is an important component of computer security mechanisms. It aims to detect computer break-ins, penetrations, and other forms of computer abuse that exploit security vulnerabilities or flaws in computer systems. Examples of these include hackers using exploit scripts to gain access to or deny the services of a computer system and insiders who misuse their privileges. Traditional security mechanisms, such as access control and information flow control, help protect systems, data, and resources. However, nothing is perfect. Even the best-protected systems must be monitored to detect successful and unsuccessful attempts to breach security. This is why intrusion detection systems (IDSs) have become an increasingly indispensable player in the arsenal against computer misuse.

IDSs were first visualized in the 1980s as a promising method for detecting and preventing intrusions and attacks. The goals of an IDS are fourfold: (1) to detect a wide variety of intrusions, including intrusions from outside and inside as well as both known and previously unknown attacks; (2) detect intrusions in a timely fashion; (3) present the analysis in a simple, easy-to-understand format; and (4) be accurate, that is, achieve a low false-alarm rate. (A false-positive occurs when an IDS raises an alarm when no attack is underway, and a false-negative occurs when an IDS fails to report an ongoing attack.) For the last two decades, three general approaches to intrusion detection have been developed, namely, anomaly detection, misuse detection, and specification-based detection [2].

An anomaly detector analyzes a set of characteristics of the monitored system (or users) and identifies activities that deviate from the normal behavior, based on the assumption that such deviations may indicate that an intrusion or attack exploiting vulnerabilities has occurred (or may still be occurring). Any observable behavior of the system can be used to build a model of the normal operation of the system. Audit logs, network traffic, user commands, and system calls are all common choices. Anomaly detection has the potential of detecting novel attacks as well as variations of known attacks. However, anomaly detection suffers from the basic difficulty of defining what is normal. When the system or user behavior varies widely, methods based on anomaly detection tend to produce many false alarms because they are not capable of discriminating between abnormal patterns triggered by an otherwise legitimate usage and those triggered by an intrusion.

In misuse detection, a user's activities are compared with the known signature patterns of attackers. Those matched are then labeled as intrusive activities. Most of today's commercial IDSs are based on misuse detection. Although misuse detection can be effective in recognizing known intrusion types, it cannot detect novel attacks.

Anomaly detection has been called the art of looking for unusual states, whereas misuse detection is the art of looking for states known to be bad. Specification-based detection, in contrast, looks for states known not to be good. It determines whether or not a sequence of instructions violates a specification of how a program or system should execute. If so, it reports a potential intrusion. Although specification-based detection has the potential for providing a very low false-positive rate while detecting a wide range of attacks, it is difficult to model complex programs or systems and write security specifications for them. Figure 5.1 illustrates the differences between the three general approaches to intrusion detection in terms of their computation and memory requirements and capability to detect novel, unseen attacks. In practice, these general approaches are often combined to detect attacks more efficiently.

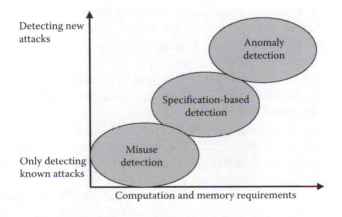

Figure 5.1   Three general approaches to intrusion detection.

5.3 Machine Learning Approaches to Anomaly Detection

5.3.1 Machine Learning and Its Problem Formulations

Learning is the process of estimating an unknown input–output dependency, i.e., a model (or hypothesis) of a system using a limited number of observations. In many learning scenarios, it has become popular to use the computer to learn the correct model based on examples of observed behavior. When computers are used to implement these learning algorithms, the discipline is termed *machine learning*. In machine learning research, a set of training data is used to search (or build or learn) for a model (or a hypothesis) in a space of possible models (hypotheses). Given some training data, machine learning is equivalent to searching the hypothesis space (or model space) for the best possible hypothesis that describes the observed training data. Evidently, a well-defined learning problem requires a well-formulated problem, a performance metric, and a source of training experience.

Depending on how the learning task is formulated in terms of the inputs that drive learning and the manner in which the learned knowledge is utilized, we can divide the machine learning tasks into three broad formulations [3]:

- *Learning for classification and regression.* This is the most common formulation of machine learning. Classification involves assigning a test case to one of a finite set of classes, whereas regression instead predicts the case's value on some continuous variable or attribute. There exist a variety of well-established methods for classification and regression, including decision trees, rule induction, neural networks, support vector machines (SVMs), nearest neighbor approaches, and probabilistic methods.
- *Learning for acting and planning.* It addresses learning of knowledge for selecting actions or plans for an agent to carry out. One well-known example is reinforcement learning, in which the agent typically carries out an action and receives some reward that indicates the desirability of the resulting states.
- *Learning for interpretation and understanding.* It focuses on learning knowledge that lets one interpret and understand situations or events. Approaches of this formulation attempt to interpret observations in a more constructive way than simple classification, by combining a number of separate knowledge elements to explain them — a process often referred to as *abduction*.

In the context of anomaly detection, it is straightforward to cast it as a classification problem (with two classes: normal and abnormal). Indeed, most existing approaches proposed for anomaly detection employ some learning mechanisms to capture the monitored object's normal usage patterns and classify new behavior as either normal or abnormal. However, one could also formulate it as a problem of understanding and explaining anomalous behavior. Yet another option would be the formulation that focuses on learning for selecting appropriate responses in the presence of intrusions. Each of these three formulations suggests different approaches to the anomaly detection task and requires different input data and prior knowledge.

5.3.2 Learning Methods for Anomaly Detection

In this section, we review the major learning methods that have been proposed for intrusion detection. Although they all represent "learning for classification," they do fall into two broad categories:

- A *generative* (also known as *profiling*) approach builds a model solely based on normal training examples and evaluates each testing instance to see how well it fits the model. Activities that deviate significantly from normal trigger an alarm.
- A *discriminative* approach attempts to learn the distinction between the normal and abnormal classes. Both normal and attack examples are used in training. New activities are classified as either normal or abnormal.

A generative approach aims to define the perimeter of "normal" and thus tends to generate more false alarms. However, it is robust over noisy training data. In contrast, a discriminative approach may give better classification performance if clean, labeled training data is available from both classes. Usually, normal examples are common, and attack examples are rare. It is common to have a training set with skewed class distributions — much more normal examples than attack examples.

Within each broad class of intrusion detection approaches, there exist many learning techniques that differ in the knowledge representations and their specific algorithms for using and learning that knowledge. Common knowledge representations include rules, decision trees, linear and nonlinear functions (including neural networks and SVMs), instance libraries, probabilistic summaries, and so on. Table 5.1 summarizes the major techniques that have been used for intrusion detection, some of which can be employed in both generative and discriminative manners.

Table 5.1 Summary of Major Machine Learning Techniques for Intrusion Detection

Style	Knowledge Representation	Learning Algorithm Examples	Features
Rule-based	Classification rules that characterize normal (and intrusive) behavior	RIPPER [4,5], time-based inductive learning [6]	Concise and intuitive rules, easy to understand and inspect
Immunological-based	Self (or nonself) model representing the set of normal (or anomalous) instances	Negative selection, positive selection [7,8]	Suitable for distributed processing
Neural nets	Linear/nonlinear classification functions	Recurrent networks [9], SVM [10,11]	High classification accuracy
Instance-based	Instance library	KNN [12,13]	No training involved, classification cost can be high when the instance library is large
Clustering and outlier detection	Clusters in input (or feature) space	KNN, one-class SVM [14], density-based local outliers [15]	Unsupervised learning, no class label required
Probabilistic learning	Probability summaries	Markov models [5,16], Mixture model [17], and Bayesian networks [18]	Robust over noisy data, require large data

It is nontrivial to compare these techniques against each other as each has its own strengths and weaknesses, let alone their different knowledge representations. In general, rule-based approaches can provide rules that are easy to understand, but they require expensive training processes as many neural nets–based learning methods do. On the other hand, the cost of classifying a new instance is high for instance-based and immunological-based approaches because the new instance is often compared with a large corpus of normal or abnormal instances. Methods based on clustering and probability-density estimation approaches usually require a larger number of samples than other approaches.

5.4 Audit Data

To detect intrusions, some source of information in which the intrusion is manifest must be observed, and some analysis that can reveal the intrusion must be performed. Systems that obtain the data to analyze from the operating system or applications subject to attack are called host-based. The events audited by operating systems usually include the use of identification and authentication mechanisms (log-in, etc.), file opens and program executions, deletion of objects, administrative actions, and other security-relevant events. The audit trail should be protected from unauthorized access or tampering. Most modern operating systems have such basic auditing capabilities. Windows NT and Solaris are examples of operating systems that support the so-called C2-level security audit. The Solaris BSM audit mechanism, in particular, provides the ability to collect detailed security-relevant data at the system call level. Most host-based systems collect data continuously as the system is operating. The substantial amount of auditing, however, could impact the host system performance and require large storage space. In addition, some intrusions may not directly manifest themselves in the audit trail.

Alternatively, network-based IDSs observe the network traffic that goes to and from the monitored systems and look for signs of intrusions in that data. The advantage of network-based data collection is that a single sensor, properly placed, can monitor a number of hosts and can look for attacks that target multiple hosts. However, the rapidly increasing network data rates and encrypted connections are the major challenges for network monitoring. Depending on the type of information that is used for intrusion detection, we can further distinguish between traffic and application models. Systems that use traffic models monitor the flow of network packets. The source and destination IP addresses and port numbers are used to determine the features such as the number of total connection arrivals in a certain period of time, the interarrival time between packets, or the number of packets to and from a certain host. These features, in turn, are used to model the normal traffic and detect attacks such as port scans or denial-of-service (DoS) attacks. In contrast, the application (or service) model attempts to incorporate application-specific knowledge of the network services (e.g., HTTP, DNS, and FTP) to detect more sophisticated attacks. The packet header, as well as the application payload information, is used to establish the normal traffic model for each service.

To facilitate quantitative evaluations of IDS performance and comparisons of different intrusion detection methods, researchers have realized the need for standardized datasets. Described in the following text are several widely cited and publicly available host-based and network-based datasets for research purposes. Without such shareable datasets, IDS researchers must either expend enormous resources creating proprietary datasets or use fairly simplistic data for their testing. To our knowledge, there are some privately owned audit datasets, including Windows NT user-profiling data and network traffic data, which are not available in the public domain.

5.4.1 DARPA/KDD Datasets

Sponsored by the Department of Defense Advanced Research Projects Agency (DARPA), the MIT Lincoln Laboratory conducted the most comprehensive evaluations of research IDSs in 1998 and 1999 [19]. In these evaluations, researchers were given sensor data in the form of sniffed network traffic (tcpdump), Solaris BSM audit data, Windows NT audit data, and file-system snapshots and asked to identify the intrusions that had been carried out during the data collection period. The 1999 evaluation effort used a test bed that generated live background traffic similar to that of an Air Force base local area network. More than 200 instances of 58 attack types (including stealthy and novel attacks) were embedded in seven weeks of training data and two weeks of test data. Automated attacks were launched against three UNIX victim machines (SunOS, Solaris, and Linux), Windows NT hosts, and a router in the presence of background traffic. Attack categories included DoS, probe, remote-to-local, and user-to-super-user attacks. The DARPA evaluations resulted in the development of an intrusion detection corpus that includes weeks of background traffic and host audit logs and hundreds of labeled and documented attacks. Part of this corpus, the preprocessed tcpdump data consisting of 41 features, was used for the 1999 KDD Cup contest, held at the fifth ACM International Conference on Knowledge Discovery and Data Mining. The DARPA corpus, especially the preprocessed KDD dataset portion, has been used extensively by researchers.

The DARPA evaluations have been criticized for their design and execution, however. As pointed out in Reference 20, the flaws in the DARPA evaluations include failures to appropriately validate the background data (especially with respect to its ability to cause false alarms), the lack of an appropriate unit of analysis for reporting false alarms, and the use of questionable or inappropriate data analysis and presentation techniques. Nevertheless, it is still possible to mix the well-behaved DARPA data with real-world data and conduct meaningful intrusion detection analyses [21].

5.4.2 UNM System Call Data

In a ground-breaking study, Forrest et al. [7] discovered that the short sequences of system calls made by a UNIX program during its normal execution are very consistent. More importantly, the sequences are different from the sequences of its abnormal, exploited executions as well as the executions of other programs. Therefore, a concise database consisting of these normal sequences can be used as the "self" definition of the normal behavior of a program and as the basis to detect anomalies (i.e., "nonself"). A number of follow-up studies, for example [4,5,9], attempted alternative models with the system call sequences including classification rules, neural nets, hidden Markov model, variable-length patterns, etc. Instead of modeling the local ordering of system calls invoked by a program, Liao and Vemuri [13] used the frequencies of system calls to characterize program behavior for intrusion detection. Their strategy allows the treatment of long stretches of system calls as one unit, thus allowing one to bypass the need to build separate databases and learn individual program profiles.

Forrest's group has collected several datasets of system calls executed by active processes and made them publicly available at the University of New Mexico [22]. These datasets include different kinds of programs (e.g., programs that run as daemons and those that do not), programs that vary widely in their size and complexity, and different kinds of intrusions (buffer overflows, symbolic link attacks, and Trojan programs). Only programs that run with privilege are included, because misuse of these programs has the greatest potential for harm to the system.

5.4.3 UNIX Command Data

User profiling has been considered as an important technique for detecting an insider's or masquerader's misuse of information systems. The underlying assumption is that hostile activity is unusual activity that will manifest as significant excursions from normal user profiles. A user profile contains information that characterizes a system user's behavior, such as commands issued, files normally accessed, resource usage, periods of time normally logged in, keystroke patterns, and a wide variety of other attributes. A popular choice has been the user commands. Lane and Brodley [12,16] modeled truncated UNIX command data (no arguments) for intrusion detection using instance-based models and hidden Markov models. Two different user populations were used in their study. The first group comprised eight different UNIX users at Purdue University, monitored over the course of more than two years. This set of UNIX command data does not appear to be publicly available now. The second group is a subset of 168 users monitored by Saul Greenberg at the University of Calgary. The original Greenberg data, documented in Reference 23, comprised full command-line entries from 168 volunteer users of the UNIX *csh* system. The data is further split into four groups: 55 novice users, 36 experienced users, 52 computer scientist users, and 25 nonprogrammer users, all of whom were affiliated with the University of Calgary (Canada) as students, faculty, researchers, or staff. This user command dataset is available for research use on request.

Schonlau and his colleagues applied a number of techniques, including Bayes 1-Step Markov, Hybrid Multi-Step Markov, IPAM, and so forth [24], to the same UNIX command dataset. The data, available online [24], contains user IDs and command names only (no arguments). This limitation was imposed for privacy reasons. The first 15,000 commands for each of about 70 users were recorded over a period of several months. Some users generated 15,000 commands in a few days; others took a few months. Some commands not explicitly typed by the user (e.g., those generated by shell files or scripts) were also included, as were names of executable programs. To evaluate the intrusion detection performance, Schonlau et al. [24] randomly selected 50 users out of the 70 from whom data were collected to serve as intrusion targets. The remaining 20 users were used as masqueraders, and their commands were interspersed into the data of the 50 intrusion targets. Each user's data was decomposed into 150 blocks of 100 commands each. The first 50 blocks (5,000 commands) of all users, free of contamination by masqueraders, were kept aside as training data. The last 10,000 (masquerader-injected with certain probability) commands were used as testing data for each user. Maxion and Townsend [25] analyzed the Schonlau data and suggested that command-line data alone, without arguments, is not enough to profile users. More recently, using the Greenberg data as the test bed, Maxion [26] demonstrated that the command data, enriched with command-line flags and arguments, facilitated masquerade detection with a significant reduction in the overall cost of errors, compared to truncated user command data.

5.5 Issues in Anomaly Detection

In addressing the anomaly detection problem with machine learning techniques, several difficult issues arise. These issues are common to all methods of anomaly detection. Even though there are many proposed methods, there are only a handful of fundamental issues.

5.5.1 Feature Selection

In anomaly detection, there are many different levels at which an IDS could monitor activities in a computer system. Anomalies may be undetectable at one level of granularity or abstraction but easy to detect at a different level. For example, a worm attack might escape detection at the level of a single host, but be detectable when the traffic of the whole network is observed and analyzed. One of the biggest challenges in anomaly detection is to choose features (i.e., attributes) that best characterize the user or system-usage patterns so that intrusive behavior will be perceived, whereas nonintrusive activities will not be classified as anomalous.

Even at a certain level of monitoring granularity, one often faces a large number of features representing the monitored object's behavior. For instance, a network connection can be characterized with numerous attributes, including basic features such as source and destination IPs, ports and protocols, and many other secondary attributes. Meanwhile, an audit trail usually consists of sequences of categorical symbols generated from a large discrete alphabet. A program may issue several hundred unique system calls. Similarly, a UNIX user's command history can contain hundreds of different commands or shell scripts. The high dimensionality of the data or the large alphabet size gives rise to a large hypothesis search space. This, in turn, not only increases the complexity of the problem of learning normal behavior, but also can lead to large classification errors. Therefore, selecting relevant features and eliminating redundant features is vital to the effectiveness of the machine learning technique employed. Similar to many other machine learning applications, anomaly detection often heavily relies on domain knowledge to manually select relevant features. Nevertheless, a few studies have attempted to automate the process of feature selection. For example, Lee et al. [4] calculated frequent patterns of the system audit data (e.g., association rules and frequent episodes of the network connection records) and then constructed predictive features based on the frequent patterns. Mukkamala and Sung [10] took a wrapper approach to feature selection; that is, features were ranked based on the performance of an SVM classifier.

5.5.2 Skewed Class Distribution

There is a fundamental asymmetry in anomaly detection problems: normal activity is common, and intrusive activity is rare. One often faces a training set consisting of a handful of attack examples and plenty of normal examples, or no attack example at all. This presents a difficult challenge to machine learning methods. Because of the lack of attack examples, discriminative approaches may not be able to generate a meaningful and general hypothesis of the intrusive behavior. Therefore, a generative approach, aiming to define the perimeter of normal with normal examples only, can play a significant role in intrusion detection.

A related issue is the base-rate fallacy in intrusion detection [27]. Because intrusive activity is relatively rare, to achieve substantial values for the intrusion detection rate — i.e., the Bayesian probability *P(Intrusion | Alarm)* — we have to achieve a very low false-positive rate. This imposes a high classification accuracy requirement on IDSs.

5.5.3 Distance Metrics

Many anomaly detection methods, including immunology-based methods, instance-based learning methods, and clustering techniques, rely on a distance measure in the event space. The degree of suspicion attached to an instance is directly proportional to the distance of the instance from, for example, the nearest normal training examples or the center of the nearest normal clusters. Common distance metrics include Euclidean distance, Manhattan distance, Hamming distance, the vector cosine measure, and so on. A major difficulty is in the construction of a distance measure that reflects a useful metric of similarity. A poor choice of distance metrics may result in meaningless classifications. However, no rationale, except empirical analysis, seems to exist in choosing distance metrics. For example, in one study, the *k*-nearest neighbor (KNN) classifier with a modified cosine metric gave far superior results when compared with the results obtained from the standard cosine metric [13,28] with comparable computational effort. Furthermore, KNN with the modified cosine metric performed competitively with SVM, a much more complex algorithm than KNN. Does the modified cosine metric capture the true nature of the problem any better than the ordinary cosine metric? Indeed, this result is rather intriguing and surprising because SVM to date provides the best combination of computational efficiency and guaranteed accuracy.

5.5.4 Window Size for Sequential Data

To learn temporal or sequential patterns of the audit data stream, a common practice is to slide a window of a certain size across the audit trace and determine whether the short sequence within the sliding window is anomalous or not. Sequences of the same length (i.e., the window size) are used for training and testing. A fundamental question is how to determine the appropriate window size for anomaly detection in a systematic way instead of an ad hoc trial-and-error fashion. Lee and Xiang [29] proposed to use several information-theoretic measures to describe the regularity of an audit dataset and determine the best sliding-window size based on the conditional entropy and information cost measures. However, Tan and Maxion [30] demonstrated that for *stide*, a simple instance-based detector that merely remembers previous training sequences (no generalization capability), the appropriate window size was influenced by the length of minimum foreign sequence in the data instead of the conditional entropy. For a general learning method for anomaly detection, choosing the optimum window size awaits further investigation.

5.5.5 IDS Performance Evaluation

It is important to quantitatively evaluate the technical performance of an IDS. Security analysts who review the output of an IDS would like to know the likelihood of an attack occurring when an alarm is issued. Moreover, acquisition managers need to compare the strengths and weaknesses of currently available IDS products and select the right system.

Quantitatively measurable IDS characteristics include the coverage (i.e., the attacks that an IDS can detect under ideal conditions), probability of false alarms, probability of detection, resistance to attacks directed at the IDS, ability to handle high-bandwidth traffic, ability to correlate events, and so on [31]. Among these measurements, probability of false alarms (i.e., false-positive rate) and probability of detection (also known as hit rate) are two of the most important characteristics of IDS and thus have gained the most attention. The receiver operating characteristic (ROC) analysis, a method from signal detection theory, is usually used to depict the trade-off between probability of false alarms and probability of intrusion detection. It can be obtained by varying the detection threshold. A variation of ROC curves, AMOC, was proposed to reflect the cost of false alarms [1].

Figure 5.2 presents two ROC curves produced by two systems in an IDS test. The x axis shows the percentage of false alarms produced during a test, and the y axis shows the corresponding percentage of detected attacks. Note that an IDS can be operated at any given point on the ROC curve. If the detection threshold of the IDS is set so low that any activity is deemed normal, the corresponding operational point is the origin (i.e., left bottom corner) of the ROC graph. Conversely, if any activity causes an alarm because of the high detection threshold, both the percentage of false alarms and the percentage of detected attacks will be 1, which corresponds to the top right corner of the graph. The line $y = x$ in Figure 5.2 represents an IDS that randomly assigns normal or intrusive (with 50-percent

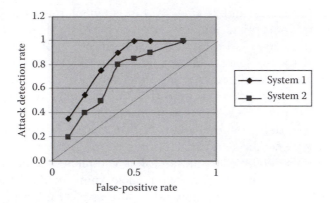

Figure 5.2   Receiver operating characteristic (ROC) curves.

probability each) for every instance. All systems should perform better than such a random-guessing–based system and appear above the $y = x$ line in the ROC graph. In this example, system 1 performs better than system 2 in that it provides higher intrusion detection probability at any given false-positive rate.

An interesting aspect of ROC curves is that there is an optimum operating point for an IDS, given a particular environment being monitored. However, to determine it, one must know the cost of a false alarm, the value of a correct detection, and the prior probabilities of normal and attack events [32].

IDS performance can be evaluated by injecting attacks into a stream of real background activity or generating background on a simulated network. It is not yet clear which approach is more effective for testing IDSs because each has unique advantages and disadvantages. For example, using real network traffic or host audit logs allows one to effectively evaluate the intrusion detection rate because the background is real, and it contains all of the anomalies and subtleties. However, it is difficult to use this technique to determine false-positive rates (and ROC curves) as it is virtually impossible to guarantee the identification of all attacks that naturally occurred in the background (unless a thorough manual analysis is performed with the real background). Other drawbacks include unrepeatability and privacy issues. In contrast, a test-bed network can provide a simulated background free of attacks and thus enable accurate measurement of false-alarm rates and intrusion detection rates. However, the difficulty of this approach lies in generating diverse background traffic and in validating it. Regardless of the approach used, a major challenge of IDS evaluation is the shortage of attack examples because of the difficulty of collecting attack scripts and other reasons.

5.5.6 Cost-Effectiveness of IDS

Cost-effectiveness is another important aspect of IDSs. An effective IDS should provide light-weighted detection of intrusions and keep up with the throughput of the audit data stream that it monitors so that intrusions can be responded to in a timely manner. A trade-off has to be made among not only the cost of damage caused by an intrusion and the cost of manual or automatic response, but also the development cost and operational cost that measures constraints on time and computing resources. Lee et al. [33] proposed to use cost-sensitive machine learning techniques that can automatically construct detection models optimized for overall cost metrics. More recently, Liao and Vemuri [34] took a game-theoretic approach to model the strategic interaction between IDS and attackers and analyze the cost-effectiveness of IDS. The main difficulty is in quantifying the site-specific cost factors.

5.6 Open Questions and Future Directions

Although a great deal of research has been done in intrusion detection, current IDSs are still plagued by excessive false alarms and poor attack detection accuracy (especially against novel attacks and insider threat). Many fundamental questions remain unanswered, and the complexity of intrusion detection problems of today presents new research challenges in the field of machine learning.

5.6.1 Theoretical Analysis

Similar to many other fields, intrusion detection has been based on a combination of intuition and ad hoc techniques. There is a lack of underlying theoretic analysis in this field.

First of all, anomaly detection assumes that intrusive activities are distinct from normal activities, and deviations from normal behaviors by users or programs are indications of intrusions. Although the assumption is intuitively appealing, there has been little theoretical support. Therefore, there is a need to address the soundness and completeness of anomaly detection methods. In other words, what types of intrusions can and cannot be detected by anomaly detection? What are the powers and limitations of a machine learning–based anomaly detection system? Is it possible to reduce the false-positive rate to, for example, 1 percent, while the attack detection rate is still high? Is it possible to distinguish anomalies related to intrusions from those related to other factors? Despite a few previous attempts [35,36], these questions remain largely open.

Second, for a particular environment, what features, metrics, and machine learning techniques provide the best performance to model the normal behavior of the environment? How many training examples are necessary to achieve the expected false-positive rate? Computational learning theory (COLT), the theoretical underpinning of machine learning, might shed light on these fundamental questions.

Last, an equally important issue is to develop some theoretical understanding of intrusive behaviors. With an abstract view of various intrusions, IDSs can better discriminate intrusive behaviors from normal and detect classes of attacks instead of individual instances.

5.6.2 Learning for Understanding and Planning

Intrusion prevention, detection, and response are three general tasks of security officers. Once an intrusion is detected, proper response should be evoked to recover and prevent future attacks. The current state-of-the-art of IDSs, mostly based on classification techniques, provides little insight on the attacker's intent (especially in the case of sophisticated attacks). Therefore, intrusion response heavily relies on manual forensic analysis. Machine learning techniques that aim to interpret observations, create situation awareness, and plan automated response can play a significant role in the progress of the IDS field.

5.6.3 Ensemble Learning

One method of improving the intrusion detection accuracy is to combine the outputs of different classifiers, a strategy known as *ensemble learning*. In practice, there are many different types of intrusions, and different methods are needed to detect them using multiple and diverse sensors. Combining the evidence from multiple classifiers can effectively improve the accuracy and trustworthiness of IDSs. There are various ways of constructing an ensemble of classifiers. For example, one can divide the original training dataset into subsets, and different classifiers are trained with each subset. This strategy works well when the hypothesis learned is fairly sensitive to small changes in training data. Another general approach is to manipulate the input features in a similar fashion. Furthermore, it is possible to build an ensemble of classifiers, each using a different learning algorithm. Learning algorithms using radically different principles probably will produce very different classifiers. The key is to correlate the outputs of these classifiers (for example, using the majority voting rule).

5.6.4 Online, Adaptive Learning

Virtually all machine learning research assumes that the training sample is drawn from a stationary data source — the distribution of the data points and the phenomena to be learned are not changing with time. In a practical environment, however, system and network behaviors as well as user activities can change for bona fide reasons. For example, the amount of traffic continues to rise. System and application programs are updated frequently. The continually changing normal behavior, a problem known as *concept drift,* presents a significant challenge in anomaly detection. An effective anomaly detection system should be capable of adapting to normal behavior changes while still recognizing anomalous activities. Otherwise, large amounts of false alarms would be generated if the model fails to change adaptively to accommodate the new patterns. A seemingly plausible solution is to update the training corpus with each new batch of audit data and rebuild the normal behavior model. However, for a continuously operating IDS, new data is available at every instant. It may not have the luxury of frequent retraining. Furthermore, it is not computationally feasible for most existing methods (e.g., rule-based methods and neural nets) because a model is expensive to generate and not suitable for incremental learning. In addition, selecting appropriate training instances without contaminating the normal behavior profile is a nontrivial issue.

The key to this difficult problem is online and adaptive learning, one of the active areas of machine learning research. In Section 5.7, we present an adaptive intrusion detection framework with the use of evolving connectionist systems.

5.7 Illustrative Example: Adaptive Anomaly Detection

In this section, we present an adaptive anomaly detection framework to address the concept drift issue. It is applicable to both host-based and network-based intrusion detection. Our framework employs unsupervised evolving connectionist systems to learn system, network, or user behavior in an online, adaptive fashion without *a priori* knowledge of the underlying data distributions. Adaptive learning and evolving connectionist systems are an active area of machine learning research. Evolving connectionist systems are artificial neural networks that resemble the human cognitive information-processing models. Because of their self-organizing and adaptive nature, they provide powerful tools for modeling evolving processes and knowledge discovery [37].

Our adaptive anomaly detection framework performs a one-pass clustering of the input data stream that represents a monitored subject's behavior patterns. Each new incoming instance is assigned to one of the three states: *normal, uncertain,* and *anomalous.* Two different alarm levels are defined to reduce the risk of false alarming. We evaluated our adaptive anomaly detection systems, based on the fuzzy adaptive resonance theory (Fuzzy ART) [38] and evolving fuzzy neural networks (EFuNN) [39], on the KDD Cup 1999 network data. Our experiments show that both evolving connectionist systems are able to adapt to network normal behavior changes and at the same time detect anomalous activities. Compared to SVM-based static learning, our adaptive anomaly detection systems significantly reduced the false-alarm rate.

5.7.1 Adaptive Anomaly Detection Framework

In addressing the problem of adaptive anomaly detection, two fundamental questions arise: (1) How do we generate a model or profile that can concisely describe a subject's normal behavior, and more importantly, can it be updated efficiently to accommodate new behavior patterns? (2) How do we select instances to update the model without introducing noise and incorporating abnormal patterns as normal? Our adaptive anomaly detection framework addresses these issues through the use of online unsupervised learning methods, under the assumption that normal instances cluster together in the input space, whereas the anomalous activities correspond to outliers that lie in sparse regions of the input space. Our framework is general in that the underlying clustering method can be any online unsupervised evolving connectionist system, and it can be used for different types of audit data. Without loss of generality, we assume that the audit data that is continuously fed into the adaptive anomaly detection system has been transformed into a stream of input vectors after preprocessing, the input features describing the monitored subject's behavior. The evolving connectionist systems are designed for modeling evolving processes. They operate continuously in time and adapt their structure and functionality through a continuous interaction with the environment. They are stable enough to retain patterns learned from previously observed data while being flexible enough to learn new patterns from new incoming data. They can learn in unsupervised, supervised, or reinforcement learning modes. The online unsupervised evolving connectionist systems provide one-pass clustering of an input data stream, there being no predefined number of different clusters that the data belongs to.

A simplified diagram of an evolving connectionist system for online unsupervised learning is given in Figure 5.3(a). Some systems such as EFuNN may have an additional fuzzy input layer, shown in Figure 5.3(b), which represents the fuzzy quantization of the original inputs with the

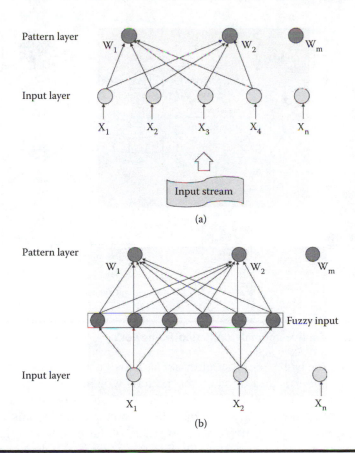

Figure 5.3 **(a) A simplified diagram of an evolving connectionist system for unsupervised learning. The system has n input nodes and m pattern nodes. There is a connection from each input node to every pattern node. Some connections are not shown in the figure. (b) An evolving connectionist system that has an additional fuzzy input layer. The task of the fuzzy input nodes is to transfer the input values into membership degrees.**

use of membership functions. A typical unsupervised evolving connectionist system consists of two layers of nodes: an *input* layer that reads the input vectors into the system continuously, and a *pattern* layer (or cluster layer) representing previously learned patterns. Each pattern node corresponds to a cluster in the input space. Each cluster, in turn, is represented by a weight vector. Then the subject's normal behavior profile is conveniently described as a set of weight vectors that represent the clustering of the previous audit data.

A distance measure has to be defined to measure the mismatch between a new instance (i.e., a new input vector) and existing patterns. Based on

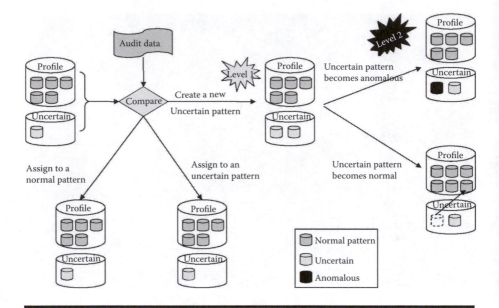

Figure 5.4   Adaptive anomaly detection framework.

the distance measure, the system either assigns an input vector to one of the existing patterns and updates the pattern weight vector to accommodate the new input, or otherwise creates a new pattern node for the input. The details of clustering vary with different evolving connectionist systems.

As described earlier, to reduce the risk of false alarms (classifying normal instances as abnormal), we define three states of behavior patterns (i.e., the pattern nodes of the evolving connectionist system): normal, uncertain, and anomalous. Accordingly, each instance is labeled as either *normal, uncertain,* or *anomalous.* In addition, the alarm is differentiated into two levels: *level-1 alarm* and *level-2 alarm*, representing different degrees of anomaly.

As illustrated in Figure 5.4, a new instance is assigned to one of the existing normal patterns and labeled *normal* if the similarity between the input vector and the normal pattern is above a threshold (the *vigilance* parameter). Otherwise, it is *uncertain*. The *uncertain* instance is either assigned to one of the existing *uncertain* patterns if it is close enough to that *uncertain* pattern, or becomes the only member of a new *uncertain* pattern. A level-1 alarm is triggered whenever a new *uncertain* pattern is created, as the new instance is different from all the learned patterns and thus deserves special attention. At this point, some preliminary security measures need to be taken. However, one cannot draw a final conclusion yet. The new instance can be truly anomalous or merely the beginning of a new normal behavior pattern, which will be determined by the subsequent instances. After the processing of a certain number (the N_{watch} parameter) of the subsequent instances in the same manner, if the number of members of an *uncertain* pattern reaches a threshold value (the Min_{count} parameter), the *uncertain* pattern becomes a *normal* pattern, and the labels of all its members are changed from *uncertain* to *normal*.

This indicates that a new behavior pattern has been developed and incorporated into the subject's normal behavior profile as enough instances have shown the same pattern. On the other hand, after N_{watch} subsequent instances, any *uncertain* pattern with less than Min_{count} members will be destroyed, and all its members are labeled *anomalous*. This will make sure that anomalous patterns, corresponding to the sparse regions in the input space, will not be included in the normal profile. A level-2 alarm is issued when an instance is labeled *anomalous*, and further response actions are expected.

The main tunable parameters of an adaptive anomaly detection system are summarized as follows:

- *Vigilance* ρ. This threshold controls the degree of mismatch between new instances and existing patterns that the system can tolerate.
- *Learning rate* β. It determines how fast the system should adapt to a new instance when it is assigned to a pattern.
- N_{watch}. It is the period that the system will wait before making a decision on a newly created *uncertain* pattern.
- Min_{count}. It is the minimum number of members that an *uncertain* pattern should have in order to be recognized as a *normal* pattern.

Our framework does not require *a priori* knowledge of the number of input features. When a new input feature is presented, the system simply adds a new input node to the input layer and connections from this newly created input node to the existing pattern nodes. This can be very important when the features that describe a subject's behavior grow over time and cannot be foreseen in a dynamic environment. Similarly, accommodation of a new pattern is efficiently realized by creating a new pattern node and adding connections from input nodes to this new pattern node. The rest of the structure remains the same.

With the framework, the learned normal profile is expressed as a set of weight vectors representing the coordinates of the cluster centers in the input space. These weight vectors can be interpreted as a knowledge presentation that can be used to describe the subject's behavior patterns and, thus, they can facilitate understanding of the subject's behavior. The weight vectors are stored in the long-term memory of the connectionist systems. Because new instances are compared to all previously learned patterns, recurring activities would be recognized easily.

Although the underlying clustering method of the adaptive anomaly detection framework can be any unsupervised evolving connectionist system, Fuzzy ART and the unsupervised learning version of EFuNN are adapted for anomaly detection in this paper. Both of them are conceptually simple and computationally fast. Furthermore, they cope well with fuzzy data, and the fuzzy distance measures help to smooth the abrupt separation of normality and abnormality of a subject's behavior. The details on Fuzzy ART and EFuNN can be seen in [38,39]. Note that the original EFuNN has a five-layer structure. Here, we only use its first three layers for unsupervised learning. In addition, the *vigilance* parameter was originally named *sensitivity threshold*.

5.7.2 Experiments

In this section, we describe some experiments. The emphasis of the experiments is on the understanding of how Fuzzy ART–based and EFuNN-based adaptive anomaly detection systems work in practice. One objective of our experiments is to observe the influence of variability of the tunable parameters on the performance of an anomaly detection system. Another objective of the experiments is to compare SVM-based static learning and evolving connectionist system–based adaptive learning.

5.7.2.1 Static Learning via SVMs

SVM is a relatively new and state-of-the-art classification method. It is based on the so-called *structural risk minimization principle,* which minimizes an upper bound on the generalization error. The method performs a mapping from the input space to a higher-dimensional feature space through the use of a kernel function. It separates the data in the feature space by means of a maximum-margin hyperplane. The SVM paradigm has been extended to the one-class problem. The origin of the coordinate system, after transforming the feature via a kernel, is treated as the only member of the second class. Training an SVM is equivalent to solving a linearly constrained quadratic programming problem.

In our experiments, we used SVM to demonstrate the weakness of static learning and the importance of adaptive learning. SVM was employed to learn a model (i.e., support vectors) that fits the training dataset. The model was then tested on the testing dataset without any update (thus, it is static learning). SVM is optimum when the data is independent and identically distributed (iid). If there was a concept drift between the training dataset and the testing dataset, SVM would generate classification errors. Adaptive learning can adapt to concept changes incrementally and learn new patterns when new testing instances are presented to the learning system. Therefore, the classification accuracy is improved.

5.7.2.2 Cost Function

To facilitate performance comparison among different methods, we used the cost function:

$$\text{Cost} = (1\text{-hit rate}) + \gamma \times \text{false-positive rate}$$

where the hit rate is the rate of detected intrusions, the false-positive rate is the probability that a normal instance is classified as *anomalous,* and the parameter represents the cost difference between a false alarm and a miss. Here, we set the value to 6. The lower the cost, the better the performance an IDS has.

5.7.2.3 Network Intrusion Detection

We conducted a series of experiments on a subset of the dataset KDD Cup 1999 [39] prepared for network intrusion detection. Many methods have been tested with this popular dataset for supervised intrusion detection. The data labels were usually used for training the learning systems. Our evolving connectionist systems, however, do not rely on the data labels. They build network connection patterns incrementally in an online, unsupervised learning mode.

The 1999 KDD Cup network traffic data is connection based. Each data record, described by 7 symbolic attributes and 34 continuous attributes, corresponds to a TCP/IP connection between two IP addresses. In addition, a label is provided, indicating whether the record is normal or it belongs to one of the four attack types (Probe, DoS, U2R, and R2L). The symbolic attributes that have two possible values (e.g., *logged in*) were represented by a binary entry with the value of 0 or 1. For symbolic attributes that have more than two possible categorical values, we used multiple entries to encode them in the vector representation, one entry for each possible value. The entry corresponding to the category value has a value of 1 while the other entries are set to 0. The attribute *service* has 41 types, and we further classified them into {*http, smtp, ftp, ftp data, and others*} to reduce the vector dimensions. The resulting feature vectors have a total of 57 dimensions.

Because different continuous attributes were measured on very different scales, the effect of some attributes might be completely dwarfed by others that have larger scales. Therefore, we scaled the attributes to the range of [0, 1] by calculating:

Table 5.2   Numbers of Normal and Attack Examples in Experiment 1 and Experiment 2

Experiment 1		Experiment 2		
Normal	Attacks	Training Normal	Testing Normal	Attacks
97,277	998	38,910	58,367	580

$$X_i = \frac{V_i - \min(V_i)}{\max(V_i) - \min(V_i)}$$

where V_i is the actual value of attribute i, and the maximum and minimum are taken over the whole dataset. However, we are aware that this scaling technique would not work if the maximum and minimum values are not known *a priori*.

We formed a subset of the original dataset consisting of 97,277 normal connections and 9,199 attacks by randomly sampling. We then conducted two experiments with this subset. The first experiment (Experiment 1) was designed to test our evolving connectionist systems. In the data stream of Experiment 1, the attack examples randomly drawn from the 9,199 attacks were inserted into the 97,277 normal examples with a 1-percent probability. Fuzzy ART and EFuNN were employed to model the network connections on the fly from an empty set of normal patterns and detect the intrusions in the data stream. For the second experiment (Experiment 2), the training dataset and testing dataset were formed to compare the performance between static learning and adaptive learning. The first 40 percent of the 97,277 normal examples was used for training, and the rest for testing. The testing dataset also included attacks interspersed into the normal examples with the probability of 1 percent. The model learned from the training examples was applied to the testing dataset. The model remained unchanged during the testing process for static learning, whereas it was updated continuously for adaptive learning methods. Table 5.2 lists the numbers of normal and attack examples in Experiment 1 and Experiment 2.

5.7.2.3.1 Effectiveness of Varying Vigilance

The *vigilance* parameter controls the degree of mismatch between new instances and previously learned patterns. The greater the value of ρ, the more similar the instances ought to be for them to be assigned to a pattern. We studied the effect of varying ρ while keeping the values of other parameters fixed. Table 5.3 presents the results when values were varied

Table 5.3   The Performance (False-Positive Rate, Hit Rate, and Cost) of Fuzzy ART and EFuNN with the Experiment 1 Data Stream

	Fuzzy ART			EFuNN		
ρ	False-Positive Rate (Percentage)	Hit Rate (Percentage)	Cost	False-Positive Rate (Percentage)	Hit Rate (Percentage)	Cost
0.90	1.82	79.8	0.311	0.259	33.4	0.682
0.91	2.07	73.6	0.389	0.340	37.2	0.649
0.92	2.06	66.3	0.460	0.421	39.3	0.632
0.93	**2.35**	**86.3**	**0.278**	0.573	66.4	0.370
0.94	2.31	66.9	0.469	0.823	57.4	0.475
0.95	3.13	66.6	0.521	1.29	74.9	0.328
0.96	3.33	64.4	0.556	**1.97**	**90.0**	**0.218**
0.97	4.42	89.7	0.369	3.30	91.7	0.281
0.98	5.81	93.2	0.417	6.99	98.7	0.433
0.99	8.84	98.1	0.549	18.3	99.6	1.10

Note: Results illustrate the impact of varying vigilance ρ on performance.

from 0.9 to 0.99 with the data stream of Experiment 1. The learning rate parameter was set to 0.1, N_{watch} was 8, and Min_{count} was 4. The false-positive rate was calculated as the percentage of normal instances that were labeled *anomalous* out of the 97,277 normal examples. Similarly, the hit rate was the percentage of detected attacks (i.e., labeled *anomalous*) out of the 998 attacks.

The results show that the false-positive rate increases monotonically as the vigilance threshold is raised. This is because of the fact that more normal instances are classified as *uncertain* and then *anomalous* when the value of ρ increases. Meanwhile, the hit rate oscillates at lower values and then approaches to 100 percent as ρ is raised nearer to 1.0. The cost of Fuzzy ART reaches the lowest value at $\rho = 0.93$ with a false-positive rate of 2.35 percent and hit rate of 86.3 percent. For EFuNN, the lowest cost is obtained at $\rho = 0.96$ while the hit rate is 90 percent and the false-positive rate is as low as 1.97 percent.

5.7.2.3.2 Effectiveness of Varying Learning Rate β

The learning rate parameter β determines how fast the system should adapt to new instances to accommodate them. A higher value of β places more

Table 5.4   The Performance of Fuzzy ART and EFuNN with the Experiment 1 Data Stream

	Fuzzy ART			EFuNN		
β	False-Positive Rate (Percentage)	Hit Rate (Percentage)	Cost	False-Positive Rate (Percentage)	Hit Rate (Percentage)	Cost
0.001	0.256	24.9	0.766	2.34	76.4	0.377
0.01	0.675	54.7	0.493	2.20	88.3	0.249
0.1	**2.35**	**86.3**	**0.278**	**1.97**	**90.0**	**0.218**
0.3	3.17	68.6	0.504	1.69	77.3	0.329
0.5	3.44	71.0	0.496	1.64	72.7	0.371
0.7	3.58	70.1	0.513	1.60	77.4	0.322
0.9	3.53	79.0	0.369	1.47	76.1	0.327
1.0	3.23	67.8	0.515	1.55	74.9	0.343

Note: Results illustrate the impact of varying learning rate β on performance.

weight on the new instance when it is assigned to a pattern and less weight on existing members of the pattern. We evaluated the performance of Fuzzy ART and EFuNN with the Experiment 1 data stream by widely varying the learning rate β. The results are described in Table 5.4. The *vigilance* parameter was set to 0.93 for Fuzzy ART and 0.96 for EFuNN because they provided the lowest cost when the effectiveness of varying vigilance was studied. N_{watch} was set to 8, and Min_{count} was 4.

It is interesting to note that for the Experiment 1 dataset, $\beta = 1$ appears to be the best choice for both Fuzzy ART and EFuNN in terms of the cost. Higher β values provide relatively stable false-positive rates and hit rates. For Fuzzy ART, lower β values ($\beta = 0.01$ or 0.001) cause much lower false-positive rates as well as lower hit rates. For EFuNN, however, the false-positive rate gets even higher at lower β values, whereas the hit rate declines slightly.

5.7.2.3.3 Effectiveness of Varying N_{watch} and Min_{count}

N_{watch} and Min_{count} are two other important parameters for an adaptive anomaly detection system. N_{watch} represents the delay the system will experience before it evaluates a newly created *uncertain* pattern. If it is too long, there is a risk that an anomalous instance cannot be handled in a timely manner. If it is too short, a large amount of false alarms may be

**Table 5.5   The Performance of Fuzzy ART and EFuNN
with the Experiment 1 Data Stream**

N_{watch}	Min_{count}	*Fuzzy ART*			*EFuNN*		
		False-Positive Rate	*Hit Rate*	*Cost*	*False-Positive Rate*	*Hit Rate*	*Cost*
4	2	1.71	74.2	0.360	**1.53**	**88.9**	**0.203**
8	4	**2.35**	**86.3**	**0.278**	1.97	90.0	0.218
12	4	1.77	77.1	0.335	1.65	89.4	0.205
12	6	4.03	70.0	0.542	3.66	92.9	0.291
12	8	6.04	95.4	0.408	5.04	95.7	0.345
16	6	2.97	61.1	0.567	2.95	92.9	0.248
16	8	4.95	72.0	0.577	4.19	94.3	0.309
16	10	6.77	84.2	0.564	6.41	96.3	0.422

Note: Results illustrate the impact of varying N_{watch} and Min_{count} on performance.

generated. Min_{count} is the minimum number of members that an *uncertain* pattern ought to have before it is changed to *normal*. We empirically studied the effect of varying N_{watch} and Min_{count} on the performance of Fuzzy ART and EFuNN. Different values of N_{watch} and $Minc_{ount}$ and the corresponding results are described in Table 5.5. The *vigilance* parameter was set to 0.93 for Fuzzy ART and 0.96 for EFuNN, and the *learning rate* was 0.1 for both.

The results show that N_{watch} = 8 and Min_{count} = 4 is a better choice than others for Fuzzy ART as it provides the lowest cost. Similarly, N_{watch} = 4 and Min_{count} = 2 gives the best performance for EFuNN. The hit rate of EFuNN is higher and more stable than that of Fuzzy ART as the values of N_{watch} and Min_{count} change. It indicates that, given the distance measure of EFuNN, the attacks are more distinguishable among the normal instances.

5.7.2.3.3 Static Learning versus Adaptive Learning

We compared Fuzzy ART and EFuNN with SVM using the Experiment 2 datasets. During the training process, Fuzzy ART and EFuNN assumed that every pattern was normal and that no instance was discarded. During the testing process, however, the task of Fuzzy ART and EFuNN became twofold: evolving their structure to accommodate new patterns and detecting anomalous instances. For simplicity, we set N_{watch} to 8 and Min_{count} to

Table 5.6   The Performance of SVM, Fuzzy ART, and EFuNN in Experiment 2

	SVM	Fuzzy ART	EFuNN
ρ		0.93	0.96
β		0.2	0.01
False-positive rate (percentage)	12.4	2.98	0.884
Hit rate (percentage)	90.7	94.0	85.0
Cost	0.836	0.239	0.203

4. We then varied the *vigilance* parameter ρ's value from 0.9 to 0.99 and the learning rate β's value from 0.01 to 0.9. The parameter settings that provide the lowest cost for Fuzzy ART and EFuNN are shown in Table 5.6. The SVM model learned from the one-class training dataset was applied to the testing dataset. Common types of kernel functions used in SVM include linear, radial-basis, and polynomial functions. In our experiments, we found that the radial-basis kernel performed better than other kernel functions for one-class learning.

Table 5.5 compares the performance of SVM, Fuzzy ART, and EFuNN. SVM was able to detect 90 percent of the attacks in the testing dataset. However, the false-positive rate was as high as 12.4 percent, which indicates the presence of concept drift between the training dataset and the testing dataset. Compared to SVM, Fuzzy ART and EFuNN generated significantly fewer false alarms. Fuzzy ART was the best in terms of hit rate, whereas EFuNN gave the lowest cost.

5.7.2.4 Discussion

Our experiments have shown that our adaptive anomaly detection systems are able to adapt to normal behavior changes while still recognizing anomalous activities. Compared to the SVM-based static learning, the adaptive anomaly detection methods can significantly reduce the false-positive rate.

Our approach assumes that normal instances vastly outnumber anomalies, and the anomalous activities appear as outliers in the data. This approach would miss the attacks or masquerades if the underlying assumptions do not hold. For example, some DoS attacks would not be identified by our adaptive anomaly detection systems. Nevertheless, our anomaly detection framework can be easily extended to incorporate signature detection. Previously learned patterns can be labeled in such a way that certain patterns may generate an alert no matter how frequently they are observed, whereas other patterns do not trigger an alarm even if they are rarely seen.

With our adaptive anomaly detection framework, it is possible that one can deliberately cover his or her malicious activities by slowly changing his or her behavior patterns without triggering a level-2 alarm. However, a level-1 alarm is issued whenever a new pattern is formed. It is then the security officer's responsibility to identify the user's intent, to distinguish malicious from benign anomalies.

To make an adaptive anomaly detection system scalable, it might be necessary to prune or aggregate pattern nodes as the system evolves, which is a significant issue for our future work. Other issues of our future work include exploring automated determination of the parameters and comparing more evolving connectionist systems, such as evolving self-organizing maps.

5.8 Summary

Over the past two decades, machine learning has played a significant role in building anomaly detection models for detecting previously unknown attacks. Yet, the current state-of-the-art of IDSs is still primitive, and much remains to be explored. In this chapter, we examined the fundamental issues involved in anomaly detection and outlined its future directions. With the ever-increasing connectivity and accessibility of computer systems, machine learning will continue to make its contribution to the development of next-generation IDSs.

References

1. Fawcett, T. and Provost, F. Activity monitoring: Noticing interesting changes in behavior. In *Proc. 5th ACM SIGKDD Int. Conf. Knowledge Discovery and Data Mining (KDD)*, 53, 1999.
2. Bishop, M. *Computer Security: Art and Science*. Pearson Education, 2003.
3. Dietterich, T. and Langley, P. Machine Learning for Cognitive Networks: Technology Assessment and Research Challenges, Draft of May 11, 2003. http://web.engr.oregonstate.edu/~tgd/kp/dl-report.pdf.
4. Lee, W. and Stolfo, S.J. A framework for constructing features and models for intrusion detection systems. *ACM Trans. Information and System Security (TISSEC)*, 3, 227, 2000.
5. Warrender, C., Forrest, S., and Pearlmutter, B. Detecting intrusions using system calls: alternative data models. In *Proc. IEEE Symp. Security and Privacy*, Oakland, CA, 1999.
6. Teng, H.S., Chen, K., and Lu, S.C. Adaptive real-time anomaly detection using inductively generated sequential patterns. *Proc. IEEE Symp. Security and Privacy*. Oakland, CA, p. 278, 1990.

7. Forrest, S. et al., A sense of self for Unix processes. In *Proc. IEEE Symp. Security and Privacy*, Oakland, CA, 120, 1996.
8. Esponda, F., Forrest, S. and Helman, P. Positive and negative detection, *IEEE Trans. Systems, Man, and Cybernetics*, 34(1), 357, 2004.
9. Ghosh, A.K. and Schwartzbard, A. A study in using neural networks for anomaly and misuse detection. In *Proc. 8th USENIX Security Symp.*, 1999.
10. Mukkamala, S. and Sung, A.H. Identifying significant features for network forensic analysis using artificial intelligent techniques. *Int. J. Digital Evidence*, 4, 1, 2003.
11. Hu, W., Liao, Y. and Vemuri, V.R. Robust support vector machines for anomaly detection in computer security. In *Proc. Int. Conf. Machine Learning and Applications*. Los Angeles, CA, 2003.
12. Lane, T. and Brodley, C.E. Temporal sequence learning and data reduction for anomaly detection. *ACM Transactions on Information and System Security (TISSEC)*, 2, 295, 1999.
13. Liao, Y. and Vemuri, V.R. Use of *k*-nearest neighbor classifier for intrusion detection, *Computers and Security*, 21, 439, 2002.
14. Eskin, E. et al. A geometric framework for unsupervised anomaly detection: Detecting intrusions in unlabeled data. In *Applications of Data Mining in Computer Security*, D. Barbara and S. Jajodia (Eds.). Kluwer, 2002.
15. Lazarevic, A. et al. A comparative study of anomaly detection schemes in network intrusion detection. In *Proc. 3rd SIAM Int. Conf. Data Mining (SDM)*, San Francisco, CA, 2003.
16. Lane, T.D. Machine Learning Techniques for the Computer Security Domain of Anomaly Detection. Ph.D. thesis, Purdue Univ., West Lafayette, IN, 2000.
17. Eskin, E. Anomaly detection over noisy data using learned probability Distributions. In *Proc. 17th Int. Conf. Machine Learning*, San Francisco, CA, 255, 2000.
18. Kruegel, C. et al. Bayesian event classification for intrusion detection. In *Proc. 19th ACSAC*, 2003.
19. Lippmann, R.P. et al. The 1999 DARPA offline intrusion detection evaluation. *Computer Networks*, 34(2), 579, 2000. DARPA Intrusion Detection datasets: http://www.ll.mit.edu/IST/ideval/data/data_index.html. KDD Cup 1999 dataset: http://kdd.ics.uci.edu/databases/kddcup99/kddcup99.html.
20. McHugh J. Testing intrusion detection systems: A critique of the 1998 and 1999 DARPA intrusion detection system evaluations as performed by Lincoln Laboratory. *ACM Trans. Information and System Security*, 3(4), 262, 2000.
21. Mahoney, M.V. and Chan, P.K. An analysis of the 1999 darpa/lincoln laboratory evaluation data for network anomaly detection. In *Proc. 6th Intl. Symp. Recent Advances in Intrusion Detection (RAID)*, Pittsburgh, PA, 220, 2003.
22. Forrest S. et al. *Sequence-Based Intrusion Detection*. Computer Immune Systems Data Sets and Software, Computer Science, The University of New Mexico. http://www.cs.unm.edu/%7Eimmsec/data-sets.htm.

23. Greenberg, S. *Using Unix: Collected traces of 168 users.* Research Report 88/333/45, Department of Computer Science, University of Calgary, Calgary, Canada, 1988.

24. Schonlau, M. et al. Computer intrusion: Detecting masqueraders. *Statistical Science,* 16(1), 58, 2001. UNIX command dataset: http://www.schon-lau.net/.

25. Maxion, R.A. and Townsend, T.N. Masquerade detection using truncated command lines. In *Proc. Int. Conf. Dependable Systems and Networks,* Washington, D.C., 219, 2002.

26. Maxion, R.A. Masquerade detection using enriched command lines. In *Proc. Int. Conf. Dependable Systems & Networks,* San Francisco, CA, 5, 2003.

27. Axelsson, S. The base-rate fallacy and the difficulty of intrusion detection. *ACM Trans. Information and System Security (TISSEC),* 3(3), 186, 2000.

28. Rawat, S. et al. Intrusion detection using text processing techniques with a binary-weighted cosine metric. *International Journal of Information Security,* Springer-Verlag, Submitted 2004.

29. Lee, W. and Xiang, D. Information-theoretic measures for anomaly detection. In *Proc. IEEE Symp. Security and Privacy,* Oakland, CA, 130, 2001.

30. Tan, K.M.C. and Maxion, R.A. Why 6? Defining the operational limit of stide, an anomaly-based intrusion detector. In *Proc. IEEE Symp. Security and Privacy,* Oakland, CA, 188, 2002.

31. Mell, P. et al. *An Overview of Issues in Testing Intrusion Detection Systems.* National Institute of Standards and Technology Interagency report 7007, June 2003. http://csrc.nist.gov/publications/nistir/nistir-7007.pdf.

32. Gaffney, J. and Ulvila, J. Evaluation of intrusion detectors: A decision theory approach. In *Proc. IEEE Symp. Security and Privacy,* Oakland, CA, 50, 2001.

33. Lee, W. et al. Toward cost-sensitive modeling for intrusion detection and response. *J. Computer Security,* 10, 5, 2002.

34. Liao, Y. and Vemuri, V.R. *Intrusion Detection and Response: A Game Theoretic Perspective.* Technical Report, Computer Science Department, University of California, Davis, 2004.

35. Helman, P. and Liepins, G., Statistical foundations of audit trail analysis for the detection of computer misuse. *IEEE Trans. Software Engineering,* 19, 9, 886, 1993.

36. Tan, K.M.C. Killourhy, K.S., and Maxion, R.A. Undermining an anomaly-based intrusion detection system using common exploits. In *Proc. 5th Int. Symp. Recent Advances in Intrusion Detection (RAID),* 2002.

37. Kasabov, N. Evolving Connectionist Systems: Methods and Applications. In *Bioinformatics, Brain Study and Intelligence Machines.* Springer-Verlag, 2002.

38. Carpenter, G.A., Grossberg, S., and Rosen, D.B. Fuzzy art: Fast stable learning and categorization of analog patterns by an adaptive resonance system. *Neural Networks,* 4, 759, 1991.

39. Kasabov, N. Evolving fuzzy neural networks for supervised/unsupervised on-line, knowledge-based learning. *IEEE Trans. Man, Machine and Cybernetics, Part B: Cybernetics,* 31(6), 902, 2001.

Chapter 6

Cyber-Security Challenges: Designing Efficient Intrusion Detection Systems and Anti-Virus Tools

Srinivas Mukkamala, Andrew Sung, and
Ajith Abraham

Several information security technologies are available today to protect information and systems against unauthorized use, duplication, alteration, destruction, and virus attacks. Intrusion detection, a key component of information security (protect, detect, and react) and network defense, provides information on successful and unsuccessful attempts to compromise information assurance (availability, integrity, and confidentiality). Intruders can broadly be categorized into two types: external intruders, who are unauthorized users of the information and systems that they attack; and internal intruders, who have permission to access information and systems, with a few restrictions. In this chapter, we first present the state-of-the-art of the evolution of intrusion detection technology and address a few intrusion detection techniques and intrusion detection system (IDS) implementations. An overview of computer attack taxonomy and computer attack demystification, along with a few detection signatures, is presented. Special emphasis is also given to the current IDS limitations. Further, we describe a few obfuscation techniques that were applied to recent viruses and used to thwart commercial-grade anti-virus tools.

6.1 Introduction to IDSs

Intrusion detection is a problem of great significance in protecting information systems security, especially in view of the worldwide increase in incidents of cyber-attacks on the critical infrastructures. Because the ability of an IDS to classify a large variety of intrusions in real-time or in near–real-time with accurate results is important. Intrusion detection, an important component of information security technology, helps in discovering, determining, and identifying unauthorized use, duplication, alteration, and destruction of information and information systems. Intrusion detection relies on the assumption that information and information systems under attack exhibit several distinguishable behavioral patterns or characteristics. Though intrusion detection technology is becoming ubiquitous in current network defense, it lacks basic definitions and mathematical understanding. Intrusion detection is subjective; each IDS has different classification and attack-labeling mechanisms. It is most common for IDSs to raise an alarm on any set of known attack behaviors. In the due course of determining whether a particular activity is normal or malicious, IDS can fail to raise alarm on an attack (false-negative) or can raise alarm on normal activity as malicious (false-positive).

The most popular way to detect intrusions has been by using the audit data generated by operating systems and by networks. Because almost all activities are logged on a system, it is possible that a manual inspection of these logs would allow intrusions to be detected. It is important to analyze the audit data even after an attack has occurred, for determining the extent of damage; this analysis helps in attack trace-back and also helps in recording the attack patterns for future prevention of such attacks. An IDS can be used to analyze audit data for such insights. This makes IDS a valuable real-time detection and prevention tool as well as a forensic analysis tool. One of the main problems with IDSs is the overhead, which can become unacceptably high. To analyze system logs, the operating system must keep information regarding all the actions performed, which invariably results in huge amounts of data, requiring disk space and CPU resources. Next, the logs must be processed and converted into a manageable format and then compared with the set of recognized misuse and attack patterns to identify possible security violations. Further, the stored patterns need to be continually updated, which would normally involve human expertise. Constructing novel attack signatures is a bit more complex as the attackers use carefully crafted packets over a period of time, making the network traffic appear to be normal.

A brief review on IDSs is given in Section 6.2. A brief introduction to computer attack taxonomy and a few common attack signatures are given in Section 6.3. Section 6.4 presents significant feature selection and three feature-ranking algorithms. Real-time data collection and feature extraction are described in Section 6.5, as well as performance evaluation of probes and DoS-attack detection. Section 6.6 describes different attacks on IDSs. In Section 6.7, we present the limitations of current anti-virus tools in detecting malware variants, with emphasis on obfuscated (polymorphic) malware and mutated (metamorphic) malware. The conclusions are given in Section 6.8.

6.2 A Review of IDSs

An *intrusion* is an activity or a sequence of activities that results in a compromise or that intends to compromise the aspects of information assurance. Intrusion detection is a security technology of great significance to critical infrastructure protection. It attempts to detect and respond to intrusions against information and information systems. IDSs that rely on audit trails (for deciding whether a particular activity is intrusive or not) compliment other security technologies (firewalls, file integrity checkers, vulnerability scanners, and anti-virus tools). IDS also provides information for forensic analysis and to detect non-repudiation activities based on the audit trails collected. An IDS that detects intrusions based on deviations from normal to abnormal state using user or systems profiles is said to perform anomaly detection. Anomaly detection tends to detect novel attacks at the expense of false-positives. Signatures are a set of actions, conditions, or activities that, when met, indicate an intrusion. IDSs that rely on signatures are defined as misuse or signature-based detection systems. Misuse detection systems tend to have higher detection rates at the expense of false-negatives.

Soft computing techniques are being widely used by the IDS community because of their generalization capabilities that help in detecting known and unknown intrusions or the attacks that have no previously described patterns. Earlier studies have utilized a rule-based approach for intrusion detection, but had difficulty in identifying new attacks or attacks that had no previously described patterns [1–4]. Lately, the emphasis is

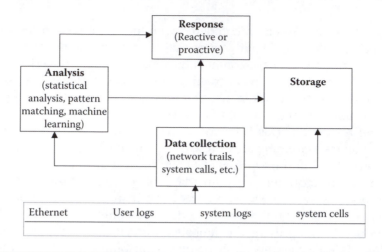

Figure 6.1   Generic intrusion detection system (IDS) model.

being shifted to learning by examples and data-mining paradigms. Neural networks have been extensively used to identify both misuse and anomalous patterns [5–9]. Recently, kernel-based methods, support vector machines, and their variants have been proposed to detect intrusions [9–13]. Several researchers have proposed data-mining techniques to identify key patterns that help in detecting intrusions [14,15]. Distributed agent technology has been proposed by a few researchers to overcome the inherent limitations of the client/server paradigm and to detect intrusions in real-time [16–19].

6.2.1 Intrusion Detection Models

Though there are several IDS implementations, most of them share the common task of detecting intrusions based on audit trails or system state. These components include the data collection module, analysis module, storage module, and response module. Most IDSs are either software packages or hardware, or a combination of both, or are part of larger systems. IDSs are built with a set of components that together define the IDS model. A generic model of IDS is illustrated in Figure 6.1.

The data collection module provides information to the rest of the system to decide whether a particular activity is intrusive or not. This module collects audit trails (user logs, network trails, system calls, etc.) for the other IDS components to make decisions. The IDS cannot function without this module. An important issue in the data collection module is audit data reduction. Instead of passing the raw data in great detail to the analysis module to decide whether a particular activity is malicious or normal, designers implement systems that eliminate audit information believed to be unimportant for intrusion analysis. The goal of audit reduction might not be limited to passing important, reduced, or summarized audit trails to the analysis module; they also help in reducing the complexity of the analysis module.

The analysis module analyzes inputs (audit trails) from the data collection module. A large chunk of IDS research is concentrated on creating novel classifiers in terms of better IDS performance (faster classification, lower false alarms, and higher accuracies). Several analysis techniques have been proposed, ranging from statistical analysis, pattern matching, machine learning, and file integrity checkers, to artificial immune system methods. The analysis module helps in automated analysis of data by reducing human intervention and speeds up the process of identifying intrusions in real-time.

The storage module provides a mechanism to store data, collected by the data collection and analysis modules, in a secure fashion. Data stored may be used for building new signatures, updating user and system profiles, forensics analysis, and identifying key audit information.

The response module can be designed in active or proactive modes. Most of the current IDSs are designed to be proactive; they set an alarm when an intrusion takes place. A significant technological advance in the field of IDSs would be to design and implement them as reactive devices rather than as a device that responds to an intrusion. Intrusion detection prevention systems (IDPSs) not only spot intrusions but also intercept and stop them.

6.2.1.1 Signature-Based or Misuse Intrusion Detection

The idea of misuse detection is to represent attacks in the form of a pattern or a signature so that the same attacks can be detected and prevented in the future [20,21]. These systems can detect many or all known attack patterns, but they are of little use for detecting naive attack methods. The main issues in misuse detection are building signatures that match possible signatures of attacks and all possible variations of the pertinent attack to avoid false-negatives, and building signatures that do not match nonintrusive activities to avoid false-positives.

6.2.1.2 Anomaly Detection

The idea here is that if we can establish a normal activity profile for a system, we can, in theory, flag all system states varying from the established profile as intrusion attempts [22–25]. However, if the set of intrusive activities is not identical to the set of anomalous activities, the situation becomes more interesting; instead of being exactly the same, we find few interesting possibilities. Anomalous activities that are not intrusive and are flagged as intrusive are called *false-positives*. Actual intrusive activities that go undetected are called *false-negatives*. This is an issue far more serious than the problem of false-positives. One of the main issues in anomaly detection systems is the selection of threshold levels such that neither of these problems is unreasonably magnified. Anomaly detection is usually computationally expensive because of the overhead associated with keeping track of and possibly updating several system profiles.

6.3 Computer Attack Taxonomy

Good attack taxonomy makes it possible to classify individual attacks into groups that share common properties. Taxonomy should be done such that classifying an attack in one category excludes all others because categories do not overlap. Good attack taxonomy should have the following characteristics:

- *Mutually exclusive:* Categories should not overlap. Classifying an attack into one category excludes it from others.
- *Exhaustive:* An attack classified into a category includes all possibilities.
- *Unambiguous:* It should be applied to all systems, irrespective of what is used or who is classifying. It should be clear and precise so that classification does not become uncertain.
- *Repeatable:* Repeated applications result in the same classification, regardless of who is classifying.
- *Acceptable:* Classifications should be logical and intuitive so that they become generally approved.

Network and computer elements identify the specific parts of software, hardware, or protocols in which the attacks take place. The view of probe and denial-of-service (DoS) characterization focuses attention on specific and tangible, as opposed to logical, elements of a system, protocol, or data packet that allows the attackers to achieve their goal of reconnaissance and denial of some service. This entity may not be the service that the attacker wishes to compromise, but instead may be the element of the network that will allow their ultimate purpose to succeed. Given that a probe and DoS attack can consist of multiple exploits, there exist multiple targets spread out over time and space. With this view of the attack space,

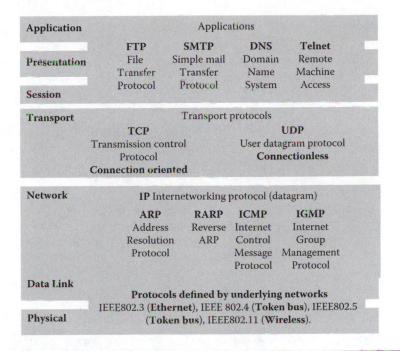

Figure 6.2 Layered approach to network and computer elements.

we recognize that attackers identify and attack real elements of networks and computers for — whether hardware, software, or firmware. Services mapped to Open Systems Interconnection (OSI) and the TCP/IP models are given in Figure 6.2. The OSI model includes two layers not often distinguished in a communication process, i.e., the presentation and session layers, whereas the TCP/IP model only utilizes four levels of granularity. OSI probe and DoS-attack views, specific to network and computer elements, are given in Figure 6.3.

6.3.1 Probing

Probing is a class of attacks in which an attacker scans a network to gather information or find known vulnerabilities. An attacker with a map of machines and services that are available on a network can use the information to cause trouble. There are different types of probes. Some of them abuse the computer's legitimate features, whereas others use social engineering techniques. This class of attacks is very common and requires very little technical expertise. Different types of probe attacks are illustrated in Table 6.1 [26,27].

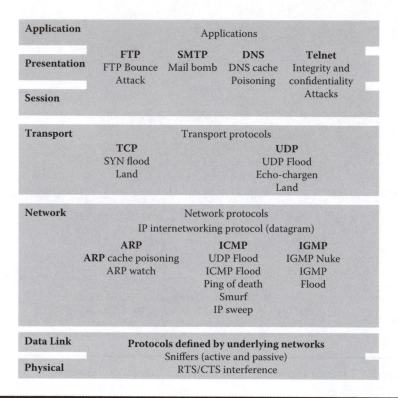

Figure 6.3   Layered attack views to network and computer elements.

- *Ipsweep:* This probing attack is one that is performed against all operating systems that use the Internet Control Message Protocol (ICMP) service, in which an attacker performs a surveillance sweep to determine which hosts are responding on a network. Information obtained from surveillance is useful in launching automated attacks or in using the vulnerable hosts as stepping stones for future distributed attacks. This attack helps the attacker identify active machines on the network and might degrade services for legitimate users. Looking for multiple ping requests that are destined for all possible machines on a network, all coming from the same host, can help detect this attack.
- *Mscan:* This is a probing tool, used to perform an attack against all operating systems that use multiple services, in which an attacker uses either DNS zone transfers or brute-force scanning of IP addresses, or both, to locate machines and look for vulnerabilities to launch future attacks. This attack helps the attacker identify known vulnerabilities on the network and the host machine. Looking for connection requests to vulnerable services from an outside

Table 6.1   Different Types of Probe Attacks

Attack Type	Service	Mechanism	Effect of the Attack
Ipsweep	ICMP	Abuse of feature	Identifies active machines
Mscan	Many	Abuse of feature	Looks for known vulnerabilities
Nmap	Many	Abuse of feature	Identifies active ports on a machine
Saint	Many	Abuse of feature	Looks for known vulnerabilities
Satan	Many	Abuse of feature	Looks for known vulnerabilities
SYN stealth	Multiple	Abuse of feature	Identifies active machines
FIN stealth	Multiple	Abuse of feature	Identifies active services
Ping sweep	ICMP	Abuse of feature	Identifies active machines
UDP scan	Multiple	Abuse of feature	Identifies active UDP services
Null scan	Multiple	Abuse of feature	Identifies active services
IP scan	Multiple	Abuse of feature	Identifies active protocols
ACK scan	Multiple	Abuse of feature	Identifies the firewall mechanism
Window scan	Multiple	Misconfiguration	Identifies active services
RCP scan	Multiple	Abuse of feature	Identifies active RPC ports

machine (NetBIOS NS, epmap, ms-sql-m, DameWare, Microsoft-ds, realsecure, domain, bind, IMAP, POP, NFS, cgi-bin, and open X servers), within a specified period of time, can help detect this attack.

- *Nmap:* This is a general-purpose probing tool used to perform network scans against all operating systems that use multiple services with user-specified time intervals; an attacker can specify which services to scan for, how much time to wait between each service, and whether the services should be scanned sequentially or in random order. This attack helps the attacker identify the running services, operating system, and known vulnerabilities on the network and the target machine. Looking for connection requests to multiple services within a specific time window can help detect this attack.

- *SAINT:* Security Administrator's Integrated Network Tool is used to gather information about remote hosts (all operating systems) that use multiple services; an attacker uses a few network services such as finger, FTP, TFTP, statd, RPC, NIS, NFS, etc. This attack helps the attacker identify the running network services, system flaws, and critical security flaws on the victim's machine. Looking for connection requests to specific network services from a machine other than an authorized machine within a specific time window can help detect this attack.

■ *Satan:* This is a probing tool used to perform scans against all operating systems that use a few network services, in which an attacker uses legitimate network services to gather information on particular vulnerabilities on the victim's machine. Looking for connection requests to specific vulnerable network services from a machine other than an authorized machine within a specific time window can help detect this attack.

■ *SYN stealth scan:* This is a probing attack performed against all operating systems that use multiple TCP services, in which an attacker performs surveillance to determine which hosts are responding to specific services on a network. Information obtained from surveillance is useful to an attacker in launching automated attacks, in using the vulnerable hosts as stepping stones for future distributed attacks, or for launching future DoS attacks. This attack helps the attacker identify active machines on the network and might degrade services for legitimate users. Looking for multiple, half-open TCP connection requests, destined for all possible machines on a network, can help detect this attack.

■ *FIN stealth scan:* This is a probing attack performed against all operating systems except Windows 95/NT when SYN scanning is not clandestine enough. In theory, closed ports are required to reply to a probe packet with an RST, whereas open ports must ignore the packets. An attacker abuses this feature to determine what services are running on a network or a host system. This scan bypasses the traditional firewalls and network filters. This attack helps the attacker identify active services and the host's operating system. Looking for connection requests to closed services within a specific time window can help detect this attack.

■ *Ping sweep:* This is a type of snooping performed against all operating systems that use ICMP, in which an attacker performs a surveillance sweep to determine which hosts are responding on a network. Information obtained from surveillance is useful to an attacker in launching automated attacks or in using the vulnerable hosts as stepping stones for future distributed attacks. This attack helps the attacker identify active machines on the network and might degrade services for legitimate users. Ping sweep, if repeated continuously or launched in a coordinated fashion, might result in a low-level DoS attack. Looking for multiple ping requests, destined for all possible machines on a network, all coming from the same host or within a specific time window from multiple hosts, can help detect this attack.

■ *UDP scan:* This is a probing attack performed against all operating systems that use UDP, in which an attacker sends 0-byte UDP packets to each UDP service on the target machine to determine which services are running on the victim's machine. This attack helps the attacker identify vulnerable UDP services on the victim's network. This information is mostly used to launch automated, distributed, and coordinated DoS attacks. Looking for multiple 0-byte UDP packets within a specific time window can help detect this attack.

■ *Null scan:* This is a probing attack performed against all operating systems except Windows 95/NT, in which an attacker turns off all flag options (FIN, URG, PUSH, etc.). This attack helps identify the victim's operating system by sending connection requests to services running on the host machine. Looking for multiple connection requests with all the flags turned off within a specific time window, destined for all possible machines on a network, can help prevent this attack.

■ *IP scan:* This is a snooping attack performed against all operating systems that use raw IP packets without any specified future protocol header. An attacker sends raw IP packets without any specific future protocol header to each specific protocol on the victim's machine. If an ICMP message stating that the protocol is unreachable is received, then it is assumed that the specific protocol is not in use. This attack helps identify all the supported protocols on a victim's network. Looking for multiple connection requests without a specific service within a specific time window can help detect this attack.

■ *ACK scan:* This is a snooping attack performed to map firewall rule sets, in which an attacker sends ACK packets (random acknowledgement/sequence numbers) to specific ports. If RST comes back, the specified port is classified as "unfiltered." If nothing comes back or an ICMP error message comes, the specified port is classified as "filtered." This attack helps identify filtered services and the type of firewall a victim's network has. Looking for random ACK packets can help detect this attack.

■ *Window scan:* This is a probing attack performed against all operating systems that use the vulnerability in TCP window–size reporting. This attack helps the attacker identify active services as well as filtered services on a victim's machine.

Table 6.2   Denial-of-Service Attacks

Attack Type	Service	Mechanism	Effect of the Attack
Apache2	HTTP	Abuse	Crashes httpd
Back	HTTP	Abuse/bug	Slows down server response
Land	HTTP	Bug	Freezes the machine
Mail bomb	N/A	Abuse	Annoyance
SYN Flood	TCP	Abuse	Denies service on one or more ports
Ping of Death	ICMP	Bug	None
Process table	TCP	Abuse	Denies new processes
Smurf	ICMP	Abuse	Slows down the network
Syslogd	Syslog	Bug	Kills Syslogd
Teardrop	N/A	Bug	Reboots the machine
Udpstrom	Echo/Chargen	Abuse	Slows down the network

■ *RCP scan:* This is a snooping attack performed against all operating systems that use multiple services to identify active remote procedure call (RPC) services. This attack helps the attacker identify active RPC services as well as the associated program and version numbers. This information is mostly used to execute arbitrary code by the attacker on a victim's machine. Looking for multiple connection requests to specific RPC services within a specific time window can help detect this attack.

6.3.2 DoS Attacks

DoS is a class of attacks in which an attacker makes the computing or memory resource too busy or too full to handle legitimate requests, thus denying legitimate users access to the machine. There are different ways to launch DoS attacks: by abusing the computer's legitimate features, by targeting the implementation bugs, or by exploiting the system's misconfigurations. DoS attacks are classified based on the services that an attacker renders unavailable to legitimate users. Some of the popular attack types are illustrated in Table 6.2 [26,27].

■ *Apache2:* This is a type of DoS attack performed against an Apache Web server, in which an attacker submits an HTTP request with several HTTP headers. In theory, if the server receives too many such requests, it will slow down the functionality of the Web server and eventually crash. This attack temporarily denies the Web service; the service can be regained with the system administrator's intervention.

■ *Back:* This is a type of DoS attack performed against an Apache Web server, in which an attacker submits a URL request with several front slashes. While trying to process these requests, the server's service becomes unavailable for legitimate users. This attack temporarily denies the Web service; the service can be regained automatically.

■ *Land:* This is a type of DoS attack performed against TCP/IP implementations, in which an attacker sends a spoofed SYN packet that has the same source and destination IP addresses. In theory, it is not possible to have the same destination and source addresses. The attacker targets the badly configured networks and uses the innocent machines as zombies for performing distributed attacks. This attack can be prevented by carefully configuring the network, which prevents requests containing the same source and destination IP addresses.

■ *Mail bomb:* This is a type of DoS attack performed against a server, in which an attacker floods the e-mail queue, possibly causing failure. The attacker tries to send thousands of e-mails to a single user. This attack denies the service permanently. The service can be regained by the system administrator's intervention; blocking the e-mails, coming from or to the same user within a short period of time, can prevent the attack.

■ *SYN flood (Neptune):* This is a type of DoS attack performed against TCP/IP implementations, in which an attacker utilizes half-open TCP connections to flood the data structure of half-open connections on an innocent server, causing it to deny access to legitimate requests. This attack, in some cases, can cause permanent failure. The service can be regained automatically. Looking for a number of simultaneous SYN packets, coming from the same host or unreachable host in a given short period of time, can prevent this attack.

■ *Ping of Death (PoD):* This is a type of DoS attack performed against older versions of operating systems, in which an attacker tries to send an oversized IP packet, and the system reacts in an unpredictable manner, causing crashing, rebooting, and even freezing in some cases. This attack causes temporary failure of services. Looking for ICMP packets that are longer than 64,000 bytes and blocking them is the way to prevent this attack.

■ *Process table:* This is a type of DoS attack performed against a variety of different UNIX systems, in which an attacker tries to allocate a new process for every incoming TCP/IP connection. When the systems process table is filled completely, legitimate commands are prevented from being executed. This attack causes temporary failure of services. Looking for a large number of active connections on a single port helps in preventing this attack.

■ *Smurf:* This is a type of DoS attack performed against all the systems connected to the Internet, in which an attacker sends ICMP echo request packets to IP broadcast addresses from remote locations to deny services. This attack causes temporary DoSs and can be automatically recovered. Looking for a large number of echo replies to the innocent machine from different places without any echo request made by the innocent machine helps in detecting this attack.

■ *Syslogd:* This is a type of DoS attack performed against Solaris servers, in which an attacker tries to kill the syslogd service remotely. The attacker exploits the DNS lookup feature; if the source IP address does match the DNS record, then syslogd crashes with a segmentation fault. This attack permanently denies services and can only be recovered with the system administrator's intervention.

■ *Teardrop:* This is a type of DoS attack performed against older versions of the TCP/IP stack, in which an attacker exploits the feature of IP fragment reassembly. This attack denies the services temporarily.

■ *Udpstorm:* This is a type of DoS attack performed against networks, in which an attacker utilizes the UDP service feature to cause congestion and slowdown. This attack denies the services permanently and can only be resumed with the system administrator's intervention. This attack can be identified by looking for spoofed packets and inside-network traffic.

6.4 Significant Feature Selection for Intrusion Detection

Feature selection and ranking is an important issue in intrusion detection [28,29]. Of the large number of features that can be monitored for intrusion detection purposes, which are truly useful? Which are less significant? And which may be useless? These questions are relevant because the elimination of useless features (the so-called audit trail reduction) enhances the accuracy of detection while speeding up the computation, thus improving the overall performance of an IDS. In cases in which there are no useless features, by concentrating on the most important ones, we may well improve the time performance of an IDS without affecting the accuracy of detection in statistically significant ways. The feature ranking and selection problem for intrusion detection is similar in nature to various engineering problems that are characterized by:

- Having a large number of input variables $x = (x_1, x_2, \ldots, x_n)$ of varying degrees of importance to the output y; i.e., some elements of x are essential, some are less important, some of them may not be mutually independent, and some may be useless or irrelevant (in determining the value of y)
- Lacking an analytical model that provides the basis for a mathematical formula that precisely describes the input–output relationship, $y = F(x)$
- Having available a finite set of experimental data, based on which a model (e.g., neural networks) can be built for simulation and prediction purposes

Because of the lack of an analytical model, one can only seek to determine the relative importance of the input variables through empirical methods. A complete analysis would require examination of all possibilities, e.g., taking two variables at a time to analyze their dependence or correlation, then taking three at a time, etc. This, however, is both infeasible (requiring 2^n experiments) and not infallible (because the available data may be of poor quality in sampling the whole input space). Features are ranked based on their influence toward the final classification.

A subset of the DARPA intrusion detection dataset is used for offline analysis. For each TCP/IP connection, 41 various quantitative and qualitative features were extracted for intrusion analysis.

The 41 features extracted fall into three categories: "intrinsic" features that describe the individual TCP/IP connections that can be obtained from network audit trails; "content-based" features that describe the payload of the network packet that can be obtained from the data portion of the network packet; and "traffic-based" features that are computed using a specific window (connection time or number of connections). Description of most important features as ranked by three feature-ranking algorithms (support vector decision function, linear genetic programming, and multivariate adaptive regression splines) is given in Table 6.3, Table 6.4, and Table 6.5.

6.4.1 SVM-Specific Feature-Ranking Method

It is of great interest and use to find exactly which features underline the nature of connections of various classes. This is precisely the goal of data

Table 6.3   Most Important Features Description as Ranked by SVDF

Ranking Algorithm	Feature Description
Normal	Destination bytes: number of bytes received by the source host from the destination host
	dst_host_count: number of connections from the same host to the destination host during a specified time window
	Logged in: binary decision (1 successfully logged in, 0 failed log-in)
	dst_host_same_srv_rate: percentage of connections to same service ports from a destination host
	Flag: normal or error status of the connection
Probe	Source bytes: number of bytes sent from the host system to the destination system
	dst_host_srv_count: number of connections from the same host with same service to the destination host during a specified time window
	Count: number of connections made to the same host system in a given interval of time
	Protocol type: type of protocol used to connect (e.g., TCP, UDP, ICMP, etc.)
	srv_count: number of connections to the same service as the current connection during a specified time window
DoS	Count: number of connections made to the same host system in a given interval of time
	srv_count: number of connections to the same service as the current connection during a specified time window
	dst_host_srv_serror_rate: percentage of connections to the same service that have SYN errors from a destination host
	serror_rate: percentage of connections that have SYN errors
	dst_host_same_src_port_rate: percentage of connections to same service ports from a destination host

Table 6.3 Most Important Features Description as Ranked by SVDF (continued)

Ranking Algorithm	Feature Description
U2Su	Source bytes: number of bytes sent from the host system to the destination system
	Duration: length of the connection
	Protocol type: type of protocol used to connect (e.g., TCP, UDP, ICMP, etc.)
	Logged in: binary decision (1 successfully logged in, 0 failed log-in)
	Flag: normal or error status of the connection
R2L	dst_host_count: number of connections from the same host to the destination host during a specified time window
	Service: type of service used to connect (e.g., finger, FTP, Telnet, SSH, etc.)
	Duration: length of the connection
	Count: number of connections made to the same host system in a given interval of time
	srv_count: number of connections to the same service as the current connection during a specified time window

visualization in data mining. The problem is that the high dimensionality of data makes it hard for human experts to gather any knowledge. If we knew the key features, we could greatly reduce the dimensionality of the data and, thus, help human experts become more efficient and productive in learning about network intrusions.

The information on which features play key roles and which is more neutral is hidden in the support vector machine (SVM) decision function. The decision function is formulated using linear kernels as follows [30,31].

$$F(X) = \langle W, X \rangle + b \qquad (6.1)$$

The point X is predicted to be in class A or positive class if F(X) is positive, and class B or negative class if F(X) is negative. We can rewrite the formula (2) to expand the dot product of W and X.

$$F(X) = \Sigma W_i X_i + b \qquad (6.2)$$

Table 6.4 Most Important Features Description as Ranked by LGPs

Ranking Algorithm	Feature Description
Normal	Hot: number of "hot" indicators
	Source bytes: number of bytes sent from the host system to the destination system
	Destination bytes: number of bytes received by the source host from the destination host
	num_compromised: number of compromised conditions
	dst_host_rerror_rate: percentage of connections that have REJ errors from a destination host
Probe	dst_host_diff_srv_rate: percentage of connections to different services from a destination host
	rerror_rate: percentage of connections that have REJ errors
	srv_diff_host_rate: percentage of connections that have same service to different hosts
	Logged in: binary decision (1 successfully logged in, 0 failed log-in)
	Service: type of service used to connect (e.g., finger, FTP, Telnet, SSH, etc.)
DoS	Count: number of connections made to the same host system in a given interval of time
	num_compromised: number of compromised conditions
	Wrong fragments: number of wrong fragments
	Land: binary decision (1 if connection is from/to the same host/port; 0 otherwise)
	Logged in: binary decision (1 successfully logged in, 0 failed log-in)

One can see that the value of $F(X)$ depends on the contribution of each factor, $W_i X_i$. Because X_i only values >0, the sign of W_i indicates whether the contribution is toward positive or negative classification. The absolute size of W_i measures the strength of this contribution. In other

**Table 6.4   Most Important Features Description
as Ranked by LGPs (continued)**

Ranking Algorithm	Feature Description
U2Su	root_shell: binary decision (1 if root shell is obtained; 0 otherwise)
	dst_host_srv_serror_rate: percentage of connections to the same service that have SYN errors from a destination host
	num_file_creations: number of file creations
	serror_rate: percentage of connections that have SYN errors
	dst_host_same_src_port_rate: percentage of connections to same service ports from a destination host
R2L	Guest log-in: binary decision (1 if the log-in is guest, 0 otherwise)
	num_file_access: number of operations on access control files
	Destination bytes: number of bytes received by the source host from the destination host
	num_failed_logins: number of failed log-in attempts
	Logged in: binary decision (1 successfully logged in, 0 failed log-in)

words, if W_i is a large positive value, then the ith feature is a key factor of the positive class or class A. Similarly, if W_i is a large negative value, then the ith feature is a key factor of the negative class or class B. Consequently, the W_i, which is close to zero, either positive or negative, carries little weight. The feature that corresponds to this W_i, is said to be the garbage feature, and removing it has very little effect on the classification. Having retrieved this information directly from the decision function of SVMs, we rank the W_i, from largest positive to largest negative. This essentially provides the soft partitioning of the features into the key features of class A, neutral features, and the key features of class B. We say soft partitioning, as it either depends on a threshold on the value of W_i, which will define the partitions, or the proportions of the features, which we want to allocate to each of the partitions. Both the threshold and the value of proportions can be set by the human expert.

**Table 6.5 Most Important Features Description
as Ranked by MARS**

Ranking Algorithm	Feature Description
Normal	Destination bytes: number of bytes received by the source host from the destination host
	Source bytes: number of bytes sent from the host system to the destination system
	Service: type of service used to connect (e.g., finger, FTP, Telnet, SSH, etc.)
	Logged in: binary decision (1 successfully logged in, 0 failed log-in)
	Hot: number of "hot" indicators
Probe	dst_host_diff_srv_rate: percentage of connections to different services from a destination host
	dst_host_srv_count: number of connections from the same host with same service to the destination host during a specified time window
	Source bytes: number of bytes sent from the host system to the destination system
	dst_host_same_srv_rate: percentage of connections to same service ports from a destination host
	srv_count: number of connections to the same service as the current connection during a specified time window
DoS	Count: number of connections made to the same host system in a given interval of time
	srv_count: number of connections to the same service as the current connection during a specified time window
	dst_host_srv_diff_host_rate: percentage of connections to the same service from different hosts to a destination host
	Source bytes: number of bytes sent from the host system to the destination system
	Destination bytes: number of bytes received by the source host from the destination host

**Table 6.5 Most Important Features Description
as Ranked by MARS (continued)**

Ranking Algorithm	Feature Description
U2Su	dst_host_srv_count: number of connections from the same host with same service to the destination host during a specified time window
	Count: number of connections made to the same host system in a given interval of time
	Duration: length of the connection
	srv_count: number of connections to the same service as the current connection during a specified time window
	dst_host_count: number of connections from the same host to the destination host during a specified time window
R2L	srv_count: : number of connections to the same service as the current connection during a specified time window
	Count: number of connections made to the same host system in a given interval of time
	Service: type of service used to connect (e.g., finger, FTP, Telnet, SSH, etc.)
	dst_host_srv_count: number of connections from the same host with same service to the destination host during a specified time window
	Logged in: binary decision (1 successfully logged in, 0 failed log-in)

6.4.1.1 Support Vector Decision Function Ranking

The input ranking is done as follows: First, the original dataset is used for the training of the classifier. Then, the classifier's decision function is used to rank the importance of the features. The procedure is:

1. Calculate the weights from the support vector decision function.
2. Rank the importance of the features by the absolute values of the weights.

6.4.2 Ranking Algorithm Using Linear Genetic Programming

The performance of each of the selected input feature subsets is measured by invoking a fitness function with the correspondingly reduced feature space and training set, and evaluating the intrusion detection accuracy. Once the required number of iterations is completed, the evolved high-ranked programs are analyzed for how many times each input appears in a way that contributes to the fitness of the programs that contain it. The best feature subset found is then output as the recommended set of features to be used in the actual input for the classifier. In the feature selection problem, the main interest is in the representation of the space of all possible subsets of the given input feature set. Each feature in the candidate feature set is considered as a binary gene, and each individual consists of a fixed-length binary string representing some subset of the given feature set. An individual of length d corresponds to a d-dimensional binary feature vector Y, in which each bit represents the elimination or inclusion of the associated feature. Then, $y_i = 0$ represents elimination, and $y_i = 1$ indicates inclusion of the *i*th feature. Fitness F of an individual program p is calculated as the mean square error (*MSE*) between the predicted output (O_{ij}^{pred}) and the desired output (O_{ij}^{des}) for all *n* training samples and *m* outputs [32,33].

$$F(p) = \frac{1}{n \cdot m} \sum_{i=1}^{n} \sum_{j=1}^{m} (O_{ij}^{pred} - O_{ij}^{des})^2 + \frac{w}{n} CE = MSE + w \cdot MCE \quad (6.3)$$

Classification error (*CE*) is computed as the number of misclassifications. Mean classification error (*MCE*) is added to the fitness function, whereas its contribution is proscribed by an absolute value of weight (W).

6.4.3 Ranking Algorithm Using Multivariate Adaptive Regression Splines

Generalized cross validation (GCV) is an estimate of the actual cross validation that involves more computationally intensive goodness-of-fit measures. Along with the multivariate adaptive regression splines (MARS) [34] procedure, a GCV procedure is used to determine the significant input features. Noncontributing input variables are thereby eliminated.

$$GCV = \frac{1}{N} \sum_{i=1}^{N} [\frac{y_i - f(x_i)^2}{1 - k/N}] \quad (6.4)$$

where N is the number of records, and x and y are independent and dependent variables, respectively. The variable k is the effective number of degrees of freedom whereby the GCV adds penalty for adding more input variables to the model. The contribution of the input variables may be ranked using the GCV with or without an input feature [35].

6.5 Detection of Probes and DoS Attacks

As DoS and probe attacks involve several connections in a short timeframe as opposed to R2L and U2Su, which are often embedded in the data portions of a single connection, traffic-based features play an important role in deciding whether a particular network activity is engaged in probing or DoS. It is shown that probe attacks can be detected at the originating hosts, and the class of DoS attacks can be detected at the network boundary.

6.5.1 Real-Time Data Collection and Feature Extraction

Experiments were performed on a real network, using two clients and the server that serves the New Mexico Tech Computer Science Department network. The network packet parser uses the WINPCAP library to capture network packets and extracts the relevant features required for classification. The output of the parser for probe classification includes seven features:

1. The duration of the connection to the target machine
2. The protocol used to connect
3. The service type
4. The number of source bytes
5. The number of destination bytes
6. The number of packets sent
7. The number of packets received

The output summary of the parser includes eleven features for DoS classification:

1. The duration of the connection to the target machine
2. The protocol used to connect
3. The service type
4. The status of the connection (normal or error)
5. The number of source bytes
6. The number of destination bytes

7. The number of connections to the same host as the current one during a specified time window (in our case, 0.01 s)
8. The number of connections to the same host as the current one using same service during the past 0.01 s
9. The percentage of connections that have SYN errors during the past 0.01 s
10. The percentage of connections that have SYN errors while using the same service during the past 0.01 s
11. The percentage of connections to the same service during the past 0.01 s

The output from the intrusion classifier is either normal or probe, or normal or DoS for each connection. A variety of probes, including SYN stealth, FIN stealth, ping sweep, UDP scan, null scan, xmas tree, IP scan, idle scan, ACK scan, window scan, RCP scan, and list scan with several options are targeted at the server. Normal data included multiple sessions of FTP, Telnet, SSH, HTTP, SMTP, POP3, and IMAP. Network data originating from a host to the server that includes both normal and probes is collected for analysis.

In the experiments performed, more than 24 types of DoS attacks are analyzed. Network data originating from a host to the server is collected for analysis. The set of features selected for stealthy probe detection and DoS detection are based on our own feature ranking algorithms and obtained using the DARPA intrusion dataset. The classifiers used in our experiments are SVMs, MARS, and linear genetic programming (LGP).

6.5.2 Performance Evaluation

Network packets contain information on the protocol and service used to establish the connection between a client and the server. Network services have an expected number of bytes of data to be passed between a client and the server. If data flow is too little or too much, it raises a suspicion about the connection, as to whether it is a case of misuse. Normal, probing, and DoS activities can be separated by using this information.

In our evaluation, we perform binary classification, normal/probe and normal/DoS. The training and testing dataset for detecting probes contains 10,369 data points generated from normal traffic and probes. The training and testing dataset for detecting DoS contains 5,385 data points generated from normal traffic and DoS-attack traffic. Table 6.6 and Table 6.7 summarize the overall classification accuracy, normal/probe and normal/DoS, using MARS, SVM, and LGP, respectively.

Table 6.6 Performance Comparison of Testing for Detecting Probes

Class\Machine	SVMs (Percentage)	LGPs (Percentage)	MARS (Percentage)
Normal	99.75	100	99.12
Probe	99.99	100	100

Table 6.7 Performance Comparison of Testing for Five-Class Classifications

Class/ Learning Machine	Normal SVM /LGP/MARS	DoS SVM/LGP/MARS	Overall Accuracy SVM/LGP/MARS
Normal	2692/2578/1730	14/128/976	99.48/95.26/63.9
DoS	538/153/0	2141/2526/2679	79.91/94.28/100
Accuracy (percentage) SVM/ LGP/ MARS	83.77/99.08/63.9	80.44/99.06/73.2	

Table 6.7 (containing three "confusion matrices" for the different classifiers used in experiments) gives the performance in terms of DoS detection accuracy.

The top-left entry in Table 6.7 shows that 2692, 2578, and 1730 of the actual normal test set were detected to be normal by SVM, LGP, and MARS, respectively; the last column indicates that 99.46, 95.26, and 63.9 percent of the actual normal data points were detected correctly by SVM, LGP, and MARS, respectively.

6.6 Attacks on IDSs

IDS plays a vital role in a security chain by alerting site administrators with all attempts to breach the information security policy of an organization. For IDS to be more useful in an information security chain, information system policy administrators need to be able to rely on the information provided by it; flawed systems not only provide false information about the current security scenario but also generate large volumes of false alarms. Moreover, the value of information from faulty systems is not only negated, but also potentially misleading [36].

Most of the IDSs rely on several components (data collection module, analysis module, storage module, and response module) to decide whether a particular activity is normal or malicious. Given the implications of malfunction of an IDS component, it is reasonable to assume that IDSs are themselves logical targets for attack. Most of the time, information security technologies become primary targets of a knowledgeable attacker.

A potential attacker targets IDS components and can make the IDS ineffective by disabling it or forcing it to provide false information (false alarms).

6.6.1 Vulnerabilities in IDSs

All the components of an IDS are vulnerable to multiple attacks and have unique security implications for the functionality of the IDS.

- The data collection module collects audit trails (user logs, network trails, system calls, etc.) for the other IDS components to decide whether a particular activity is malicious or normal. If an attacker targets this module, the IDS becomes nonfunctional.
- The analysis module analyzes inputs (audit trails) from the data collection module to decide whether a particular activity is normal or malicious. If an attacker knows the analysis technique, he or she can mislead and circumvent the IDS from being functional.
- The storage module provides a mechanism to store the data collected by data collection and analysis modules in a secure fashion. Data stored might be used for building new signatures, updating user and system profiles, forensics analysis, and identifying key audit information. An attacker who can compromise the storage module can prevent the IDS from logging the attack information, insertion, or deletion of audit trails. A more advanced attacker can also change the profiles and intrusion detection signatures of the IDS.
- The response module provides a mechanism for aftermath operations. A compromise on a response module will allow the attacker to continuously attack the system without generating an alarm. In case of reactive devices, rather than aftermath devices, an attacker can make the system deny legitimate activity and accept malicious activity.

6.6.2 Insertion and Evasion Attacks

Insertion attacks are caused by inserting malfunction packets that an end system rejects but an IDS accepts [13]. An attacker exploits this feature by sending packets that an end system will reject but an IDS will still accept and inspect for malicious activity. Attacks range from insertion of malfunction packets to data modification. Evasion attacks are caused by inserting legitimate packets that an IDS rejects but an end system accepts. An attacker exploits this feature by sending packets that an end system will accept but an IDS will reject. This will cause an IDS to generate false alarms and deny legitimate packets.

- *Bad header fields:* End systems reject packets that have invalid header fields. Network peripheral devices do not route the packets with invalid header fields, but if the IDS is on the same local network as the attacker's, it is still subject to insertion attacks. Most of the IP implementations do not process packets with a bad checksum. An IDS that does not check the packets for correct checksums is thus vulnerable to simple insertion attacks. Every packet requires a time to live (TTL) field to be routed by the routers. The router decrements the TTL value as it routes the packet to the next hop. An attacker can exploit this property by specifying a time that is just enough for the packets to reach the IDS but not the end system.

- *IP options:* Lack of proper knowledge of end-system implementations might lead an IDS to take ambiguous actions. Parsing of IP options varies from system to system; an IDS requires special processing capabilities for proper and correct interpretations. Most end systems drop the packets if the IP checksum is wrong. An IDS without the knowledge of the end system's actions on wrong IP checksums might lead to ambiguity in taking proper action.

- *Media access control (MAC) address spoofing:* Most of the network peripheral devices do not check for matching the IP address and MAC address. Because of the use of complex dynamic protocols such as Dynamic Host Control Protocol (DHCP) and virtual private networks (VPNs), network address translators (NATs), etc., it becomes even harder to verify the legitimacy. An attacker who knows the MAC address of the IDS sends packets to it. An IDS that does not have the capability to check for legitimate IP and MAC address pairs is subject to simple insertion attacks.

6.6.3 Availability Attacks

The recent trend of the attackers — "if I can't have it, nobody can" — has changed the emphasis of information assurance with respect to information security. Legitimate networks packets consume various kinds of shared resources, such as bandwidth, memory, processing power, and operating system structures. Most of the IDS components require system and network resources to process the information passed by the network. An attacker identifies a few activities that are resource intensive and targets the IDS with such activity, making it nonfunctional. A few possible scenarios of resource exhaustion are: buffers exhausted, file descriptors exhausted, address space exhausted, disk space exhausted, CPU cycle exhausted, and bandwidth exhausted.

6.7 Attacks on Anti-Virus Tools

Software security assurance and malware detection are important aspects of information system assurance. Software obfuscation is a general technique that is used to protect the software from reverse engineering techniques and is being used by malware writers to circumvent the current detection mechanisms (anti-virus tools). Current static scanning techniques for malware detection have serious limitations; on the other hand, neither does sandbox testing provide a complete solution because of time constraints (e.g., time bombs cannot be detected before their preset times expire). In this section, we describe a few obfuscation techniques that were applied to recent viruses and were used to thwart commercial-grade anti-virus tools.

6.7.1 Malware Used for Analysis

Several recent viruses (executables) are being used for analysis. We describe the analysis of four viruses. The description of the virus is given based on the payload, enabling vulnerability, propagation medium, and the systems infected.

- *W32.Mydoom:* A mass-mailing worm and a blended backdoor that arrives as an attachment with file extensions such as .bat, .cmd, .exe, .pif, .scr, or .zip [37]. The payload performs a DoS against www.sco.com and creates a proxy server for remote access using TCP ports 3127 through 3198. Infects all Windows systems.
- *W32.Blaster:* Exploits Windows DCOM RPC vulnerability using TCP port 135. The payload launches a DoS attack against windowsupdate.com, causing systems to crash and opening a hidden remote cmd.exe shell. Propagates via TCP ports 135 and 4444 and UDP port 69. Infects only Windows 2000 and Windows XP systems.
- *W32.Beagle:* A mass-mailing worm blended with a backdoor. The worm contains large-scale e-mail with extensions .wab, .htm, .xml, .nch, .mmf, .cfg, .asp, etc. [38]. Uses its own SMTP engine and TCP port 2745 to spread, and also tries to spread via file-sharing networks such as Kazaa. Infects all Windows systems.
- *Win32.Bika:* According to the virus library, it is a harmless, per-process, memory-resident, parasitic Win32 virus. It infects only Win32 applications [39]. The virus writes itself to the end of the

file while infecting an application. Once the host program is infected, it starts the virus hooks "set current directory" Win32 API functions (SetCurrentDirectoryA, SetCurrentDirectoryW) that are imported by the host program and stays as a background thread of infected process, and then infects files in the directories when the current directory is being changed. The virus does not manifest itself.

6.7.2 Obfuscation

In its simplest form, *obfuscation* is defined as obscuring some information such that another person cannot construe its true meaning. This is certainly true for code obfuscation, in which the objective is to hide the underlying logic of a program.

Code obfuscation has been compared to code optimization, which is some transformation that will minimize a program's metric, such as execution time or execution size; code obfuscation has the additional requirement that the code transformation also maximizes obscurity [40]. When we optimize for speed, we generally try to take advantage of hardware pipelines, memory buffers, etc., while leaving the program essentially the same. Any optimization that changes the program's functionality or logic cannot be applied blindly and is generally avoided.

Obfuscation has also been applied to program watermarking and is a well-known technique to prevent reverse engineering [41]. In general, obfuscating a program to prevent reverse engineering is similar to a classic cryptography game: you try and make reversing your obfuscation hard enough such that it is impractical to attack. Given enough time and resources, any obfuscation can be reversed but as long as the reverse engineering takes 100,000 years it is considered pretty secure. By obfuscating, you can prevent another individual from gaining knowledge about your program. With respect to malware, code obfuscation is an appealing technique to hinder detection. A simple obfuscation technique may render a known virus completely invisible to conventional scanners with very little effort on the part of the virus writer.

Applying an obfuscation transformation to a program has the advantage that it is essentially a self-decrypting encryption. Although the code is rendered incomprehensible, the program remains viable.

6.7.2.1 Data Obfuscation

Data obfuscation changes the look of a program by modifying the constants or encapsulated bits of data. An example would be to split the string "hello world" into smaller strings, such as *he*, *ll*, and *o*. Another method would be to separate a Boolean variable into two integers and use comparisons between the two to emulate the true/false properties of the original.

In general, complex data transformations require the addition of helper code if the original functionality is to be maintained. In the example given in the preceding text, we would need to generate code to concatenate the small strings together to get the original "hello world" before using it.

6.7.2.2 Control Flow Obfuscation

Control flow transformations focus on obscuring how the program runs. For example, inserting junk code into a program changes its appearance considerably but does not change the logic. A more complex example would be to use global pointers for control flow. If we used pointers *p* and *q* and inserted a statement such as *if (p == q) then,* it is nearly impossible to determine if this statement is true or false by using static analysis. Such a combination of pointers and control flow statements is considered opaque because of the difficulty inherent in pointer alias analysis.

This type of obfuscation is particularly appealing to malware authors because of its strength. We see control flow transformations implemented in polymorphic and metamorphic engines in which the code changes with each infected host.

6.7.2.3 Other Techniques

Data and control flow are not the only techniques that can be used to obscure a program's meaning or prevent reverse engineering. Many software authors make use of *antidisassembly* and *antidebugging* techniques to hinder analysis. In general, these are tricks that slow down automated tools such as disassembles. Bytecode scramblers are also used to obfuscate strongly typed bytecode such as that of Java. All of these techniques, combined with a generous helping of data and control flow obfuscation, help make code analysis exorbitantly difficult.

6.7.2.4 Classification

For simplicity, we have separated obfuscation techniques into six general categories. Because of the complexity in implementing and detecting pointer aliases, we gave them their own category. As a general rule, the complexity and robustness of the technique increases with the type level.

Table 6.8   Null Operations Obfuscation

Original Code	
Mov	eax, -44(ebp)
Mov	-44(ebp), ebx
Sub	12, esp
Lea	-24(ebp)
Push	eax
After Transformation	
Mov	eax, -44(ebp)
Mov	-44(ebp), ebx
Nop	
Sub	12, esp
Lea	-24(ebp)
Nop	Null operation
Push	eax

Straight control flow obfuscation is (in general) not as robust as both data and control flow obfuscation together. These types assume a low-level language such as x86 assembly.

- *Type 0: None* — Program is left unmodified and functions exactly the same as before.
- *Type 1: Null operations* — NOPs are inserted into the code. There is virtually no modification to data or control flow. An example of a type-1 transformation is presented in Table 6.8. On the left, we have the original code, and on the right, we have the modified code with null operations inserted every second operation. Inserting null operations is essentially the same as inserting white space in a document: it may take longer to read but the content is exactly the same.
- *Type 2: Data* — Some data obfuscation transformation is applied, such as string splitting or variable-type replacement. For example, we could replace a Boolean variable with two integers. If they are equal, the statement is true; otherwise it is false. In Table 6.9, *x* is a Boolean variable, and *a* and *b* are integers. The code on the left is the original control flow, and the code on the right performs exactly the same but has a different signature.

Table 6.9   Data Obfuscation

Original Code and Meaning			Transformed Code and Meaning		
cmpb	0, x	if (x == true)	mov	a, eax	if (a < b)
je	.sub	goto sub	cmpl	b, eax	goto sub
			jge	.sub	

Table 6.10   Control Flow Obfuscation

Original Code	
Cmp	24, eax
Jne	.sub
Sub	12, eax
Push	eax
After Transformation	
Jmp	[shift]
Nop	Helper code
Nop	
Push	eax Original execution path resumes
Cmp	24, eax
Jne	.sub − [shift]
Sub	12, eax
Jmp	-[shift] Helper code

■ *Type 3: Control flow* — Control flow transformations are applied. Code is swapped around, and jump instructions are inserted. For example, we could copy the contents of a subroutine to another location in the file and add jumps to and from the subroutine. The code would function in exactly the same manner but look quite different. In Table 6.10, three lines of code have been shifted to some location (denoted as [shift]), and helper code has been inserted.

Table 6.11 Combination of Null Operations and Control Flow Obfuscation

Original Code	
cmp	24, eax
jne	.sub
sub	12, eax
push	eax
After Transformation	
jmp	[shift]
nop	Helper code
nop	
push	eax Original execution path resumes
mov	24, eax data obfuscation
cmpl	b, eax data obfuscation
jle	.dead_code
jne	.sub – **[shift]**
sub	12, eax
jmp	-[shift] Helper code

- *Type 4: Combination of 2 and 3* — We pull out all the stops and combine data and control flow transformations. At this level, junk code is inserted, and variables can be completely replaced with large sections of needless code. For example, we can modify all integer variables as given in the preceding text and transpose the program's entry point as in Table 6.11.
- *Type 5: Pointer aliasing* — The final step is to introduce pointer aliasing. Variables are replaced with global pointers, and functions are referred to by arrays of function pointers. This type of transformation is relatively easy to implement using high-level languages that allow pointer references but tricky (at best) using assembly languages. Pointer aliasing can be as simple as changing $a = b$ into $*a = **b$ or as complex as converting all variables and functions into an array of pointers referenced by pointers to pointers.

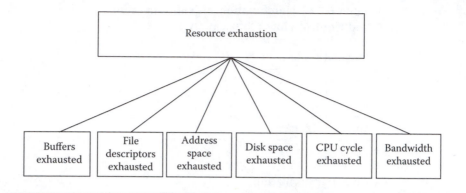

Figure 6.4   Resource exhaustion scenarios of an IDS.

6.7.3 Obfuscation Used for Defeating Commercial Scanners

In our research, we discovered that most commercial virus scanners could be defeated with very simple obfuscation techniques. For example, simple program entry point modifications consisting of two extra jump instructions effectively defeated most scanners. Therefore, we only used the bare minimum level of obfuscation needed to prevent detection. Our goal was to show how trivial it is to modify recent malware to defeat existing scanning techniques using only the compiled executable and a few tools.

The obfuscation process is presented in Figure 6.4. The binary code is disassembled into a more readable format so that we may understand what the program is doing. Someone with foreknowledge about malware need not spend so much time analyzing the program. Once we have the disassembled program and have studied it, we pick out an area to attack. The first target when applying a control flow transformation is to attack the program's entry point, but when using data transformation we generally have to guess. We decide where and what modifications need to be performed and change the binary file directly, using the disassembled version as a guide or map. Once all modifications have been made, the file is examined using the anti-virus scanners.

All variants, with the exception of the MyDoom virus, were generated using off-the-shelf hex-editing tools. We were fortunate enough to have a copy of the MyDoom.A source code and made all our modifications using the Microsoft .net environment. The Hackman hex-editing utility was used to generate all other variants [41].

Table 6.12 shows the preliminary results of New Mexico Tech's recent investigation of the MyDoom worm and several other recent worms and viruses, using eight different (commercial) scanners and proxy services

Table 6.12 Obfuscation Attacks on Commercial Scanners

	N	M¹	M²	D	P	K	F	A
W32.Mydoom.A	✔	✔	✔	✔	✔	✔	✔	✔
W32.Mydoom.A V1	✗	✔	✔	✗	✗	✔	✔	✗
W32.Mydoom.A V2	✔	✗	✗	✗	✗	✗	✗	✗
W32.Mydoom.A V3	✗	✗	✗	✗	✗	✗	✗	✗
W32.Mydoom.A V4	✗	✗	✗	✗	✗	✗	✗	✗
W32.Mydoom.A V5	✗	?	✗	✗	✗	✗	✗	✗
W32.Mydoom.A V6	✗	✗	✗	✗	✗	✗	✗	✗
W32.Mydoom.A V7	✗	✗	✗	✗	✗	✗	✗	✗
W32.Bika	✔	✔	✔	✔	✔	✔	✔	✔
W32.Bika V1	✗	✗	✗	✔	✗	✔	✔	✔
W32.Bika V2	✗	✗	✗	✔	✗	✔	✔	✔
W32.Bika V3	✗	✗	✗	✔	✗	✔	✔	✔
W32.Beagle.B	✔	✔	✔	✔	✔	✔	✔	✔
W32.Beagle.B V1	✔	✔	✔	✗	✗	✔	✔	✗
W32.Beagle.B V2	✔	✗	✗	✗	✗	✗	✗	✗
W32. Blaster.Worm	✔	✔	✔	✔	✔	✔	✔	✔
W32. Blaster.Worm V1	✗	✔	✔	✔	✔	✔	✔	✗
W32. Blaster.Worm V2	✔	✔	✔	✗	✗	✔	✔	✗
W32. Blaster.Worm V3	✔	✔	✔	✔	✔	✗	✗	✗
W32. Blaster.Worm V4	✗	✗	✗	✗	✗	✔	✔	✗

Note: N = Norton, M¹ = McAfee UNIX Scanner, M² = McAfee, D = Dr. Web, P = Panda, K = Kaspersky, F = F-Secure, A = Antiy Ghostbusters.

(✔ indicates detection, ✗ indicates failure to detect, and **?** indicates only an alert; all scanners used are most current and updated versions) [42,43].

The obfuscation techniques (Figure 6.5) used to produce the polymorphic versions of different malware tested in the experiments include control flow modification (e.g., MyDoom V2 and Beagle V2), data segment modification (e.g., MyDoom V1 and Beagle V1), and insertion of dead code (e.g., Bika V1).

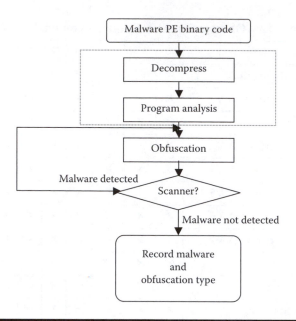

Figure 6.5 Obfuscation attack process on commercial scanners.

In our recent work, we developed robust and unique signature-based malware (viruses, worms, trojans, etc.) detection, with emphasis on detecting obfuscated (or polymorphic) malware and mutated (or metamorphic) malware. The hypothesis is that all versions of the same malware share a common or core signature — possibly a second-order signature that is a combination of several features of the code. After a particular malware has been first identified (through sandbox testing or other means), it can be analyzed to extract the signature that provides a basis for detecting variants and mutants of the same malware in the future. The detection algorithm is based on calculating the similarity of the code under scanning and the signatures; for more details of the detection algorithm, see Reference 42 and Reference 43.

6.8 Conclusions

In this chapter, we attempted to present the current cyber-security challenges from an IDS and anti-virus tools perspective. The state-of-the-art of the evolution of intrusion detection technology with an overview of computer attack taxonomy and computer attack demystification, along with a few detection signatures, is presented.

Because malware is expected to become more lethal (third-generation worms using multiple attack vectors to exploit both known and unknown vulnerabilities) and spread even faster (attacking prescanned targets with lightning speed) in the future, it is important that the scanners be capable of detecting polymorphic (obfuscated or variant) versions of known malware. The currently available scanners, however, are grossly inadequate because they are not able to detect even slightly obfuscated versions of known malware.

Acknowledgments

The authors would like to thank Professor Rao Vemuri for the editorial comments, which improved the presentation of this chapter. Support for this research, received from ICASA (Institute for Complex Additive Systems Analysis, a division of New Mexico Tech), a Department of Defense IASP Capacity Building grant, and an NSF SFS Capacity Building grant, is gratefully acknowledged. We would also like to acknowledge the assistance of Dennis Xu, Patrick Chavez, Authonis Suliman, Karthikeyan Ramamoorthy, and Xie Tao for assisting in carrying out some experiments.

References

1. Lunt, T., Tamaru, A., Gilham, F., Jagannathan, R., Jalali, C., Neumann, P.G., Javitz, H.S., Valdes, A., and Garvey, T.D. (1992). A Real Time Intrusion Detection Expert System (IDES) — Final Report, SRI International, Menlo Park, CA.
2. Ilgun, K. (1993). USTAT: A real-time intrusion detection system for UNIX. *Proceedings of the 1993 Computer Society Symposium on Research in Security and Privacy*, IEEE Computer Society Press, pp. 16–29.
3. Anderson, D., Lunt, T.F., Javitz, H., and Tamaru, V.A. (1995). A. Detecting Unusual Program Behavior Using the Statistical Component of the Next-generation Intrusion Detection Expert System (NIDES), SRI-CSL-95-06. SRI International, Menlo Park, CA.
4. Porras, A. and Neumann, P. (1997). Event monitoring enabling responses to anomalous live disturbances. In *Proceedings of the National Information Systems Security Conference*, pp. 353–365.
5. Debar, H. and Dorizzi, B. (1992). An application of a recurrent network to an intrusion detection system. *Proceedings of the International Joint Conference on Neural Networks*, pp. 78–83.
6. Debar, H., Becke, B., and Siboni, D. (1992). A neural network component for an intrusion detection system. *Proceedings of the IEEE Computer Society Symposium on Research in Security and Privacy*, pp. 240–250.
7. Ryan, J., Lin, M-J., and Miikkulainen, R. (1997). Intrusion detection with neural networks. *Advances in Neural Information Processing Systems 10*, Cambridge, MA: MIT Press.
8. Cannady, J. (1998). Artificial neural networks for misuse detection. *Proceedings of National Information Systems Security Conference*, pp. 368–381.

9. Mukkamala, S., Janowski, G., and Sung, A.H. (2001). Intrusion detection using neural networks and support vector machines. *Proceedings of hybrid information systems advances in soft computing*, Physica Verlag, Springer-Verlag, ISBN 3790814806, pp. 121–138.

10. Fugate, M. and Gattiker, J.R. (2003). Computer intrusion detection with classification and anomaly detection, using SVMs. *International Journal of Pattern Recognition and Artificial Intelligence* 17(3): 441–458.

11. Hu, W., Liao, Y., and Vemuri, V R. (2003). Robust support vector machines for anamoly detection in computer security. *International Conference on Machine Learning*, pp. 168–174.

12. Heller, K.A., Svore, K.M., Keromytis, A.D., and Stolfo, S. J. (2003). One class support vector machines for detecting anomalous window registry accesses. In *3rd IEEE Conference Data Mining Workshop on Data Mining for Computer Security*.

13. Lazarevic, A., Ertoz, L., Ozgur, A., Srivastava, J., and Kumar, V. (2003). A comparative study of anomaly detection schemes in network intrusion detection. In *Third SIAM Conference on Data Mining*.

14. Stolfo, J., Fan, W., Lee, W., Prodromidis A., and Chan, P.K. (2000). Cost-based modeling and evaluation for data mining with application to fraud and intrusion detection. *Results from the JAM Project by Salvatore*.

15. Jianxiong, L. and Bridges, S.M. (2000). Mining fuzzy association rules and fuzzy frequency episodes for intrusion detection. *International Journal of Intelligent Systems*, Vol. 15, No. 8, pp. 687–704.

16. Crosbie, M. and Spafford, E.H. (1995). Defending a Computer System Using Autonomous Agents. Technical Report CSD-TR-95-022.

17. Prodromidis, L. and Stolfo, S.J. (1999). Agent-Based Distributed Learning Applied to Fraud Detection. Technical Report, CUCS-014-99.

18. Dasgupta, D. (1999). Immunity-based intrusion detection system: A general framework. *Proceedings of 22nd National Information Systems Security Conference (NISSC)*, pp. 147–160.

19. Helmer, G., Wong, J., Honavar, V., and Miller, L. (2003). Lightweight agents for intrusion detection. *Journal of Systems and Software*, pp. 109–122.

20. Kumar, S. and Spafford, E.H. (1994). An Application of Pattern Matching in Intrusion Detection, Technical Report CSD-TR-94-013. Purdue University.

21. Kumar, S. and Spafford, E.H. (1994). A pattern matching model for misuse intrusion detection. In *Proceedings of the 17th National Computer Security Conference*, pp. 11–21.

22. Denning, D. (1987). An intrusion-detection model. *IEEE Transactions on Software Engineering*, SE-13 (2): 222–232.

23. Lee, W. and Stolfo, S.J. (2000). A framework for constructing features and models for intrusion detection systems. *ACM Transactions on Information and System Security,* Vol. 3, No. 4, pp. 227–261.

24. Mahoney, M. and Chan, P.K. (2003). An analysis of the 1999 DARPA/Lincoln laboratory evaluation data for network anomaly detection. *6th International Symposium on Recent Advances in Intrusion Detection*, pp. 220–237.

25. Chan, P.K., Mahoney, M., and Arshad, M. (2003). Learning rules and clusters for anomaly detection in network traffic. *Managing Cyber Threats: Issues, Approaches and Challenges*, Kluwer (to appear).

26. Kendall, K. (1998). A Database of Computer Attacks for the Evaluation of Intrusion Detection Systems. Master's thesis, Massachusetts Institute of Technology.

27. Webster, S.E. (1998). The Development and Analysis of Intrusion Detection Algorithms. Master's thesis, Massachusetts Institute of Technology.

28. Mukkamala, S. and Sung, A.H. (2003). Feature Selection for Intrusion Detection Using Neural Networks and Support Vector Machines. *Journal of the Transportation Research Board of the National Academics,* Transportation Research Record No 1822; 1822: 33–39.

29. Mukkamala, S. and Sung, A.H. (2003). Identifying significant features for network forensic analysis using artificial intelligence techniques. In *International Journal on Digital Evidence,* IJDE; 1.

30. Vladimir, V.N. (1995). *The Nature of Statistical Learning Theory.* Springer-Verlag, Berlin.

31. Joachims, T. (2000). Making Large-Scale SVM Learning Practical. LS8-Report, University of Dortmund.

32. Banzhaf, W., Nordin, P., Keller, E.R., and Francone, F.D. (1998). *Genetic Programming: An Introduction on the Automatic Evolution of Computer Programs and Its Applications.* Morgan Kaufmann.

33. Brameier, M. and Banzhaf, W. (2001). A comparison of linear genetic programming and neural networks in medical data mining, *IEEE Transactions on Evolutionary Computation,* 5(1): 17–26.

34. Friedman, J.H. (1991). Multivariate Adaptive Regression Splines. *Annals of Statistics,* 19: 1–141.

35. Steinberg, D., Colla, P.L., and Martin, K. (1999). *MARS User Guide,* Salford Systems, San Diego.

36. Ptacek, H.T. and Newsham, N.T. (1998). Insertion, Evasion and Denial of Service: Eluding Network Intrusion Detection. Secure Networks.

37. Symantec Corporation. http://securityresponse.symantec.com/avcenter/ (accessed on September 16, 2004).

38. Virus Library. http://www.viruslibrary.com/virusinfo/Win32.Bika.htm (accessed on September 16, 2004).

39. Collberg, C.S. and Thomborson, C. (2002). Watermarking, tamper-proofing, and obfuscation — tools for software protection, *IEEE Transactions on Software Engineering* 28: 8, 735–746.

40. Krishnaswamy, S., Kwon, M., Ma, D., Shao, Q., and Zhang, Y. (2000). Experience with software watermarking. In the *Proceedings of 16th Annual Computer Security Applications Conference,* pp. 308–316.

41. Hex, H. (Ed.). http://www.technologismiki.com/en/index-h.html.

42. Sung, A.H., Xu, J., Ramamurthy, K., Chavez, P., Mukkamala, S., Sulaiman, T., and Xie, T. (2004). Static Analyzer for Vicious Executables (SAVE). *Presented in Work-in-progress Section of IEEE Symposium on Security and Privacy.*

43. Sung, A.H., Xu, J., Chavez, P., and Mukkamala, S. (2004). Static Analyzer for Vicious Executables (SAVE). *Proceedings of 20th Annual Computer Security Applications Conference* (to appear).

Chapter 7

Artificial Immune Systems in Intrusion Detection

Dipankar Dasgupta and Fabio Gonzalez

7.1 Introduction

The biological immune system (BIS) is a complex network of specialized tissues, organs, cells, and chemicals. Its main function is to recognize the presence of strange elements in the body and respond to eliminate or neutralize the foreign invaders. All living organisms are exposed to many different microorganisms and viruses that are capable of causing illness. These microorganisms are called *pathogens*. In general, organisms try to protect against pathogens using different mechanisms including high temperature, low pH, and chemicals that repel or kill the invaders. More advanced organisms (vertebrates) have developed an efficient defense mechanism called the *immune system* [26]. Substances that can stimulate specific responses of the immune system are commonly referred to as *antigens* (pathogens usually act as antigens).

To be effective, the immune system must respond only to foreign antigens; therefore, it should be able to distinguish between the self (cells, proteins, and in general, any molecule that belongs to or is produced by the body) and the nonself (antigens) [7]. The self/nonself discrimination is an essential characteristic of the immune system because the outcome of an inappropriate response to self-molecules can be fatal.

The immune system generates a large variety of cells and molecules for defensive purposes. These cells and molecules interact with each other and form a dynamic network of active immune cells while detecting and eliminating antigens. It is difficult to give a concise picture of such a complex system, as many of the mechanisms are not completely understood. Detailed review of the natural immune system and its functionalities may be found elsewhere [26,27,33].

7.1.1 Multilayered Protection

The immune system can be envisioned as a multilayer system with defense mechanisms in several layers [24]. The three main layers include the anatomic barrier, innate immunity, and adaptive immunity. They are described as follows:

■ *Anatomic barrier:* The first layer is the anatomic barrier, composed of the skin and the surface of mucous membranes. Intact skin prevents the penetration of most pathogens and also inhibits most bacterial growth because of its low pH. On the other hand, many pathogens enter the body by binding or penetrating through the mucous membranes; these membranes provide a number of nonspecific mechanisms that help to prevent such entry. Saliva, tears, and some mucous secretions act to wash away potential invaders and also contain antibacterial and antiviral substances [33].

■ *Innate immunity:* Innate immunity [26], which is also known as nonspecific immunity, refers to the defense mechanism against foreign invaders that individuals are born with. Innate immunity is mainly composed of the following mechanisms:

  – *Physiologic barriers:* This includes mechanisms such as temperature, pH, oxygen tension, and various soluble chemicals. The purpose of these mechanisms is to provide detrimental living conditions for foreign pathogens. For instance, the low acidity of the gastric system acts as a barrier to infection by ingested microorganisms because they cannot survive the low pH of the stomach.

  – *Phagocytic barriers:* Some specialized cells (such as macrophages, neutrophils, and natural killer cells) are able to ingest specific material, including whole pathogenic microorganisms. This ingestion has two purposes: to kill the antigen and to present fragments of the invader's proteins to other immune cells and molecules.

  – *Inflammatory response:* Activated macrophages produce proteins called *cytokines*. They work as hormone-like messengers that induce the inflammatory response, which is characterized by vasodilation and rise in capillary permeability. These changes allow a large number of circulating immune cells to be recruited to the site of the infection. Cytokines are also produced by other immune cells and nonimmune cells, for example, those that secrete cytokines when damaged [26].

■ *Adaptive immunity:* This layer is described in detail in the following subsections.

7.1.2 Adaptive Immunity

It is also called acquired or specific immunity, which represents the part of the immune system that is able to specifically recognize and selectively eliminate foreign microorganisms and molecules. It is important to note that acquired immunity does not act independently of innate immunity; on the contrary, they work together to eliminate foreign invaders. For instance, phagocytic cells (innate immunity) are involved in the activation of adaptive immune response. Also, some soluble factors, produced during a specific immune response, have been found to augment the activity of these phagocytic cells [33].

7.1.2.1 Characteristics of Adaptive Immunity

An important part of the adaptive immune system is managed by white blood cells, called *lymphocytes.* These cells are produced in the bone marrow, circulate in the blood and lymph system, and reside in various lymphoid organs to perform immunological functions.

■ *B-cells and T-cells:* They represent the major population of lymphocytes. These cells are produced in the bone marrow and are inert initially, i.e., they are not capable of executing their functions. To become immune competent, they have to go through a maturation process. In the case of B-cells, the maturation process occurs in the bone marrow itself. For T-cells, they have to migrate first to the thymus, where they mature. In general, a mature lymphocyte can be considered as a detector that can detect specific antigens. There are billions of these detectors that circulate in the body, constituting an effective, distributed anomaly detection and response system [33].

■ *Humoral immunity:* Mature B-cells express unique antigen-binding receptors (ABR) on their surface. The interaction of ABR with specific antigens induces proliferation and differentiation of B-cells into antibody-secreting plasma cells. An antibody is a molecule that binds to antigens and neutralizes them or facilitates their elimination. Antigens coated with antibodies can be eliminated in multiple ways: by phagocytic cells, by the complement system, or by preventing them from performing any damaging functions (e.g., binding of viral particles to host cells) [40].

■ *Cellular immunity:* During their maturation, T-cells express a unique ABR on their surface, called the T-cell receptor. Unlike B-cell ABR that can recognize antigens alone, T-cell receptors can only recognize antigenic peptides that are presented by cell-membrane proteins known as major histocompatibility complex (MHC) molecules. When a T-cell encounters antigens associated with an MHC molecule on a cell,* the T-cell proliferates and differentiates into memory T-cells and various effector T-cells. The cellular immunity is accomplished by these generated effector T-cells. There are different types of T-cells that interact in a complex way to kill altered self-cells (for instance, virus-infected cells) or to activate phagocytic cells [36].

■ *Self/nonself discrimination:* The immune system can distinguish its own cells from foreign antigens, and so responds only to the dangerous nonself molecules. As was mentioned before, T-cells mature in the thymus. There, they go through a process of selection that ensures that they are able to recognize nonself peptides presented by MHC [7].

■ *Negative selection:* The purpose of negative selection is to test for tolerance of self-cells. T-cells that recognize the combination of MHC and self-peptides fail this test. This process can be seen as a filtering of a large diversity of T-cells; only those T-cells that do not recognize self-peptides are retained [30].

■ *Immune memory:* The immune system can "remember" a previous encounter with an antigen. This helps to deliver a quick response in subsequent encounters. In particular, immune-competent lymphocytes are able to recognize specific antigens through their ABR. The specificity of each T-cell and B-cell is determined prior to its contact with the antigen through random gene rearrangements in the bone marrow (or thymus) during the maturation process [32]. The presence of an antigen in the system and its subsequent interaction with mature lymphocytes trigger an immune response, resulting in the proliferation of lymphocytes with a unique antigenic

---

* In general, T-cells do not recognize whole antigen molecules; instead, their receptors detect fragments of the antigen called *peptides,* which are processed and presented by antigen-presenting cells (APCs).

specificity. This process of population expansion of particular T-cells and B-cells is called *clonal selection*. Clonal selection contributes to the specificity of adaptive immunity response because only lymphocytes whose receptors are specific to a given antigen will be cloned and, thus, mobilized for an immune response.

Another important consequence of clonal selection is immune memory [33]. The first encounter of naive immune-competent lymphocytes with an antigen generates the primary response, which, as discussed before, results in the proliferation of the lymphocytes that can recognize this specific antigen. Most of these lymphocytes die when the antigen is eliminated; however, some are kept as memory cells. The next occurrence of the same antigen can be detected quickly, activating a secondary response. This response is faster and more intense because of the availability of such memory cells.

7.1.3 Computational Aspects of the Immune System

From the point of view of information processing, the natural immune system exhibits many interesting characteristics. The following is a list of these characteristics [12,20]:

- *Pattern matching:* The immune system is able to recognize specific antigens and generate appropriate responses. This is accomplished by a recognition mechanism based on chemical binding of receptors and antigens. This binding depends on the molecular shape and on the electrostatic charge.
- *Feature extraction:* In general, immune receptors do not bind to the complete antigen but to peptides. In this way, the immune system can recognize an antigen just by matching segments of it. Antigenic features are extracted (called peptides) and presented to the lymphocyte receptors by antigen-presenting cells (APC). These APCs act as filters that can extract the important information and remove the molecular noise.
- *Learning and memory:* The main characteristic of the adaptive immune system is that it is able to learn through interaction with the environment. The first time an antigen is detected, a primary response is induced that includes the proliferation of lymphocytes and a subsequent reduction. Some of these lymphocytes are kept as memory cells. The next time the same antigen is detected, the memory cells generate a faster and more intense response (secondary response). Memory cells work as an associative (highly) distributed memory.

■ *Diversity:* The adaptive immune system can generate billions of different recognition molecules that are able to uniquely recognize different structures of foreign antigens. Clonal selection and hyper-mutation mechanisms constantly test different detector configurations for known and unknown antigens. This is a highly combinatorial process that explores the space of possible configurations for close-to-optimum receptors that can cope with the different types of antigens. Exploration is balanced with exploitation by favoring the reproduction of promising individuals.

■ *Distributed processing:* Unlike the nervous system, the immune system does not possess a central controller. Detection and response can be executed locally and immediately without communicating with any central organ. This distributed behavior is accomplished by billions of immune molecules and cells that circulate in the blood and lymph systems and are capable of making decisions in a local collaborative environment.

■ *Self-regulation:* Depending on the severity of the attack, the response of the immune system can range from very light and almost imperceptible to very strong. A stronger response uses a lot of resources to help repel the attacker. Once the invader is eliminated, the immune system regulates itself to stop the delivery of new resources and to release the used ones. Programmed cell death and clonal expansions are parts of this self-regulatory process.

7.2 Artificial Immune Systems

The study and design of artificial immune systems (AISs) is a relatively new area of research that tries to build computational systems that are inspired by the BIS [14]. There are many desirable computational features in the BIS that can be used to solve computational problems. In many respects, AISs are abstract computational models of the immune system; in fact, some AIS techniques are based on theoretical models of the BIS. However, the main difference lies in the use of AISs as a problem-solving technique.

A theoretical model that has served as a basis for some AISs is the idiotypic network theory proposed by Jerne [29]. This theory proposed that the BIS regulates itself by forming a network of B-cells that can enhance or suppress the expression of specific antibody types. This self-regulatory mechanism maintains a stable immune memory. The formation of such a network is only possible by the presence of paratopes on the B-cells that can be recognized by other B-cell epitopes. This recognition usually extends to more than one level, resulting in the formation of complex reaction networks. This model is a simplification of the BIS that ignores important elements such as T-lymphocytes and macrophages and concentrates on the modeling of the idiotypic networks.

Forrest and her group [21] proposed the negative-selection algorithm (NSA), which is inspired by the mechanism used by the immune system to train the T-cells to recognize antigens (nonself) and to prevent them from recognizing the body's own cells (self). Different variations of this algorithm have been applied to problems in anomaly detection [14,25], fault detection [13,41], and computer intrusion detection [15,21,24]. The rest of this chapter describes in detail the NSA, its versions, and applications to intrusion detection.

7.2.1 NSA

The immune system can recognize and classify different novel patterns (pathogenic patterns of interest) and generate selective responses in nonself space. Self/nonself (or danger) discrimination may be one of the important tasks of the immune system during the process of pathogenic recognition.

This discrimination is achieved in part by T-cells, which have receptors on their surface that can detect foreign proteins (antigens). During the generation of T-cells, receptors are made by a pseudorandom genetic rearrangement process. Then they undergo a censoring process in the thymus, called *negative selection,* in which T-cells that react against self-proteins are destroyed; hence, only those that do not bind to self-proteins are allowed to leave the thymus. These matured T-cells then circulate throughout the body to perform immunological functions to protect against foreign antigens. Forrest et al. [21] proposed the NSA based on self/nonself discrimination in the immune system.

The NSA is based on the principles of self/nonself discrimination in the immune system (Figure 7.1 shows the concept of self and nonself space). This can be summarized as follows [16]:

■ Define self as a collection S of elements in a feature space U, a collection that needs to be monitored. For instance, if U corresponds to the space of states of a system represented by a list of features, S can represent the subset of states that are considered normal for the system.
■ Generate a set F of detectors, each of which fails to match any string in S. An approach that mimics the immune system generates random detectors and discards those that match any element in

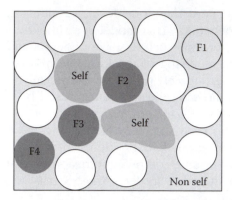

Figure 7.1 Conceptual view of self and nonself. Here, F1, F2, and F3 indicate different known attack types.

the self set. However, a more efficient approach [17] tries to minimize the number of generated detectors while maximizing the coverage of the nonself space.

■ Monitor *S* for changes by continually matching the detectors in *F* against *S*. If any detector ever matches, then a change is known to have occurred, as the detectors are designed not to match any representative samples of *S*.

This description is very general and does not say anything about the representation of the problem space and the type of matching rule that is used. It is, however, clear that the algorithmic complexity of generating good detectors can vary significantly, which depends on the type of problem space (continuous, discrete, mixed, etc.), detector-encoding scheme, and the matching rule (which determines if a detector matches an element or not). Most of the past works on the NSA had been restricted to the binary matching rules like *r*-contiguous, hamming distance, r-chunk, etc. The primary reason for this choice is the ease of use, and there exist efficient algorithms that exploit the properties of the binary representation and its matching rules [17]. However, there are practical issues that prevent the binary NSA from being applied more extensively:

■ Scalability is one such issue. To guarantee good levels of detection, a large number of detectors have to be generated (depending on the size of the self). For some problems, the number of detectors could be unmanageable.

■ The low-level detector representation prevents the extraction of meaningful domain knowledge. This makes it difficult to analyze reasons for reporting an anomaly in a monitored system or process.

▪ A sharp distinction exists between the normal and abnormal. This divides the space into two subsets: self (the normal) and the nonself (abnormal). An element in the space is considered to be abnormal if there exists a detector that matches it. In reality, normalcy is not a crisp concept. A natural way to characterize the self space is to define a degree of normalcy; this can be accomplished, for instance, by defining the self as a fuzzy set.

▪ Other immune-inspired algorithms use higher-level representation (e.g., real-valued vectors). A low-level representation, such as binary, makes it difficult to integrate the NS algorithm with other immune algorithms.

The following sections describe a real-valued negative-selection (RNS) algorithm, which uses different encoding schemes to speed up the detector generation process and to alleviate the limitations previously mentioned.

7.3 Real-Valued Negative Selection (RNS)

The RNS algorithm applies a heuristic process that iteratively changes the position of the detectors. It is driven by two goals: to maximize the coverage of the nonself subspace and to minimize the coverage of the self samples. Different versions of RNS algorithms are being studied for the generation of variably sized and shaped detectors, including spherical, hyper-rectangular, and fuzzy-rule detectors [11,23]. In all these cases, the self/nonself space, U, corresponds to a subset of R^n, unitary hypercube $[0,1]^n$, and each detector covers some nonself area in this high-dimensional space.

7.3.1 Negative Selection with Detection Rules (NSDR)

The first approach uses real-valued representation to characterize the self/nonself space and evolves a set of detectors that can cover the (nonself) complementary subspace (as shown in Figure 7.2). The structure of these detection rules is $(R^1, R^2, \ldots, R^m)$:

where,

▪ $Cond_i = x_1 \in [\text{low}_1^i, \text{high}_1^i]$ and $\ldots$ and $x_n \in [\text{low}_n^i, \text{high}_n^i]$
▪ $(x_1, \ldots, x_n)$ is a feature vector
▪ $[\text{low}_i^j, \text{high}_i^j]$ specifies the lower and upper values for the feature x_i in the condition part of the rule R^j

The condition part of each rule defines hyper-rectangle in the self/nonself space, $[0.0, 1.0]^n$. A set of these rules tries to cover the nonself space

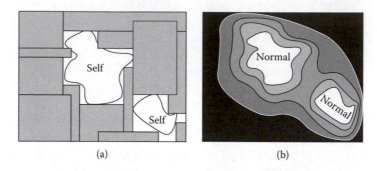

(a)   (b)

Figure 7.2 Self/nonself space. (a) Approximation of the nonself space by rectangular interval rules. (b) Levels of deviation from the normal in the nonself space.

with hyper-rectangles. For the case $n = 2$, the condition part of a rule represents a rectangle. Figure 7.2(a) illustrates an example of such a coverage for $n = 2$.

The nonself characteristic function (crisp version) generated by a set of rules $R = \{R^1, \ldots, R^m\}$ is defined as follows:

$$X_{non\_self,R}(\vec{x}) = \begin{cases} 1 & \text{if } \exists R^j \in R \text{ such that } \vec{x} \in R^j \\ 0 & \text{otherwise} \end{cases}$$

Alternatively, the nonself space can be divided into different levels of deviation. In Figure 7.2(b), these levels of deviation are shown as concentric regions around the self regions.

To characterize the different levels of abnormality, we considered a variability parameter (v) to the set of normal descriptor samples, in which v represents the level of variability that we allow in the normal (self) space. A higher value of v means more variability (allows larger variation in self characterization); a lower value of v represents less variability (a smaller self space). Figure 7.3 shows two sets of rules that characterize self subspaces with large and small values of v. Figure 7.3(a) shows coverage using a smaller v. Figure 7.3(b) shows coverage using a larger value of v. The variability parameter can be assumed as the radius of a hypersphere around the self samples. Figure 7.3(c) shows the levels of deviation defined by two coverings.

In the nonself space, different values of v are used to generate a set of rules that can provide maximum coverage. An example of such a set of rules is as follows:

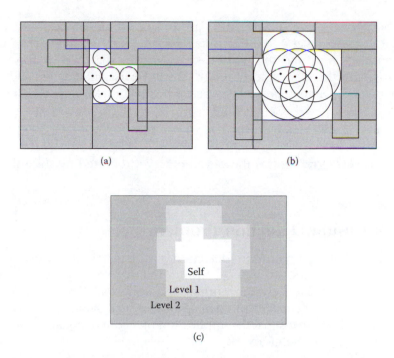

(a)

(b)

(c)

Figure 7.3 A set of normal samples is represented as points in 2-D space. The circle around each sample point represents the allowable deviation. (a) Rectangular rules cover the nonself (abnormal) space using a small value of *v*. (b) Rectangular rules cover the nonself space using a large value of *v*. (c) Level of deviation defined by each *v*, in which level 1 corresponds to nonself cover in (a) and level 2 corresponds to nonself cover in (b).

R^1:   If $Cond_1$ then   **Level 1**

.   .   .

.   .   .

.   .   .

R^i: If $Cond_i$ then   **Level 1**

R^{i+1}: If $Condi_{+1}$ then   **Level 2**

.   .   .

.   .   .

.   .   .

R^j: If $Cond_j$ then   **Level 2**

.   .   .

.   .   .

.   .   .

The different levels of deviation are organized hierarchically such that level 1 contains level 2, level 2 contains level 3, and so forth. This means that an element in the self/nonself space can be matched by more than one rule, but the highest level reported will be assigned as its level. This set of rules generates a graded characteristic function for the nonself space:

$$\mu_{non\_self}(\vec{x}) = \max(\{l \mid \exists R^j \in R, \vec{x} \in R^j \text{ and } l = \text{level}(R^j)\} \cup \{0\}),$$

where *level* (R^j) represents the deviation level reported by the rule R^j.

7.4 Intrusion Detection Problem

The anomaly-based intrusion detection problem can be viewed as a learning task that tries to induce, from a training set, a general function that can discriminate between normal and abnormal samples. However, in many anomaly detection problems, only normal samples are available for training. This means that the application of a conventional classification algorithm is not straightforward.

7.4.1 Positive or Negative Characterization?

Normal behavior or normal data patterns will be represented by a subspace S (called SELF) of the feature space, X. On the other hand, the complement of S, $N = X–S$, will be referred to as NON_SELF. The techniques to generate detectors can be classified as follows [19]:

- *Positive characterization (PC):* All the representative patterns are chosen from the set of normal patterns, i.e., normal entities of the system, denoted by S.
- *Negative characterization:* All the representative patterns are chosen from the set of patterns in $X–S$, i.e., abnormal entities of the system.

Negative characterization does not seem to be as natural as PC in cases in which the normal space is relatively small. So, what is the justification for negative characterization? Esponda and Forrest [18] provided three main reasons:

- There is practical evidence that the negative-detection approach works, because it has been applied with some success to solve practical problems.
- From an information theory point of view, characterizing the normal space is equivalent to characterizing the abnormal space.

■ Negative characterization is more suitable for distributed anomaly detection. That is, it is possible to divide a set of negative detectors into subsets and apply them in a distributed fashion, because the activation of only one negative detector is enough to classify a sample as abnormal. If we use positive detection, it is necessary to apply all the positive detectors before it can be concluded that a sample is abnormal.

The third reason appears to be the strongest. However, if the description of the normal set is compact enough, it would be more efficient to have multiple, redundant copies of positive detectors perform distributed anomaly detection. Accordingly, negative detection is more suitable than positive detection for performing distributed detection, but only if the normal subspace is not very small.

Keogh et al. [31] argued that "a major limitation of the approach (negative selection) is that it is only defined when the self space is not exhaustive." The authors provided an example of random walk data series, in which the self set can have all possible patterns, causing the nonself set to be empty. Notice that this is also a possible issue for the positive detection strategy and, in general, for any learning strategy that tries to induce a model of the normal profile from samples. So, the problem is not associated with the algorithm itself, but with the set of features selected to represent the system behavior, which are not useful to characterize the system or process normalcy. For instance, in the case of the random walk time series, a set of features that includes high-level statistical characteristics of the time series may perform better than a set of features based on a sliding-window scheme.

Once a uniform representation for the parameter space is chosen, a set of patterns that correspond to normal entities is presented to the NSA. Such a set is called the *set of self patterns,* and it is used during the learning process to determine a set of representative elements that will be used to detect novelties in the system. Depending on the context, a representative pattern is called a *detector* or a *classification rule.* We use these terms interchangeably. In the next section, we test the proposed approach with network traffic data.

7.5 Experimentation

7.5.1 Dataset

We tested the proposed approaches with network traffic data. The idea was to examine if the system is able to detect some attacks after it is trained with normal traffic patterns. This dataset is a version of the 1999

Table 7.1   Second-Week Attack Description

Day	Attack Name	Attack Type	Start	Duration
1	Back	DoS	9:39:16	00:59
2	Portsweep	Probe	8:44:17	26:56
3	Satan	Probe	12:02:13	02:29
4	Portsweep	Probe	10:50:11	17:29
5	Neptune	DoS	11:20:15	04:00

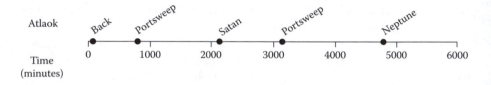

Figure 7.4   Network attacks on the second week.

DARPA intrusion detection evaluation dataset generated and managed by MIT Lincoln Labs [35]. This data represents both normal and abnormal information collected in a test network, in which simulated attacks were performed. The purpose of this data is to test the performance of intrusion detection systems. The datasets contain normal data (not mixed with attacks) obtained over a period of several weeks. This provides enough samples to train the detection system.

The dataset is composed of network traffic data (tcpdump, inside and outside network traffic), audit data (BSM), and file systems data. For our initial set of experiments, we used only the outside tcpdump network data for a specific computer (e.g., hostname: marx), and then we applied the tool tcpstat to get traffic statistics. We used the first week's data for training (attack free), and the second week's data for testing, which included some attacks. Some of these were network attacks, and the others were inside attacks. Only network attacks were considered for our testing. These attacks are described in Table 7.1, and the attack timeline is shown in Figure 7.4.

Three parameters were selected to detect some specific types of attacks. These parameters were sampled each minute (using tcpstat) and normalized. Table 7.2 lists six time series S_i and T_i for training and testing, respectively.

The set S of normal descriptors is generated from a time series $\{r_1, r_2, \ldots, r_n\}$ in an overlapping–sliding-window fashion:

Table 7.2 Time Series for Different Parameters Used for Training and Testing

Name	Description	Week	Type
S1	Number of bytes per second	1	Training
S2	Number of packets per second	1	Training
S3	Number of ICMP packets per second	1	Training
T1	Number of bytes per second	2	Testing
T2	Number of packets per second	2	Testing
T3	Number of ICMP packets per second	2	Testing

$$S = \left\{ \left(r_1, \ldots, r_w \right), \left(r_2, \ldots, r_{w+1} \right), \ldots, \left(r_{n-w+1}, \ldots, r_n \right) \right\}$$

where w is the window size. In general, from a time series with n points, a set of $n - w + 1$ of w-dimensional descriptors can be generated. In some cases, we used more than one time series to generate the feature vectors. In those cases, the descriptors were put side by side to produce the final feature vector. For instance, if we used the three time series S1, S2, and S3 with a window size of 3, a set of 9-dimensional feature vectors was generated.

To evaluate the ability of the proposed approach to produce a good estimation of the level of deviation, we implemented a simple (but inefficient) anomaly detection mechanism. It uses the actual distance of an element to the nearest neighbor in the self set as an estimation of the degree of abnormality.

7.5.2 PC Approach

In this approach, we used the positive samples to build a characterization of the self space, *Self*. In particular, we did not assume a model for the self set. Instead, we used the positive sample set itself for a representation of the self space. The degree of abnormality of an element is calculated as the distance from itself to the nearest neighbor in the self set. We chose to define the characteristic function of the nonself set, *non_self*, because its definition is more natural, and the derivation of the self set characteristic function is straightforward.

$$\mu_{non\_self}\left(\vec{x} \right) = D\left(\vec{x}, Self \right) = \min \left\{ d\left(\vec{x}, \vec{s} \right) : \vec{s} \in Self \right\}$$

Here, $d(x, s)$ is a Euclidean distance metric (or any Minkowski metric). $D(\vec{x}, Self)$ is the nearest-neighbor distance, that is, the distance from $\vec{x}$ to the closest point in *Self*. Then, the closer an element x is to the self set, the closer the value of $\mu_{non\_self}(x)$ is to 0.

The crisp version of the characteristic function is the following:

$$\mu_{non\_self,t}\left(\vec{x}\right) = \begin{cases} 1 & \text{if} \quad \mu_{non\_self}\left(\vec{x}\right) > t \\ 0 & \text{if} \quad \mu_{non\_self}\left(\vec{x}\right) \le t \end{cases} = \begin{cases} 1 & \text{if} \quad D\left(\vec{x}, Self\right) \\ 0 & \text{if} \quad D\left(\vec{x}, Self\right) \end{cases}$$

In a dynamic environment, the parameter values that characterize normal system behavior may vary within a certain range over a period of time. The term $(1 - t)$ represents the amount of allowable variability in the self space (the maximum distance that a point can be from the self-samples to be considered normal). This PC can be implemented efficiently by using spatial trees. In our implementation, a KD-tree [5,6] was used. A KD-tree represents a set of k-dimensional points and is a generalization of the standard one-dimensional binary search tree. The nodes of a KD-tree are divided into two classes: internal nodes, which partition the space with a cut plane defined by a value in one of the k dimensions, and external nodes (leaves), which define "buckets" (resulting in hyper-rectangles) in which the points are stored.

This representation allows answering queries in an efficient way. The amortized cost of a nearest-neighbor query is $O(log\ N)$ [6]. We used a library (which implements the KD-tree structure) developed at the University of Maryland [37].

7.5.2.1 PC Experiments

In each experiment, the training set was used to build a KD-tree to represent the self set. Then, the distance (nearest neighbor) from each point in the testing set to the self set was measured to determine deviations. For this set of experiments, the variables were considered independently; that is, the feature vectors were built using only one variable (time series) each time. Figure 7.5 shows an example of the training and testing datasets for the parameter *number of packets per second*. Figure 7.6(a) represents the nonself characteristic function $\mu_{non\_self}(\vec{x})$, that is, the distance from the test set to the training set for the same parameter. In this case, the window size used to build the descriptors was 1. Figure 7.6(b) and Figure 7.6(c) show $\mu_{non\_self}(\vec{x})$ when a window size of 3 is used.

In Figure 7.6(b), the Euclidean distance is used, and in Figure 7.6(c), the D_∞ distance is used.

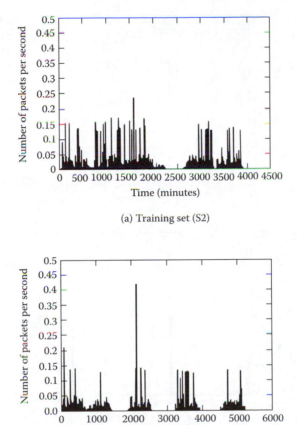

(a) Training set (S2)

(b) Testing set (T2)

Figure 7.5 **Behavior of the parameter** *number of packets per second.* **(a) Training (self) set corresponding to the first week. (b) Testing set corresponding to the second week.**

The plots (in Figure 7.6) of the nonself characteristic function show some peaks that correspond to significant deviations from the normal. It is easy to check that these peaks coincide with the network attacks present on the testing data (Table 7.1 and Figure 7.6). We conclude the following from these results:

■ Using only one parameter is not enough to detect all five attacks. Figure 7.8 shows how the function $\mu_{non\_self}(\bar{x})$ detects deviations that correspond to attacks; however, none of the parameters is able to independently detect all five attacks.

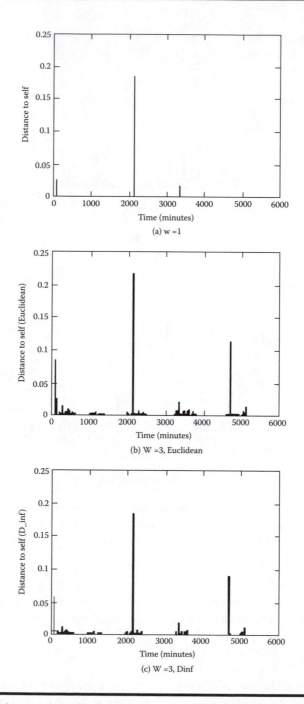

Figure 7.6 **Distance from the testing set (T2) to the self set (S2) ($\mu_{non\_self}(x)$). (a) Using window size 1. (b) Using window size 3 and Euclidean distance. (c) Using window size 3 and D_∞ distance.**

- A higher window size increases the sensitivity; this is reflected in the higher values of deviation.
- A higher window size allows for the detection of temporal patterns. For the time series T1 and T3, increasing the window size does not modify the number of detected anomalies. But, for the time series T2, when the window size is increased from 1 in Figure 7.6(a) to 3 in Figure 7.6(b) and Figure 7.6(c), one additional deviation (corresponding to attack 5) is detected. Clearly, this deviation was not caused by a value of this parameter (number of bytes per second) out of range; otherwise, it would be detected by the window size 1. There was a temporal pattern that was not seen in the training set, and that might be the reason why it was reported as an anomaly.
- The change of the distance metric from Euclidean in Figure 7.6(b) to D_∞ in Figure 7.6(c) does not modify the number and type of deviations detected.

As we found in previous experiments, to detect the four attacks, it is necessary to take into account more than one parameter. In the following experiments, we used three parameters to build the feature vector to test whether the PC technique can detect all the attacks. Accordingly, we performed two experiments by varying the sliding-window size.

Figure 7.7 shows the nonself characteristic function for feature vectors conformed to samples of three time series. In all cases, there are five remarkable anomalies that correspond to five attacks. Similar to previous experiments, an increase in the size of the window increases the sensitivity of the anomaly detection function. However, this could generate more false-positives. To measure the accuracy of the anomaly detection function,

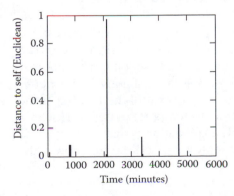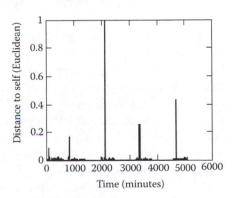

Figure 7.7 Distance from test sets to the self set ($\mu_{non\_self}(\overline{x})$) using S1, S2, and S3. (a) Window size 1. (b) Window size 3.

it is necessary to convert them to a crisp version. In this case, the output of the function will be normal or abnormal. This output can be compared with attack information to calculate how many anomalies (caused by an attack) were detected accurately.

The crisp version of the anomaly detection function $\mu_{non\_self}(x)$ is generated by specifying a threshold (t), indicating the frontier between normal and abnormal. Clearly, the value of t will affect the capabilities of the system to detect accurately. A very large value of t will allow large variability on the normal (self), increasing the rate of false-negatives; a very small value of t will restrict the normal set, causing an increase in the number of detections, but also increasing the number of false-positives (false alarms). To show this trade-off between the false-alarm rate and the detection rate, receiver operating characteristics (ROC) diagrams [39] are drawn. The anomaly detection function $\mu_{non\_self}, t(x)$ is tested with different values of t, the detection and false-alarm rates are calculated, and this generates a set of points that constitute the ROC diagram. The detection and false-alarm rates are calculated using the following equations:

$$\text{Detection rate} = \frac{TP}{TP + FN} \tag{7.1}$$

$$\text{False-alarm rate} = \frac{FP}{TN + FP}, \tag{7.2}$$

where:

TP: true positives, anomalous elements identified as anomalous
TN: true negatives, normal elements identified as normal
FP: false-positives, normal elements identified as anomalous
FN: false-negatives, anomalous elements identified as normal

Figure 7.8 shows the ROC diagrams for the $\mu_{non\_self}(x)$ functions shown in Figure 7.9. In general, the behavior of these four functions is very similar: high detection rates with a low false-alarm rate. The anomaly detection functions that use window size 3 show a slightly better performance in terms of detection rates. This could be attributed to the higher sensitivity, produced by a larger window, to temporal patterns. However, this causes more false alarms. A possible explanation is that after an attack, some disturbance may still remain in the system, and the function with a larger window size was able to detect it.

The PC technique has been shown to work well on the performed experiments. The main drawback of this technique is its memory requirements, because it is necessary to store the samples that constitute the normal profile. The amount of data generated by network traffic can be

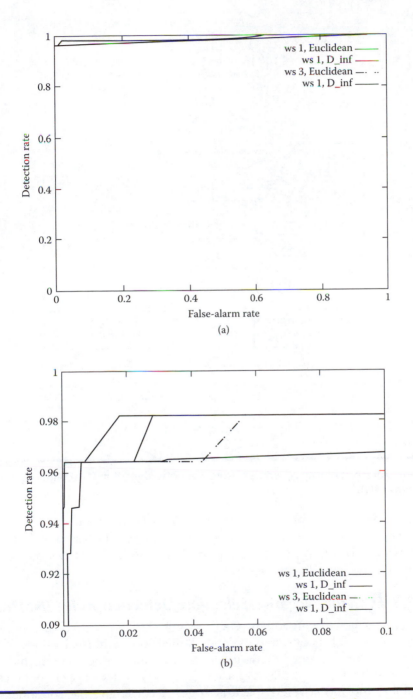

Figure 7.8 ROC diagrams for the $\mu_{non\_self}(x)$ function shown in Figure 7.7. (a) Full scale. (b) Detail of the upper-left corner.

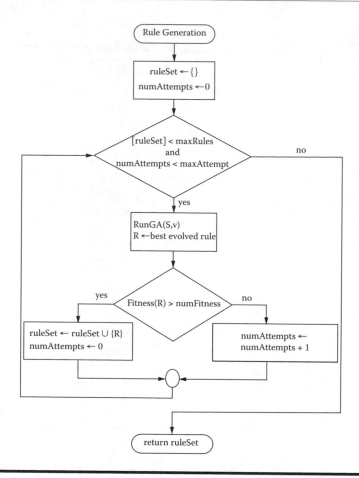

Figure 7.9   NSDR rule generation using a genetic algorithm (GA) with sequential niching (SN).

large, making this approach unfeasible. This is the main motivation for the negative characterization approach, e.g., NSDR (discussed in the following subsection), compressing the information of the normal profile without significant loss in accuracy.

7.5.3 Evolving Negative-Selection Detection Rules (NSDR)

We used a genetic algorithm (GA) to evolve rules to cover the nonself space. These rules constitute the complement of the normal values of the feature vectors. Several criteria guide the evolution process performed by the GA [9,10]. Hence, a rule is considered good if it does not cover positive samples, and the covered space is large. Accordingly, the soundness of a rule is determined by various factors: the number of normal samples that it covers, its coverage, and the overlap with other rules. This is a multiobjective, multimodal optimization problem, because a set of rules (solutions) that can collectively solve the problem (covering of the nonself region) is desired.

A niching technique is used with GAs to generate different rules. The input to the GA is a set of feature vectors $S' = \{x^1, \ldots, x^l\}$, which indicate normal behavior. Each element x^j in S' is an n-dimensional vector $x^j = (x_1^j, \ldots, x_n^j)$. The algorithm for the rule generation is shown in Figure 7.9, where:

S':	self-samples training set
v:	level of variability
maxRules:	maximum number of rules in the solution set
minFitness:	minimum fitness allowed for a rule to be included in the solution set
maxAttempts:	maximum number of attempts to try to evolve a rule with a fitness greater or equal to *minFitness*

The algorithm tries to generate a set of rules (*ruleSet*) using a GA (procedure *RunGA( )*). Each rule in the *ruleSet* is generated with different runs of the GA. The rule must have a fitness value of at least *minFitness*. If after a maximum number of attempts (*maxAttempts*) it cannot generate a good rule, the algorithm stops (typical values for *maxAttempts* lie between 3 and 5 runs).

The procedure *RunGA( )* executes a tournament-selection–based GA. Its execution time is $(O\ num\_gen * pop\_size * f_{time})$, where num_gen is the number of generations, pop_size is the population size, and f_{time} is the execution time of the fitness evaluation. In this case, $f_{time} = O(|S'|)$, where $|S'|$ is the size of the self sample set. Therefore, the execution time of the NSDR algorithm is $O(m * num\_gen * pop\_size * |S'|)$, where m is the number of generated rules.

Each individual (chromosome) in the GA represents the condition part of a rule because the consequent part is the same for all the rules (the descriptor belongs to the nonself). However, the levels of deviation in the nonself space are determined by the variability factor (v). The condition part of the rule is determined by the low and high limits for each dimension. The chromosome that represents these values consists of an array of float numbers. Uniform crossover and Gaussian mutation operators are used.

Given a rule R with a condition part ($x_1 \in [low_1, high_1]$ AND …AND $x_n \in [low_n, high_n]$), we say that a feature vector $x^j = (x_1^j, \ldots, x_n^j)$ satisfies the rule R (represented as $x^j \in R$) if the hypersphere with center x^j and radius v intercepts the hyper-rectangle defined by the points ($low_1, \ldots, low_n$) and ($high_1, \ldots, high_n$).

The raw fitness of a rule is calculated considering the following two factors:

1. The number of elements in the training set S' that are covered by the rule:

$$\text{num\_elements}\ (R) = \{x^i \in S \mid x^i \in R\}$$

2. The volume of the subspace represented by the rule:

$$\text{volume}(R) = \prod_{i=1}^{n} (\text{high}_i - \text{low}_i)$$

The raw fitness is defined as:

$$\text{raw\_fitness}_R = \text{volume}(R) = C * \text{num\_elements}(R)$$

where C is the coefficient of sensitivity. It specifies the amount of penalization that a rule suffers if it covers some normal samples. So, the larger the coefficient (C), the higher is the imposed penalty. Raw fitness can also take negative values.

The idea is to run the GA multiple times [4] to generate different rules so as to cover the entire nonself region. In each run, we want to generate a new rule, that is, a rule that can cover a portion of the nonself region. The raw fitness of each rule is modified according to the overlap with the previously chosen rules. The following pseudocode segment shows how the final fitness of the rule R is calculated.

```
fitness ← raw_ fitness_R
for each R^j ∈ ruleSet do
fitness_R ← raw_ fitness_R – volume(RR^j)
end-For
```

where *volume*( ) calculates the volume of the subspace specified by the argument.

Because the coverage of the nonself space is accomplished by a set of rules, it is necessary to evolve multiple rules. To evolve different rules, a sequential niching (SN) algorithm is applied.

7.5.3.1 Experiments: NSDR-GA with SN

To test the negative characterization approach (NSDR), we used the MIT DARPA 99 dataset (mentioned in Section 7.4) [35]. We used as training set the time series S1, S2, and S3, and as testing set the time series T1, T2, and T3, with window sizes of 3 and 1, respectively (the time series are described in Table 7.2).

Table 7.3   Number of Generated Rules for Each Deviation Level

Level	Radius	Average Number Rules (Window Size = 1)	Average Number Rules (Window Size = 3)
1	0.05	1.1	19.5
2	0.1	1.1	20.7
3	0.15	1	26
4	0.2	1.1	28

The parameters for the GA were population size 100, number of generations 1500, mutation rate 0.2, crossover rate 1.0, and coefficient of sensitivity 1.0 (high sensitivity).

The GA was run with variability parameter (v) equal to 0.05, 0.1, 0.15, and 0.2, respectively. Then, the elements in the testing set were classified using rules generated for each level (different values of v). This process was repeated ten times, and the results reported corresponded to the average of these runs.

Table 7.3 shows the number of rules generated by the GA for each level. There is a clear difference between the number of rules when the window size changes; the number of rules changes with the size of the window as the pattern space becomes larger.

Figure 7.10 shows two typical attack profiles produced by evolved rules applied to the testing set. With a window size of 1, three out of five attacks are detected, whereas with a window size of 3, four out of five attacks are detected.

The negative characterization technique (NSDR) is more efficient (in time and space) compared to the PC technique. In the case of a window size of 1, the PC needs to store $5,202 \times 3 = 15,606$ floating-point values; the NSDR technique only has to store $4 \times 6 = 24$ floating-point values, so the compression ratio is approximately 1000:1.5. In the case of the window size of 3, the ratio is 46,728:1,698,* approximately 100:8. It seems to be a trade-off between compactness of the rule set representation and accuracy. Validity of these arguments is observed in our results. Figure 7.11 shows how the rate of true positives (detection rate) changes according to the value of the threshold t. In both cases, the PC technique has better performance than the NSDR technique, but only by a small difference. In general, the NSDR technique shows detection rates similar to the

---

* The number of floating point numbers needed by the positive characterization is equal to (5192 samples) * (9 dimensions) = 46,728. The number of floating points numbers needed by the negative characterization is (94 rules) * (18 floating values per rule) = 1,698.

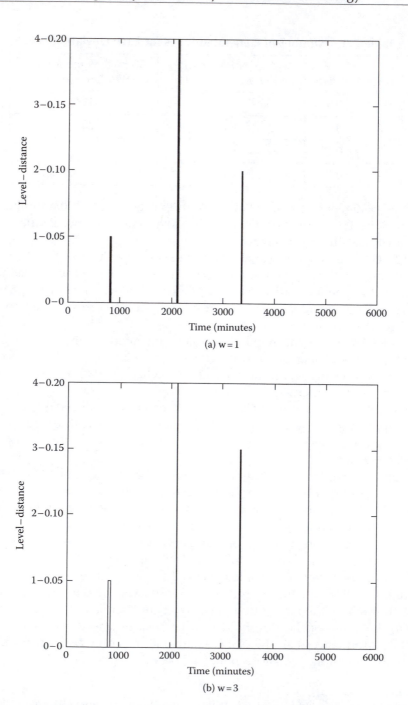

Figure 7.10 Indicates the deviations in the testing set detected by the evolved rule set. (a) For window size 1. (b) For window size 3.

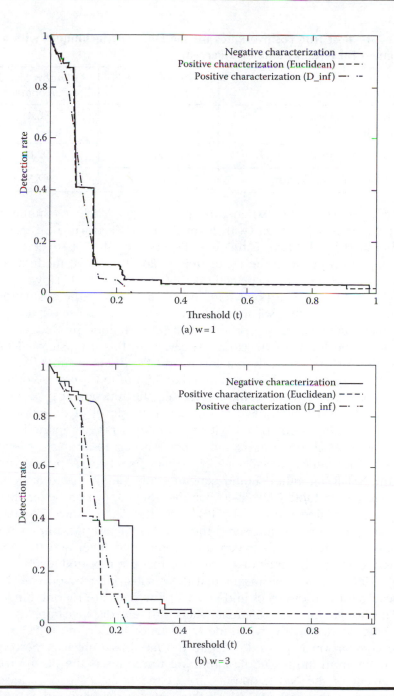

Figure 7.11   Comparison of the true positives rate of the detection function μ_{non_self}, $t(x)$ **generated by positive characterization (PC) and negative characterization (NSDR) for different values of** t. **(a) Window size 1. (b) Window size 3.**

Table 7.4   Best True Positive Rates for the Different Techniques with a Maximum False-Alarm Rate of 1 Percent

Detection Technique	Window Size 1 (Percentage)	Window Size 3 (Percentage)
Positive characterization (Euclidean)	92.8	96.4
Positive characterization (*D*)	92.8	92.8
Negative characterization	82.1	87.5

more accurate (but more expensive) PC technique. Table 7.4 summarizes the best true positive rates (with a maximum false alarm of 1 percent) accomplished by the two techniques. Esponda et al. [19] suggested that this comparison between the PC technique and the NSDR method is not meaningful, because the two methods are quite different. However, the PC technique provides a point reference that facilitates the evaluation of the performance of the NSDR technique.

As mentioned earlier, the proposed NSDR technique produces a good estimate of the levels of deviation. To evaluate this estimate, a detailed comparison of the NSDR output levels and PC distance range was performed. The results are illustrated in Table 7.5 in the form of a confusion matrix. For each element in the testing set, the function $\mu_{non\_self}(x)$ generated by the NSDR is applied to determine the level of deviation. This level of deviation is compared with the distance range reported by the PC algorithm. Each row (and column) corresponds to a range or level of deviation. The ranges are specified in square brackets. A perfect output from the NSDR algorithm should generate only values in the diagonal.

The results in Table 7.5 suggest that the NSDR approach better approximates the deviation reported by PC using the D_∞ distance. To support this claim precisely, we measured the number of testing samples for all the possible differences between the PC-reported level and the NSDR-reported level. A difference of zero means that the reported levels are the same, a difference of one means that the results differ by one level, etc. The results for two distances and two window sizes are reported in Table 7.6. The results are very different when different distances are used for the PC algorithm. Clearly, when the D_∞ distance is used in the PC, results of the comparison improved. Despite the fact that only 50.3 percent of the outputs from the NSDR algorithm are the same as the PC approach, 100 percent of the NSDR outputs are in the range of 0 or 1 level of difference from that of the PC. The distance metric determines the structure of a metric space. For instance, in a Euclidean space, the set of points that are at the same distance from a fixed point corresponds to a circle

Table 7.5   Confusion Matrix for PC- and NSDR-Reported Deviations

PC Output Level	NSDR Output Level				
Euclidean	No Deviation [0.0,0.05]	Level 1 [0.05,0.1]	Level 2 [0.1,0.15]	Level 3 [0.15,0.2]	Level 4 [0.2,1]
[0.0,0.05]	5131	0	0	0	0
[0.05,0.1]	4	1	0	0	0
[0.1,0.15]	0	2.9	2.1	0	0
[0.15,0.2]	0	22	2	0	0
[0.2,1]	0	0	6.9	10.5	9.6
D					
[0.0,0.05]	5132	0	0	0	0
[0.05,0.1]	3	7.8	0.2	0	0
[0.1,0.15]	0	18.1	3.9	0	0
[0.15,0.2]	0	0	6.9	9.5	0.6
[0.2,1]	0	0	0	1	9

Note: The values of the matrix elements correspond to the number of testing samples in each class, and the diagonal values represent correct classification.

Table 7.6   The Difference between PC- and NSDR-Reported Levels for Test Dataset

Difference	Euclidean Distance (Percentage)	D_∞ Distance (Percentage)
0	20.8	50.3
1	31.8	49.7
2	47.3	0.0
3	0.0	0.0
4	0.0	0.0

Note: The difference is expressed as a percentage of the abnormal feature vectors (distance greater than 0.05). A difference of 0 means that the levels reported by PC and NSDR are the same; a difference of 1 means that the results differ by 1 level, etc.

(a hypersphere in higher dimensions). In the D_∞ metric space, this set of points corresponds to a rectangle (hyper-rectangle). Therefore, the rectangular rules used by the NSDR approach are better suited to approximate the structure of the D_∞ metric space, and this is reflected in the experimental results.

We investigated GAs to evolve detectors in the complement pattern space to identify any changes in the normal behavior of monitored behavior patterns. This technique (NSDR) is used to characterize and identify different intrusive activities by monitoring network traffic, and is compared with the other approach (PC). We used a real-world dataset (MIT Lincoln Labs) that has been used by other researchers for testing different approaches. The following are some preliminary observations from these experiments:

- When PC and NSDR approaches are compared, PC appears to be more precise, but it requires more time and space resources. The negative characterization is less precise but requires fewer resources.
- Results demonstrate that the NSDR approach to detector generation is feasible. It was able to detect four of the five attacks detected by the PC (with a detection rate of 87.5 percent and a maximum false-alarm rate of 1 percent).
- The best results were produced when we used a window size of 3. We observed that a larger window size makes the system more sensitive to deviations.

7.5.3.2 NSDR-GA Using Deterministic Crowding

The main drawback of the SN approach is that the GA must be run multiple times to generate multiple rules. The deterministic crowding (DC) [34] approach allows the generation of multiple rules in a single run. The NSDR algorithm using DC [23] is shown in Figure 7.12. The main inputs to the algorithm are a set of n-dimensional feature vectors $S = \{x^1, \ldots, x^l\}$, which represents samples of the normal behavior of the parameter, the number of different levels of deviation (*num_levels*), and the allowed variability for each level $\{v_1, \ldots, v_{numLevels}\}$. Additional parameters to the algorithm are the population size (*pop_size*) and number of generations (*num_gen*).

The execution time of this algorithm is $O(num\_levels * num\_gen * pop\_size |S'|)$, where $|S'|$ is the number of self-samples, which is included in the expression because the time complexity of the fitness calculation is $O(|S'|)$. Notice that the time complexity depends on the number of levels and not on the number of rules; this makes this algorithm more efficient than the NSDR algorithm based on SN. A good measure of distance between

```
NS-DETECTOR-RULES(S', num_levels,{ v1,.............,vnumLevels})
S : set of self samples
num_levels : number of deviation levels
{ v1,.............,vnumLevels}: allowed variability for each level
1:for i = 1 to num_levels
2: initialize population with random individuals
3: For j = 1 to num_gen
4: For k = 1 to pop_size/2
5: select two individuals,(parent1 parent2) , with uniform probability
and without replacement
6: apply crossover to generate an offspring(child)
7: mutate child
8: If dist ( child, parent1) < dist( child, parent2)
∧ fitness(child)> fitness( parent1)

10: Then parent1 ← child
11: ElseIf dist(child, parent1)>= dist(child, parent2)
12: ∧ fitness(child)> fitness(parent2)

13: Then parent2 ← child
14: EndIf
15: EndFor
16: EndFor
17: extract the best individuals from the population and add them to
the final solution
18:EndFor
```

Figure 7.12   Evolving negative-selection detection rules (NSDR) using deterministic crowding (DC).

individuals is important for DC niching, because it allows the algorithm to replace individuals with closer individuals. This allows the algorithm to preserve niche formation. The distance measure used in this work is the following:

$$dist\left(c,p\right) = \frac{volume\left(p\right) - volume\left(p \cap c\right)}{volume\left(p\right)},$$

where c is a child, and p is its parent.

Note that the distance measure is not symmetric. The purpose is to give more importance to the area of the parent that is not covered. The justification is as follows: if the child covers a high proportion of the parent, that means that the child is a good generalization of it, but if the child covers only a small portion, then it is not so. We used the same dataset as before as the training set time series S1, S2, and S3 for training, and time series T1, T2, and T3 for testing, with a window size of 3. This means that the size of the feature vectors was 9.

The parameters for the GA were population size 200, number of generations 2000, mutation rate 0.1, and coefficient of sensitivity 1.0 (high sensitivity). The GA was run with variability for each level equal to 0.05, 0.1,

Table 7.7 Number of Generated Rules for Each Deviation Level

		Average Number Rules	
Level	*Radius*	*Sequential Niching*	*Deterministic Crowding*
1	0.05	19.5	7.75
2	0.1	20.7	8.25
3	0.15	26	10
4	0.2	28	10

0.15, and 0.2, respectively. Then, the elements in the testing set are classified using rules generated for each level (radius). This process is repeated ten times, and the results reported correspond to the average of these runs.

Table 7.7 shows the number of rules NSDR generated by the GA with two niching techniques (NSDR with SN and NSDR with DC). The DC technique produces less rules, which suggests the possibility that the DC technique is discarding some good rules and, therefore, ignoring some niches. However, the performance of the set of rules generated by each technique is apparently similar. This shows that the DC technique is able to find a set of more compact rules producing the same performance. This can be explained by the fact that SN is more sensitive to the definition of the distance between individuals than DC.

Another notable point is the efficiency of the DC technique, as it only needs four runs (one per level) to generate a rule set. For the SN technique, it is necessary to run the GA as many times as the number of rules we want to generate. This is a clear improvement on computational time.

In Section 7.5.3.1, it is shown that the NSDR with SN technique produces a good estimate of the level of deviation when this is calculated using the D_∞ distance. Table 7.8 shows the confusion matrix for the NSDR technique using SN and DC. For each element in the testing set, the function $\mu_{non\_self}(x)$ generated by the NSDR is applied to determine the level of deviation. This level of deviation is compared with the distance range reported by the PC algorithm (using the D_∞ distance). Each row (and column) corresponds to a range or level of deviation. The ranges are specified on square brackets. A perfect output from the NSDR algorithm will generate values only in the diagonal.

In both cases, the values are concentrated around the diagonal, indicating that the two techniques produced a good estimate of the distance to the self set. However, the NSDR approach with DC appears to be more precise. One possible explanation for this performance difference seems to be the fact that the SN requires derating the fitness function for each evolved rule. This arbitrary modification in the fitness landscape can prevent evolving better rules in subsequent runs.

Table 7.8 The Values of the Matrix Elements Correspond to the Number of Testing Samples in Each Class

PC Output Level	NSDR Output Level				
	Sequential Niching				
	0	1	2	3	4
1: [0.0,0.05]	5132	0	0	0	0
2: [0.05,0.1]	3	7.8	0.2	0	0
3: [0.1,0.15]	0	18.1	3.9	0	0
4: [0.15,0.2]	0	0	6.9	9.5	0.6
5: [0.2,1]	0	0	0	1	9
	Deterministic Crowding				
	0	1	2	3	0
1: [0.0,0.05]	5132	0	0	0	0
2: [0.05,0.1]	3	4	4	0	0
3: [0.1,0.15]	0	0	22	0	0
4: [0.15,0.2]	0	0	0	17	0
5: [0.2,1]	0	0	0	0	10

Note: The diagonal values represent correct classification.

7.5.4 Extending NSDR to Use Fuzzy Rules

We next extended the NSDR algorithm to evolve fuzzy rules instead of crisp rules [23]. That is, given a set of self-samples, the algorithm will generate fuzzy detection rules in the nonself space that can determine if a new sample is normal or abnormal. The use of fuzzy rules appears to further improve the accuracy of the method and produces a measure of deviation from the normal that does not need to partition the nonself space.

The normal and the abnormal behaviors in networked computers are hard to predict, as the boundaries cannot be well defined. Hence, fuzzy logic can provide varying degrees of normalcy in system behavior.

A fuzzy detection rule has the following structure:

$$\textbf{If } x_1 \in T_1 \wedge \ldots x_n \in T_n \textbf{ then } \text{non\_self,}$$

where
$(x_1, \ldots, x_n)$: elements of the self/nonself space being evaluated

T_i: fuzzy set

∧:   fuzzy conjunction operator (in this case, min ())

The fuzzy set T_i is defined by a combination of basic fuzzy sets (linguistic values).

Given a set of linguistic values $S = \{S_1, \ldots, S_m\}$ and a subset T_i S associated with each fuzzy set T_i,

$$T_i = \bigcup_{S_j \in \hat{T}_i} S_j,$$

where $\cup$ corresponds to a fuzzy disjunction operator, which is defined as follows:

$$\mu_{A \cup B}(x) = \min\{\mu_A(x) + \mu_B(x), 1\}$$

An example of fuzzy detection rules in the self/nonself space with dimension $n = 3$ and linguistic values $S = \{L, M, H\}$:

If $x_1 \in L \wedge x_2 \in (L \cup M) \wedge x_3 \in (M \cup H)$ **then** non_self,

In our experiments, the basic fuzzy sets correspond to a fuzzy division of the real interval [0.0,1.0] using triangular and trapezoidal fuzzy membership functions. Figure 7.13 shows an example of such a division using five basic fuzzy sets representing the linguistic values low, medium-low, medium, medium-high, and high.

Given a set of rules $\{R^1, \ldots, R^k\}$, each one with a condition part $Cond_i$, the degree of abnormality of a sample x is defined by

$$\mu_{\text{non\_self}}(x) = \max_{i=1,\ldots k}\{Cond_i(x)\},$$

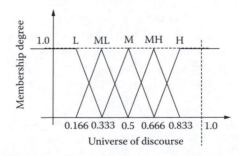

Figure 7.13   Partition of the interval [0,1] in basic fuzzy sets.

```
NS-FUZZY-DETECTOR-RULES(Self')

    Self'  :  set of self samples

 1:  initialize population with random individuals
 2:  For j = 1 to num_gen
 3:   For k = 1 to pop_size/2
 4:    select two individuals,(parent1,parent2),  with uniform
       probability and without replacement
 5:    apply crossover to generate an offspring (child)
 6:    mutate child
 7:    If dist(child,parent1) < dist(child,parent2)
          ∧fitness(child) > fitness(parent1)
 8:     Then parent1 ← child
 9:    ElseIf dist(child,parent1) ≥ dist(child,parent2)
              ∧fitness(child) > fitness(parent2)
11:     Then parent2 ← child
12:    EndIf
13:   EndFor
14:  EndFor
15:  extract the best individuals from the population
     and add them to the final solution
```

Figure 7.14   Negative selection with fuzzy detection rules (NSFDR) algorithm.

where $Cond_i(x)$ represents the fuzzy true value produced by the evaluation of $Cond_i$ in x, and $\mu_{non\_self}(x)$ represents the degree of membership of x to the nonself set; thus, a value close to 0 means that x is normal, and a value close to 1 indicates that x is abnormal.

To generate the fuzzy-rule detectors, we will use the same evolutionary algorithm described in NSDR with DC. However, the use of fuzzy rules does not require the generation of rules for different levels of deviation. Thus, all the rules are generated in a simple run of the DC algorithm. Figure 7.14 shows the NSFDR algorithm. The time complexity of the algorithm is $O(num\_gen * pop\_size * |Self'|)$.

The use of fuzzy rules requires changes in GA implementation such as chromosome representation, fitness evaluation, and distance calculation.

Each individual (chromosome) in the GA represents the condition part of a rule, because the consequent part is the same for all rules (the sample belongs to nonself). As was described before, a condition is a conjunction of atomic conditions. Each atomic condition, x_i, T_i, corresponds to a gene in the chromosome that is represented by a sequence $(s_1^i, ..., s_m^i)$ of bits, where $m = |S|$ (the size of the set of linguistic values), and $s_j^i = 1$ if and only if $S_j \subseteq T_i$. That is, the bit s_j^i is "on" if and only if the corresponding basic fuzzy set S_j is part of the composite fuzzy set T_j. Figure 7.14 shows the structure of a chromosome that is $n \times m$ bits long (n is the dimension of the space and m is the number of basic fuzzy sets).

$s_1^1, \ldots, s_m^1$	$\cdots$	$s_1^n, \ldots, s_m^n$
gene 1		gene n

Given here is the structure of the chromosome representing the condition part of a rule. The fitness of a rule R^i is calculated by taking into account the following two factors:

■ The fuzzy true value produced when the condition part of a rule, $Cond_i$, is evaluated for each element x from the self set:

$$selfCovering(R) = \frac{\displaystyle\sum_{x \in Self} Cond_i(x)}{|Self|}$$

■ The fuzzy measure of the volume of the subspace represented by the rule:

$$volume(R) = \prod_{i=1}^{n} measure(T_i),$$

where $measure(T_i)$ corresponds to the area under the membership function of the fuzzy set T_i.

The fitness is defined as follows:

$$fitness(R) = C * (1 - selfCovering(R)) + (1 - C) * volume(R)$$

where C, $0\ C\ 1$, is a coefficient that determines the amount of penalization that a rule suffers if it covers normal samples. The closer the value of the coefficient to 1, higher is the penalization. In our experiment, we used values between 0.8 and 0.9.

In this work, we used Hamming distance because there is a strong relation between each bit in the chromosome with a single fuzzy set of some particular attribute in the search space. For example, if the s_i^j bit in both parent and child fuzzy-rule detectors is set to 1, both individuals include the atomic sentence $x_i \in s_j$, i.e., they use the jth fuzzy set to cover some part of the ith attribute. Then, the more bits the parent and the child have in common, the more common area they will cover.

7.5.4.1 NSFDR Experimentation

We applied the fuzzy algorithm (negative selection with fuzzy detection rules—NSFDR) and the crisp version (NSDR using DC) to three different

Table 7.9 Datasets Used for Experimentation

Dataset	Training	Testing	
		Normal	Abnormal
Mackey-Glass	497	396	101
MIT DARPA 99	4,000	5,136	56
MIT DARPA 98	1,474	19,056	396,745

datasets as shown in Table 7.9 (two of these are considered here). The algorithms were run 1000 iterations with a population size of 200 individuals. The mutation probability was fixed to 0.1, and the NSDR algorithm was run four times, each time with a different level of deviation (0.1, 0.2, 0.3, and 0.4). The crisp detectors (hyper-rectangles) generated by each run were combined to define the final set of detectors produced by the NSDR.

To access the performance of both methods, we calculate the detection rate (DR, Equation 7.1) and false-alarm rate (FA, Equation 7.2) and plot the result using ROC curves. Also, the reported DR was obtained for each algorithm when the FA was fixed to 3 percent.

We used the same MIT DARPA 99 dataset described in Section 7.4. Additionally, we used the dataset corresponding to the 1998 version of the DARPA intrusion detection evaluation, also prepared and managed by MIT Lincoln Labs [34]. The dataset was generated by processing the original tcpdump data to extract 42 attributes (33 of them numerical) that characterize the network traffic. This set was used in the *KDD Cup 99* competition and is available at the University of California Machine Learning repository [35]. Even though the dataset corresponds to 10 percent of the original data, its size is still considerably large (492,021 records).

We generated a reduced version of the 10-percent dataset, taking only the numerical attributes. Therefore, the reduced 10-percent dataset is composed of 33 attributes. The attributes were normalized between 0 and 1 using the maximum and minimum values found. Of the normal samples, 80 percent were picked randomly and used as training datasets, whereas the remaining 20 percent were used along with the abnormal samples as a testing set. Five fuzzy sets were defined for the 33 attributes. One percent of the normal dataset (randomly generated) was used as a training dataset (MIT DARPA 98 dataset).

The NSFDR algorithm shows a better performance than the NSDR algorithm (Figure 7.15) with the MIT DARPA 98 dataset. The results of the NSDR algorithm are competitive only for a high FA rate (greater than 4 percent). Table 7.10 compares the performance of the tested algorithms and some results reported in the literature. The result produced by the

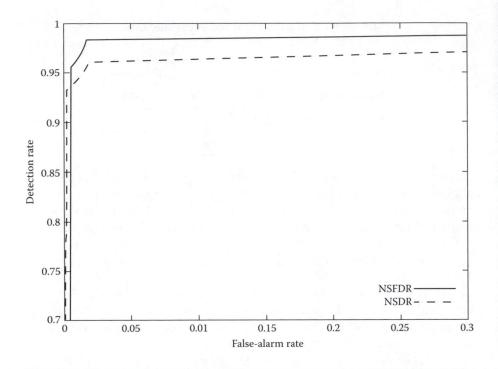

Figure 7.15 ROC curves generated by the two algorithms tested with the MIT DARPA 98 dataset.

Table 7.10 Comparative Performance in the MIT DARPA 98 Dataset

Algorithm	DR (Percentage)	FA (Percentage)	Number of Detectors
NSFDR	98.22	1.9	14
NSDR	96.02	1.9	699
EFRID[64]	98.95	7.0	—
RIPPER-AA[53]	94.26	2.02	—

NSFDR algorithm and reported in Table 7.10 is the closest value to the optimum point (0,1). Amazingly, the number of detectors using fuzzyfication is very small compared to the number of detectors using the crisp characterization. This suggests that the fuzzy representation can handle high dimensionality better (the dimensionality of this dataset is 33 attributes).

According to Table 7.10, the performance of NSFDR is comparable with the performance of other approaches reported in the literature and in many cases is better. For example, when NSFDR is compared with

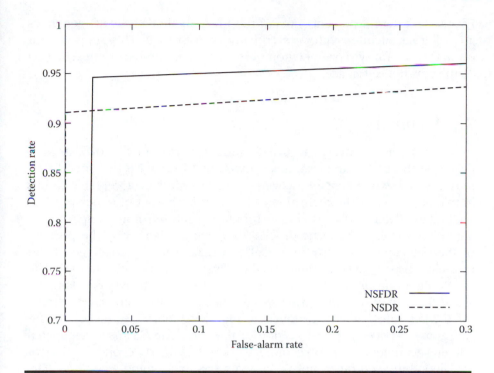

Figure 7.16   ROC curves generated by the two algorithms tested with the MIT DARPA 99 dataset.

Table 7.11   Comparative Performance in the MIT DARPA 99 Problem

Algorithm	DR (Percentage)	Number of Detectors
NSFDR	94.63	7
NSDR	89.37	35

RIPPER-AA, the FA rate is almost the same (close to 2 percent), but NSFDR has a higher DR (4 percent more abnormal samples detected). Now, compared with the crisp approach (NSDR), the performance is also superior (2.2 percent more abnormal samples detected). Clearly, the fuzzy characterization of abnormal space reduces the number of false alarms while the detection rate is increased.

When the MIT DARPA 99 dataset is used, the performance of the NSDR algorithm is better than that of the NSFDR algorithm for very small values of the FA rate. However, if the FA rate is allowed to be at most 2 percent, the NSFDR is clearly superior (Figure 7.16). Table 7.11 compares the performance of the tested algorithms over the MIT DARPA 99 dataset (for

FA rate less than 3 percent). Again, the fuzzy method (NSFDR) generates a smaller set of rules without sacrificing performance. This supports our claim that the fuzzy representation permits a more compact representation of the self/nonself space.

7.6 Summary

In this chapter, we investigate a technique to perform intrusion detection based on the NSA. Earlier studies showed that binary NS performed well in two of the experiments; however, it failed to produce acceptable results in two other cases. The real-valued NSA starts with a set of hyperspherical antibodies (detectors) randomly distributed in the self/nonself space. The algorithm applies a heuristic process that changes iteratively the position of the detectors driven by two goals: to maximize the coverage of the nonself subspace and to minimize the coverage of the self-samples. The NSDR algorithm uses a GA to evolve detectors with a hyper-rectangular shape that can cover the nonself space. These detectors can be interpreted as *If-Then* rules, which produce a high-level characterization of the self/nonself space. The first version of the algorithm [11] used sequential nitching technique to evolve multiple detectors. The second version of the algorithm used deterministic crowding as the niching technique. The algorithm was applied to detect attacks in network traffic data. We further extended the NSDR algorithm to use fuzzy rules, which is called NSFDR. This improves the accuracy of the method and produces a measure of deviation from the normal that does not need a discrete division of the nonself space.

The real-valued NSDR technique uses a GA to generate good anomaly detector rules. To test this technique, a set of experiments to detect anomalies in network traffic data was performed. We used a real-world dataset (MIT Lincoln Labs), used by different researchers in computer security, for testing. The following are some preliminary observations:

■ The immunogenetic algorithm was able to produce good detectors that gave a good estimation of the amount of deviation from the normal. This shows that it is possible to apply the NSA to detect anomalies on real network traffic data. The real representation of the detectors was very useful in this work.

■ The proposed algorithm is efficient; it was able to detect four of the five attacks detected by the PC (with a detection rate of 87.5 percent and a maximum false-alarm rate of 1 percent), while only using a fraction of the space (when compared to PC).

■ The use of DC as a niching technique improved the results obtained using SN. While retaining the performance, in terms of a high detection rate, the new algorithm generated a smaller set of rules that estimated the amount of deviation in a more precise way. The new technique is also more efficient in terms of computational power because it is able to generate multiple rules for each individual run of the GA.

When NSFDR technique was used to evolve fuzzy rules for negative detection, it performed better than NSDR approach and was comparable with other results reported in the literature. The following are the main advantages of the NSFDR approach:

- It provides a better definition of the boundary between normal and abnormal. The previous approach used a discrete division of the nonself space, whereas the new approach does not need such a division because the fuzzy character of the rules provide a natural estimate of the amount of deviation from the normal.
- It shows an improved accuracy in the anomaly detection problem. This can be attributed to the fuzzy representation of the rules that reduce the search space, allowing the evolutionary algorithm to find better solutions.
- It generates a more compact representation of the nonself space by reducing the number of detectors. This is also a consequence of the expressiveness of the fuzzy rules.

Bibliography

1. M. Ayara, J. Timmis, L. de Lemos, R. de Castro, and R. Duncan, Negative selection: how to generate detectors, in *Proceedings of the 1st International Conference on Artificial Immune Systems (ICARIS)*, Canterbury, UK: University of Kent at Canterbury Printing Unit, September 2002, pp. 89–98.
2. J. Balthrop, F. Esponda, S. Forrest, and M. Glickman, Coverage and generalization in an artificial immune system, in *Proceedings of the Genetic and Evolutionary Computation Conference (GECCO)*, San Francisco, CA: Morgan Kaufmann Publishers, July 9–13, 2002, pp. 3–10.
3. J. Balthrop, S. Forrest, and M.R. Glickman, Revisiting LISYS: Parameters and normal behavior," in *Proceedings of the 2002 Congress on Evolutionary Computation (CEC)*, USA: IEEE Press, 2002, pp. 1045–1050.
4. D. Beasley, D. Bull, and R. Martin, A sequential niche technique for multimodal function optimization, *Evolutionary Computation*, Vol. 1, No. 2, pp. 101–125, 1993.
5. J.L. Bentley, Multidimensional binary search trees used for associative searching, *Communications of the ACM*, Vol. 18, No. 9, pp. 509–517, 1975.
6. J.L. Bentley, K-D trees for semidynamic point sets, in *Proceedings of the 6th Annual ACM Symposium Computational Geome*try, 1990, pp. 187–197.

7. A. Coutinho, The self non-self discrimination and the nature and acquisition of the antibody repertoire, *Annals of Immunology. (Inst. Past.)*, Vol. 131D, 1980.

8. T.M. Cover and P.E. Hart, Nearest neighbor pattern classification, *IEEE Transactions on Information Theory*, Vol. 13, pp. 21–27, 1967.

9. M. Crosbie and E. Spafford, Applying genetic programming to intrusion detection, in *Working Notes for the AAAI Symposium on Genetic Programming*, MIT, Cambridge, MA: AAAI, November 10–12, 1995, pp. 1–8.

10. D. Dasgupta and F. González, Evolving complex fuzzy classifier rules using a linear genetic representation, in *Proceedings of the Genetic and Evolutionary Computation Conference (GECCO)*, San Francisco, CA: Morgan Kaufmann, July 2001, pp. 299–305.

11. D. Dasgupta and F. Gonzalez, An immunity-based technique to characterize intrusions in computer networks, *IEEE Transactions on Evolutionary Computation*, Vol. 6, No. 3, pp. 281–291, June 2002.

12. D. Dasgupta, An overview of artificial immune systems and their applications, in *Artificial Immune Systems and Their Applications*, D. Dasgupta, Ed. Springer-Verlag, Berlin, 1999, pp. 3–23.

13. D. Dasgupta and S. Forrest, Tool Breakage Detection in Milling Operations Using a Negative Selection Algorithm, Department of Computer Science, University of New Mexico, Technical Report CS95-5, 1995.

14. D. Dasgupta, *Artificial immune systems and their applications*. Springer-Verlag, Berlin, January 1999.

15. D. Dasgupta, Immunity-based intrusion detection system: a general framework, in *Proceedings of the 22nd National Information Systems Security Conference (NISSC)*, October 1999, pp. 147–160.

16. D. Dasgupta and S. Forrest, Novelty detection in time series data using ideas from immunology, in *Proceedings of the 5th International Conference on Intelligent Systems (ISCA)*, June 1996, pp. 82–87.

17. P. D'haeseleer, S. Forrest, and P. Helman, An immunological approach to change detection: algorithms, analysis and implications, in *Proceedings of the 1996 IEEE Symposium on Computer Security and Privacy*, USA: IEEE Press, 1996, pp. 110–119.

18. F. Esponda and S. Forrest, Detector coverage under the r-contiguous bits matching rule, Department of Computer Science, University of New Mexico, Technical Report TRCS-2002-03, 2002.

19. F. Esponda, S. Forrest, and P. Helman, A formal framework for positive and negative detection schemes, July 2002.

20. S. Forrest and S.A. Hofmeyr, Immunology as information processing, in *Design Principles for the Immune System and Other Distributed Autonomous Systems*, L.A. Segel and I. Cohen, Eds. New York: Oxford University Press, 2000.

21. S. Forrest, A. Perelson, L. Allen, and R. Cherukuri, Self-nonself discrimination in a computer, in *Proceedings IEEE Symposium on Research in Security and Privacy*. Los Alamitos, CA: IEEE Computer Society Press, 1994, pp. 202–212.

22. J. Friedman, J. Bentley, and R. Finkel, An algorithm for finding best matches in logarithmic expected time, *ACM Transactions on Mathematical Software*, Vol. 3, No. 3, pp. 209–226, 1977.

23. F. Gonzalez, *A Study of Artificial Immune Systems Applied to Anomoly Detection*, Ph.D. thesis, The University of Memphis, May, 2003.

24. S.A. Hofmeyr, An interpretative introduction to the immune system, in *Design Principles for the Immune System and Other Distributed Autonomous Systems*, I. Cohen and L.A. Segel, Eds. New York: Oxford University Press, 2000.

25. S. Hofmeyr and S. Forrest, Architecture for an artificial immune system, *Evolutionary Computation*, Vol. 8, No. 4, pp. 443–473, 2000.

26. C.A. Janeway, How the immune system recognizes invaders, *Scientific American*, Vol. 269, No. 3, pp. 72–79, 1993.

27. C.A. Janeway, P. Travers, S. Hunt, and M. Walport, *Immunobiology: The immune system in Health and Disease*, Garland Pub., New York, 1997.

28. N.K. Jerne, Clonal selection in a lymphocyte network, in *Cellular Selection and Regulation in the Immune Response*, Raven Press, New York, 1974, pp. 39–48.

29. N.K. Jerne, Towards a network theory of the immune system, *Ann. Immunol. (Inst. Pasteur)*, Vol. 125C, pp. 373–389, 1974.

30. J. Kappler, N. Roehm, and P. Marrack, T cell tolerance by clonal elimination in the thymus, *Cell*, No. 49, pp. 273–280, 1987.

31. E. Keogh, S. Lonardi, and B. Chiu, Finding surprising patterns in a time series database in linear time and space, in *Proceedings of the 8th ACM SIGKDD International Conference on Knowledge Discovery and Data Mining (KDD)*, USA: ACM Press, 2002, pp. 550–556.

32. T.B. Kepler and A.S. Perelson, Somatic hypermutation in B-cells: an optimal control treatment, *Journal of Theoretical Biology*, Vol. 164, pp. 37–64, 1993.

33. J. Kuby, *Immunology*, 3rd ed., W.H. Freeman and Co., New York, 1997.

34. S.W. Mahfoud, Crowding and preselection revisited, in *Parallel Problem Solving From Nature 2*, Amsterdam: North-Holland, 1992, pp. 27–36.

35. 1999 Darpa intrusion detection evaluation, MIT Lincoln Labs, 1999. [Online]. Available: http://www.ll.mit.edu/IST/ideval/index.html.

36. P.A. Moss, W.M. Rosenberg, and J.I. Bell, The human T-cell receptor in health and disease, *Annu. Rev. Immunol.*, Vol. 10, No. 71, 1993.

37. D. Mount and S. Arya, ANN: a library for approximate nearest neighbor searching, in *2nd Annual CGC Workshop on Computational Geometry*, 1997. [Online]. Available: http://www.cs.umd.edu/mount/ANN.

38. P. Murphy and D. Aha, UCI Repository of machine learning databases, Irvine, CA: University of California, Department of Information and Computer Science, 1992. [Online]. Available: http://www.ics.uci.edu/~mlearn/MLRepository.html.

39. F. Provost, T. Fawcett, and R. Kohavi, The case against accuracy estimation for comparing induction algorithms, in *Proceedings of 15th International Conference on Machine Learning*, CA: Morgan Kaufmann, 1998, pp. 445–453.

40. I. Tizzard, The response of B-cells to antigen, in *Immunology: An Introduction*, 2nd ed., Saunders College Publishing, 1988, pp. 199–223.
41. A. Tyrrell, Computer know thy self: a biological way to look at fault tolerance, in *Proceedings of the 2nd Euromicro/IEEE workshop on Dependable Computing Systems*, Milan, 1999, pp. 129–135.
42. J. Kim and P. Bentley, An evaluation of negative selection in an artificial immune system for network intrusion detection, in *Proceedings of the Genetic and Evolutionary Computation Conference (GECCO)*, San Francisco, CA: Morgan Kaufmann, 2001, pp. 1330–1337.
43. J. Kim and P.J. Bentley, Toward an artificial immune system for network intrusion detection: An investigation of dynamic clonal selection, in *Proceedings of the 2002 Congress on Evolutionary Computation (CEC)*, USA: IEEE press, May 2002, pp. 1015–1020.

Chapter 8

Application of Wavelets in Network Security

Challa S. Sastry and Sanjay Rawat

8.1 Introduction

Design of intrusion detection systems (IDSs) has been an active area of research for more than a decade because of the increasing rate of attacks on computer systems. There are two families of techniques to build an IDS: The first is misuse-based IDS, which works on the signatures of known attacks and, thus, cannot capture new attacks. The second is anomaly-based IDS, which learns the normal behavior of a system (viz., users, computer networks, or programs), and any deviation from this behavior is considered as a probable attack. IDSs based on the latter technique are generally capable of detecting new attacks. Based on the data being analyzed by the IDS to detect an intrusion, there are host-based IDSs (HIDSs) and network-based IDSs (NIDSs). An HIDS collects data from the system it is protecting, whereas NIDS collects data from the network, usually in the form of packets.

It has been observed that Internet traffic is self-similar in nature. *Self-similarity* is the property that is associated with objects whose structure is unchanged on different scales. It is pointed out [9] that the self-similarity of Internet traffic distributions can often be accounted for by a mixture of the actions of a number of individual users, and hardware and software behaviors at their originating hosts, multiplexed through an interconnection network. It has been observed that the traffic related to attacks, especially denial-of-service (DoS) attacks, is bursty in nature. Traffic that is bursty on many or all timescales can be described statistically using the notion of self-similarity.

In view of its multiscale framework and localization aspects, the wavelet technique is capable of being used for the analysis of scaling and local "burstiness" features of a function. In recent literature on wavelet-based IDS, wavelet analysis has been used both to describe and analyze network data traffic. In addition, it has been used to characterize network-related problems such as congestion, device failure, etc. [6]. The basic philosophy in wavelet-based IDS is that self-similarity is prevalent in the network traffic under normal conditions and, therefore, can be considered as a signature for normal behavior. The loss of self-similarity, signifying a possible attack, can be taken as a deviation from normal behavior.

Wavelets do seem to have some merit for various applications in data mining [1,15,18,22] and therefore are useful in IDS. In reality, as far as the method is concerned, there is no difference between HIDS and NIDS. In view of the use of the self-similarity property in NIDS (and not in HIDS), it seems appropriate to study the applicability of wavelets in HIDS and NIDS separately. As this chapter, which deals with the application of wavelets in IDS, is primarily tutorial in nature, it discusses some of the applications of wavelets in HIDS separately and concentrates more on NIDS, presenting some computational results.

The rest of the chapter is organized as follows: In Section 8.2 and Section 8.3, we discuss the notion of self-similarity and give a brief introduction to wavelets, respectively. Section 8.4 talks about the usability of wavelets in different applications, including those in IDS. A motivation is presented in Section 8.5 for the applicability of wavelets in HIDS. Following this, Section 8.6 discusses the application of wavelets in NIDS. In Section 8.7, we provide some simulation work to illustrate the relationship between self-similarity and network traffic anomaly. In addition to presenting the concluding remarks, Section 8.8 suggests a different use of wavelet coefficients for the detection of not only the presence of anomaly in data, but also the time instances in which anomalies occur. A detailed treatment of the fundamentals of wavelet theory is provided in the appendix at the end of the chapter.

8.2 A Brief Introduction to Self-Similarity

In this section, we present the definition of self-similarity and the basic concepts associated with it, followed by a brief introduction to wavelets. Formally, we can define self-similarity as follows [11]:

Definition: A process or function $\{f(t) : t \in (-\infty, \infty)\}$ is said to be self-similar with self-similarity parameter H, if and only if $\{c^{-H} f(ct) : t \in (-\infty, \infty)\}$ and $\{f(t) : t \in (-\infty, \infty)\}$, $\forall$ $c > 0$ and $t \in (-\infty, \infty)$ have the same distributions, which is referred to as the *scaling property* of the process f. To say that a time series or a process or a measure displays the scaling property means many different things, depending on the context and the definition of scaling properties [11]. Underlying all such definitions is the intuitive notion that the process being considered has no inherent characteristic scale, i.e., it enjoys scale invariance.

The high variability in network data traffic is because of the long-range dependence (LRD) property of the traffic processes. It is commonly accepted [25] that, by definition, the LRD property means that the autocorrelation function $r(k)$ of a wide-sense-stationary process X_n slowly decreases according to a power law such as $r(k) \sim c_r k^{-(2-2H)}$ as $k \to \infty$, where $c_r > 0$ and $H \in (0.5, 1)$. The parameter H is called the *Hurst parameter*. For a general self-similar process, the parameter H measures the degree of self-similarity. For random processes suitable for modeling network traffic, H is basically a measure of the speed of decay of the tail of the autocorrelation function. If H lies between 0.5 and 1, the process is LRD, and if it lies between 0 and 0.5, the corresponding process is said to have short-range dependence (SRD). Hence, H is widely used to capture the intensity of LRD. In traffic modeling, however, the term "self-similar" is usually used to refer to the asymptotically second-order self-similar process [25]. Hence, in the study of anomalous behavior of traffic data, any deviation of H from the 0.5 to 1 range signifies the presence of anomaly in the data [2,11]. Throughout this chapter, we use this observation for the detection of intrusion present in the data. From now on, we consider f to be a finite-variance self-similar process with the self-similarity parameter $H \in (0.5, 1)$. In mathematical terms, however, we treat the function f as being a self-similar finite energy function possessing finite (support) duration.

8.3 A Brief Introduction to Wavelet Analysis

A *wavelet* is a "little wave" that is both localized and oscillatory. The representation of a function in terms of wavelet basis functions (generated by dyadic scaling and integer translates of the wavelet) involves a low-frequency block containing the identity of the function and several high-frequency blocks containing the visually important features or "flavors" (such as edges or lines). Therefore, the wavelet transform is expected to provide economical and informative mathematical representation of many objects of interest [16]. Because of the easy accessibility of many software packages that contain fast and efficient algorithms [8] to perform wavelet transforms, wavelets have quickly gained in popularity among scientists and engineers working on both theoretical issues and applications. Above all, wavelets have been widely applied in such computer science areas as image processing, computer vision, network management, and data mining.

Wavelets have many favorable properties, such as compact support, and can generate different classes of (wavelet) bases. The property of wavelets being compactly supported implies their localization feature. The main advantage of this feature is that the presence of local error (noise) in the data reflects local changes in wavelet coefficients, unlike the Fourier technique, in which a local change in data has a global effect on the Fourier coefficients. This feature, along with the multiresolution feature, is being widely used in image/signal/pattern analysis [21]. To add to this, in contrast to the Fourier technique (in which one uses the sine and cosine functions to generate a representation of a suitable function), in wavelet technique, different wavelet bases such as orthonormal, biorthogonal (symmetric), multiwavelets, wavelet packets, M-band wavelets, etc., are constructed [10] to tackle various applications. The choice of wavelet basis can be made depending on the requirement. For example, in image compression and boundary value problems, biorthogonal (symmetric) wavelets are found to be useful. In some of the feature extraction algorithms, orthonormal wavelets are found to be useful [21]. Although one can use different types of wavelets in IDS, throughout this chapter we use orthonormal Daubechies wavelets. Besides the properties stated earlier, wavelet bases possess other properties such as zero moments, hierarchical and multiresolution frameworks, and decorrelated coefficients. These features could provide considerably more efficient and effective solutions to many practical problems. A fairly detailed mathematical description of wavelets and their properties is given in the appendix.

8.4 Application of Wavelets

This section studies the application of wavelets in a two-tier pattern. Considering some of the problems associated with IDS, in the first part we concentrate on the application of wavelets to dimension reduction, clustering, and similarity search, whereas in the other part we review the application of wavelets in NIDS.

8.4.1 Some Applications in Data Mining

In this subsection, we briefly talk about some applications of wavelets in data mining, which, as we will see later on, are useful in IDS.

The basic objective in dimensionality reduction is to retain the information content of a larger dataset in a smaller dataset. As the wavelet transform breaks up a function or a dataset into different frequency components, wavelets can achieve [1,18] dimensionality reduction by projecting the dataset into frequency spaces of lower dimension or by retaining significant wavelet coefficients. The first case, involving the projection of data into lower-resolution spaces, is equivalent to taking the first few coefficients in the wavelet representation of a dataset. Although this approach is useful for easy indexing, it works well when the information content of the dataset is present in the first few levels and that in higher-resolution levels is insignificant. The second case, which involves retaining few larger coefficients in the wavelet domain, results in very little loss of information in data (because of Equation 8.19). This process involves arranging coefficients in decreasing order and then taking the first few, as dictated by the preassigned error tolerance between the energy of the dataset and that of the retained coefficients. One may use datasets in the wavelet domain after reducing the dimension for similarity search. An excellent overview of the application of wavelets to similarity search has been given in Reference 15.

The aim of data clustering methods is to group objects in databases into meaningful subclasses. Because of the huge amount of data in use, an important challenge for clustering algorithms is to achieve good time efficiency. Using the multiresolution property of wavelet transforms, Sheikholeslami et al. [22] proposed an algorithm called *WaveCluster* for clustering very large databases. WaveCluster considers multidimensional data as a multidimensional signal and applies wavelet transform to convert data into the frequency domain. It then convolves the wavelet domain data with an appropriate kernel function, which results in a transformed space in which the natural clusters in the data become more distinguishable. Finally, it identifies the clusters by finding the dense regions in the transformed domain. It has been experimentally observed that WaveCluster [22] outperforms some of the standard clustering algorithms.

8.4.2 Some Applications in IDS

Wavelet-based network traffic data analysis has been drawing the attention of many researchers. A detailed bibliography regarding the work in this direction can be found in Reference 24.

The study by Gilbert [11] discusses the theoretical and implementation issues of wavelet-based scaling analysis for network traffic. Network traffic is characterized by packets per second and user-requested-page per session for the demonstration of the presence of self-similarity in the traffic.

Energy plots and partition functions are calculated using wavelet coefficients. The presence of self-similarity in data is inferred from the straight-line behavior of energy plots.

In another work, Nash and Ragsdale [17] propose that self-similarity be used to generate network traffic for IDS evaluation. They observe that it is difficult both to produce traffic that includes a large number of intrusions and to analyze such huge traffic for signs of intrusions. They use self-similarity to reproduce real traffic and the wavelet coefficients to decompose the data for analysis. Using the Hurst parameter that is estimated through Mandelbrot's method, they demonstrate the self-similarity of network data.

Along similar lines, Huang et al [12] propose the use of energy plots to analyze the network (FDDI ring ISP network and Internet traffic from a research lab) in terms of round-trip time (RTT) and retransmission timeout (RTO). A tool named *WIND* has been built to analyze the packets collected from the *tcpdump* tool. TCP/IP packets can be analyzed across different time periods and across the part of traffic destined for different subnets by exploiting the built-in scale-localization ability of wavelets.

In Reference 6, the use of wavelet coefficients is proposed to analyze various network-related anomalies. These anomalies are grouped into three categories: *network operation anomalies*, which include network device outages and change in traffic because of configurational changes; *flash crowd anomalies*, which include traffic because of some software release or external interest in some specific Web site; and *network abuse anomalies*, which include DoS or scans. Recent work of William and Marlin [4] shows that the DARPA 98 dataset shows self-similarity, but within a certain interval of time, i.e., from 8 AM to 6 PM. The periodogram method is used to estimate the Hurst parameter H. The methodology involves the plotting of periodograms for each two-hr period of each attack-free day in the DARPA data. The Hurst parameter is estimated from each plot by performing a least-square fit to the lowest ten percent of the frequencies to determine the behavior of the spectral energy as it approaches the origin. The importance of their study is the observation that other methods that use temporal distribution for their model should concentrate only on the data between 8 AM and 6 PM of each day. The authors of Reference 5 use the loss of self-similarity (LoSS technique) to characterize many DoS attacks whose effectiveness depends on a continuing stream of attack traffic (termed as *DoS-TE*). In Reference 5, self-similarity is established by calculating the Hurst parameter H, using the Whittle and periodogram approaches [8], and using the following conditions to decide the loss of self-similarity:

$$MIN(periodogram, Whittle) \le 0.05$$

or

$$MAX(periodogram, Whittle) \ge 0.99$$

A time series of packets' arrival count per unit time is constructed to calculate the periodogram and Whittle estimates of the Hurst parameter. A sliding window, ranging from 10 to 30 min, is used to construct the time series. Datasets from other sources are used as normal background traffic, and DARPA data is used for attacks. To capture burstiness, peak packets per second (pps) rate of each attack is calculated for each window. This pps value is compared to the background traffic pps rate to detect the attack. Out of 23 chosen attacks, 21 are detected using the LoSS technique. It is important to note that such a technique is useful only if there is a very high intensity of pps during the attack.

8.5 Wavelets for HIDS

In this section, we consider studying briefly the applicability of wavelets in HIDS. There are many approaches proposed in the literature to build an HIDS. The following is the methodology that is commonly used to monitor processes in terms of the system calls invoked by them: Various processes under the UNIX system are converted into vectors using the frequencies of various system calls invoked by those processes under normal conditions. Depending on the applications, the number of system calls under normal conditions may vary from 30 to 70 and more, per application. Therefore, each process is represented as a vector of dimension, say, 50. Then a similarity metric (e.g., cosine metric) is used to calculate the similarity among processes for classification.

The time taken by an IDS to analyze the data and detect malicious activity is as important as the IDS itself. Consequently, the data to be analyzed by an IDS should be as small in amount as possible, containing as much information of the attack traces as possible. With the reduced vectors, the similarity calculation takes less time. In Reference 20, based on the work of Liao and Vemuri [14], an attempt has been made in this direction, using singular value decomposition (SVD) as a suitable candidate for reducing the dimension. In Reference 20, the empirical results show that the reduction in dimension by SVD does not degrade the performance of an IDS. SVD, however, has several drawbacks as an indexing scheme. The most important of these relates to its complexity. The classic algorithms computing SVD require $O(mn^2)$ time and $O(mn)$ space, with m and n being the number of processes and the dimension, respectively.

In view of the applicability of wavelets to dimension reduction and similarity measure, as discussed in Subsection 8.4.1, one may conclude that such wavelet-based algorithms can be used for HIDSs. In contrast to SVD's $O(mn^2)$ computations, for the m, n defined earlier, the discrete Haar wavelet transform [10] can be carried out in $O(mn)$ computations, thereby achieving faster dimension reduction.

In practical situations, we may not obtain labeled data to train IDSs. For HIDS, the processes collected for training are either abnormal or normal and, therefore, difficult to label manually. In such situations, it is desirable to have some techniques to cluster data into different (normal and abnormal) parts. As we have seen in Subsection 8.4.1, the wavelet-based clustering algorithm, namely WaveCluster, is shown to be efficient. One may use it, as and when required, to cluster the data for HIDS.

8.6 Wavelets for Network-Based IDS

In this section, using the properties of wavelet bases and self-similar functions, we present the methodology described in Reference 2 and Reference 11 for the detection of anomalies in the data.

The coefficients in the wavelet representation of a self-similar function satisfy the following simple relation: For any integers j,m,n such that $j = m + n$, we have

$$
\begin{aligned}
d_{j,k} &= 2^{\frac{j}{2}} \int_{-\infty}^{\infty} f(t)\psi(2^j t - k)dt \\
&= 2^{\frac{j}{2}} \int_{-\infty}^{\infty} f(2^{-n}t)\psi(2^m t - k)2^{-n}\,dt \\
&= 2^{\frac{j}{2}}2^{-nH-n} \int_{-\infty}^{\infty} f(t)\psi(2^m t - k)dt \because c^H(-H)f(ct) = f(t) \\
&= 2^{\frac{-n(2H+1)}{2}} d_{m,k}
\end{aligned}
$$

(8.1)

Taking $m = 0$ and computing the energy E_j at the jth scale of wavelet coefficients, we get

$$
\begin{aligned}
E_j &:= \frac{1}{N_j}\sum_k |d_{j,k}|^2 \\
&= \frac{2^{-j(2H+1)}}{N_j}\sum_k |d_{0,k}|^2 = 2^{-j(2H+1)}E_0
\end{aligned}
$$

(8.2)

In this equation, N_j represents the number of wavelet coefficients at scale j. From Equation 8.1, it may be noted that N_j is the same at all levels. Consequently, the Hurst parameter H can be computed using

$$H = \frac{1}{2}\left[\frac{1}{j}log_2\left(\frac{E_0}{E_j}\right) - 1\right] \tag{8.3}$$

In actual simulations, however, the plot of logarithm of energies at various levels is considered [3,11] using the following log-scale formula:

$$log_2 E_j = -j(2H+1) + log_2 E_0 \tag{8.4}$$

The scales over which the plot is a straight line are determined first to identify the scale interval over which the self-similarity possibly holds. Then, from the slope of the line, i.e., $-(2H+1)$, H is computed. If the Hurst parameter falls between 0.5 and 1, the data is a self-similar LRD process. In the event of either H not lying between 0.5 and 1 or in the absence of straight-line behavior in the log-scale plot, the data is said to possess anomaly.

Note 1: It may be noted that the energy plots can be linear for some functions and, in spite of it, the corresponding function f in question may not satisfy the scaling property. For example, suppose f is a polynomial of some degree N over the interval $[-2^J, 2^J]$ and 0 outside it, for some positive integers J, N. When we use the wavelet basis possessing zero moments up to order N−1 (i.e., $m \leq N-1$ in Equation 8.18), the energy plot is a straight line between the levels 0 and J, and the slope of the line, as dictated by the choice of N, can take arbitrary values. This is, of course, a hypothetical function, chosen as an example to justify that the straight-line behavior of the log-scale plot does not necessarily imply self-similarity.

Note 2: Suppose f is a self-similar and LRD stationary process. The explanation given in the foregoing paragraphs concludes that the energy plot is a straight line, and the H determined from the slope of the energy plot falls in (0.5,1). It may be noted that the converse is not necessarily true, because of the following reason: Suppose the energy plot of a function g is a straight line over scale interval $[j_1, j_2]$ with the corresponding H falling in the desired interval. Then g need not be self-similar, as follows. So for any noise function $\eta(x)$ (for example, $\eta \in V_l$ for $l < j_1$ or $\eta \in W_l$ for $l > j_2$; see the appendix for details), that is orthogonal to $\psi_{j,k}$, $\forall k$ and $j \in [j_1, j_2]$, we have

Table 8.1   Self-Similar Test Data

1,2,2,4,2,4,4,8,2,4,4,8,4,8,8,16,2,4,4,8,4,8,8,16, 4,8 8, 16,8,16,16,32, 2,4,4,8,4,8,8, 16,4,8,8,16,8,16,16,32,4 8,8,16,8,16,16,32,8,16,16,32, 16,32, 32,64,2,4,4,8, 4,8,8 16,4,8,8,16,8,16,16,32,4,8,8,16,8,16,16,32

$$< f + \eta, \psi_{j,k} > = < f, \psi_{j,k} > + < \eta, \psi_{j,k} > = < f, \psi_{j,k} > \qquad (8.5)$$

Hence, the energy plots of f and $g = f + \eta$ are exactly the same. But the function $f + \eta$, because of the presence of the noise factor η, may not be a self-similar process. This problem, however, can be overcome by replacing f with $f - Proj_{V_{j_1}} f - \sum_{j \geq j_2} Proj_{W_j} f$. In the case of no noise factor, the projection factors become zero, and hence up to the additive noise factor, we can conclude from the straight-line behavior that self-similarity is present in the data. Here, $Proj_X f$ stands for the projection of f onto X.

8.7 Simulation Results

In this section, we demonstrate the applicability of the approach presented in the earlier section. We use the self-similar data shown in Table 8.1 and plotted in Figure 8.1(a), as well as its disturbed version, shown in Figure 8.1(b), and compute the energies at different scales.

The corresponding log-scale diagrams are shown in Figure 8.2 and Figure 8.3. As an example, we have disturbed the data by replacing the entries indexed from 10 to 20 with 0 and entries from 50 to 60 with 100 in the data. We observe that the loss of self-similarity in data changes the Hurst parameter value from 0.8058 to 1.410. This justifies the applicability of the method. In Figure 8.2 and Figure 8.3, the level parameter j is taken along the x direction, whereas the logarithm of energy, i.e., $log_2 E_j$, is taken along the y direction. Throughout our simulation work, we have used the Daubechies orthonormal wavelet db2 as an example. It may be noted that one can as well use other choices of wavelets. In the computation of the Hurst parameter from energy plots, and the scale interval over which self-similarity holds, we have adopted the strategy presented in Reference 3.

Note 3: In view of the availability of different classes of wavelets, the choice of wavelet may be a matter of concern when it comes to implementing wavelet-based algorithms. Because the higher-order orthonormal (Daubechies) wavelets, possessing a large number of zero moments, have the capacity to provide energy compaction (because of faster convergence

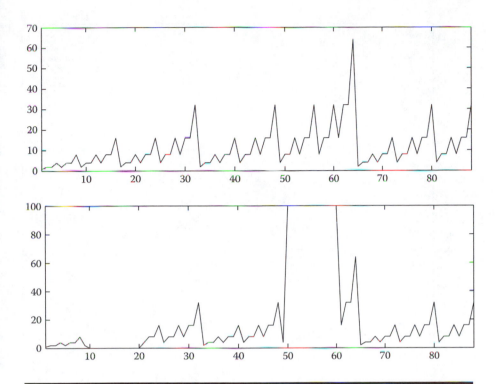

Figure 8.1 Plots of (a) data shown in Table 8.1 and (b) disturbed data.

in Equation 8.14; see the appendix for details) over a few scales when the data is sufficiently smooth, in such situations, one has to deal with a smaller number of levels. Because of this, as one may not be able to figure out the appropriate scale interval, the lower-order wavelets, possessing a smaller number of zero moments, may be preferable to higher-order wavelets in simulations.

8.8 An Observation for Future Work and Conclusion

As the energy computed is global in nature, in the sense that both the location and strength of the anomaly are hidden by the averaging performed in Equation 8.2, instead of computing H using energy plots one may use Equation 8.1 differently for the determination of possible presence of anomaly in the data as follows:

$$H = \frac{1}{2}\left[\frac{2}{n}log_2\left(\frac{d_{m,k}}{d_{m+n,k}}\right) - 1\right] \tag{8.6}$$

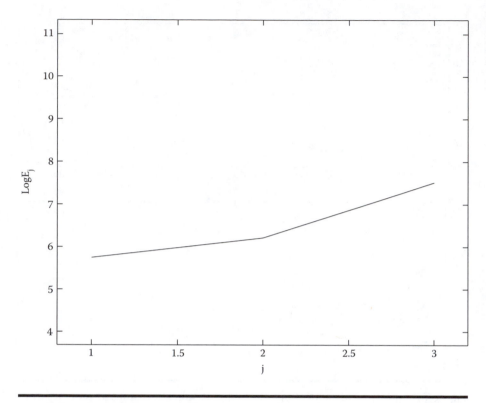

Figure 8.2 **Log-scale plot of Figure 8.1(a). It can be seen that the plot is almost a straight line.**

The Hurst parameter H, computed for different m,n, and k, reveals not only the scale interval over which H falls in the desired range, but also the time instances in which H goes out of range at different scales of f, in the event of presence of anomalies in the data. We believe that this observation helps us detect the possible presence of anomaly and the corresponding time locations. The method is discussed in Reference 19 and is, nevertheless, yet to be justified experimentally.

This chapter presented a tutorial on wavelets and reviewed the application of wavelets in IDS, highlighting some of the important points as Notes.

Appendix

The key idea in wavelet technique is to start with a function ϕ that is made up of a smaller version of itself, i.e.:

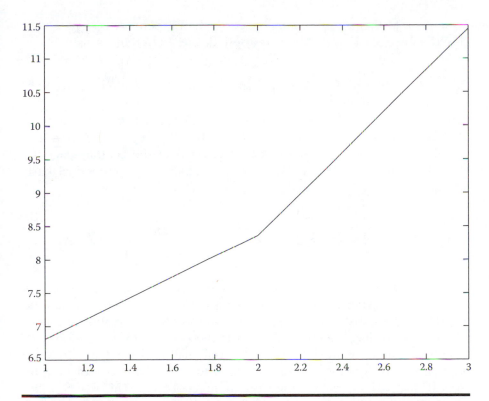

Figure 8.3 **Log-scale plot of Figure 8.1(b). The line behavior is not straight as compared to Figure 8.2. It is, however, less evident because of high variation along the *y* direction.**

$$\phi(x) = \sum_{k=-\infty}^{\infty} b_k \phi(2x - k) \tag{8.7}$$

which is called the refinement (or two-scale) equation. The coefficients b_k are called filter coefficients or masks. The function ϕ is called the scaling (or father wavelet) function.

To compute the wavelet transform of a function efficiently, the concept of multiresolution analysis (MRA) was introduced [10]. Associated with MRA, there is a family of algorithms that can be computed fast. The motivation of MRA is to use a sequence of embedded subspaces to approximate $L^2(IR)$, the space of all finite energy functions defined over the real line $IR = (-\infty, \infty)$, so that one can choose a proper subspace for a specific application task to get a balance between accuracy and efficiency (bigger spaces can contribute better accuracy at the expense of computational resources). Mathematically, MRA concerns the property of a sequence of closed subspaces $V_j, j \in Z$, which approximate $L^2(IR)$ and satisfy

$$\{0\} = V_{-\infty} \subset \ldots \subset V_{-1} \subset V_0 \subset V_1 \subset \ldots \subset V_{\infty} = L^2(IR) \qquad (8.8)$$

which confirms that the closure of union of all V_j is $L^2(IR)$. The multiresolution property is reflected by the property: $f(.) \in V_j \iff f(2.) \in V_{j+1}$, meaning that all the spaces are scaled versions of the central space V_0. First, the translates of ϕ, i.e., $\{\phi(x-k)\}_{k \in Z}$, generate an orthogonal basis for V_0, i.e.:

$$\int_{-\infty}^{\infty} \phi(x-n)\phi(x-m)dx = \begin{cases} 1 \text{ when } m = n \\ 0 \text{ when } m \neq n \end{cases}$$

The nestedness property of V_j spaces ensures that the functions $\{\phi(2^j x - k)\}_{k \in Z}$ generate an orthogonal basis for V_j for each j. It may be noted that the translation parameter k controls the observation location, whereas the scaling parameter j controls the observation resolution.

Having an orthonormal basis of V_j is only half of the picture. To solve problems such as noise filtering, we need to have a way of isolating the "spikes" that belong to V_j but are not members of V_{j-1}. This is where the wavelet ψ enters the picture. Let W_0 be the complement of V_0 in V_1, i.e., $W_0 = V_1 \ominus V_0$ or $V_1 = V_0 \oplus W_0$. The symbols $\ominus$ and $\oplus$ have the following meaning: If every function in V_1 is uniquely written as a sum of the orthogonal components of it in V_0 and W_0 (i.e., $b \in V_1$ implies $b = b_1 + b_2$ for unique $b_1 \in V_0$, $b_2 \in W_0$, and $\int_{-\infty}^{\infty} b_1(x)b_2(x)dx = 0$), we write $V_1 = V_0 \oplus W_0$ or $W_0 = V_1 \ominus V_0$. The question as to how the information in W_0 can be studied is answered by the wavelet function ψ, called the *mother wavelet*, which is defined [10] by

$$\psi(x) = \sum_{k=-\infty}^{\infty} (-1)^k \overline{b_{1-k}}\phi(2x-k) \qquad (8.9)$$

From the definition of W_0, it can be concluded that $\psi \in V_1$, but $\psi \notin V_0$. Consequently, ψ is orthogonal to ϕ and, hence, it is easy to conclude that an arbitrary translation of the father wavelet (or scaling function) ϕ is orthogonal to an arbitrary translation of the mother wavelet ψ, i.e.:

$$\int_{-\infty}^{\infty} \phi(x-n)\psi(x-m)dx = 0 \text{ for all } m,n$$

If $\{\psi(x-k)\}_{k\in Z}$ generates an orthonormal basis of W_0, for any j, translates of $\psi(2^j)$ generate a basis of W_j, which is $V_{j+1} \ominus V_j$. Using the definition of V_j and W_j spaces, for some $J \geq 0$, we have

$$V_J = V_{J-1} \oplus W_{J-1}$$
$$= V_{J-2} \oplus W_{J-2} \oplus W_{J-1}$$
$$= ... \tag{8.10}$$
$$= V_0 \oplus W_0 \oplus ... \oplus W_{J-1}$$

Decomposing V_0 further, we have

$$V_J = W_{-\infty} \oplus ... W_0 \oplus ... \oplus W_{J-1} \tag{8.11}$$

Letting $J \to \infty$, we get

$$L^2 \leftarrow V_J = W_{-\infty} \oplus ... W_0 \oplus ... \oplus W_{J-1} \to \oplus_{j=-\infty}^{\infty} W_j \tag{8.12}$$

In Equation 8.12, L^2 space is partitioned into different subspaces that are orthogonal to each other. Hence, a function $f \in L^2$ can be divided into different orthogonal pieces, g_j's, that capture the edges or singularities of f of different strengths as follows:

$$f = \sum_{j\in Z} g_j \quad \text{for } g_j \in W_j \tag{8.13}$$

In Equation 8.13, $g_j = \sum_{k\in Z} \langle f, \psi_{j,k} \rangle \psi_{j,k}$ and $\langle f, \psi_{j,k} \rangle = \int_{-\infty}^{\infty} f(x)\psi_{j,k}(x)dx$, the inner product of f and $\psi_{j,k}$, where $\psi_{j,k}(t) = 2^{\frac{j}{2}}\psi(2^j t - k)$. The factor $2^{\frac{j}{2}}$ in the definition of $\psi_{j,k}$ is taken to normalize its energy. In actual computational work, using Equation 8.8, a function $f \in L^2$ is approximated by $f_J \in V_J$ for a fair choice of J. Then, using Equation 8.10, we take the wavelet representation of f as

$$f \approx f_J = f_0 + g_0 + ... + g_{J-1} \tag{8.14}$$

Here, $f_0 \in V_0$ and, hence, $f_0 = \sum_k < f, \phi_{0,k} > \phi_{0,k}$, and $g_i \in W_i$. In Equation 8.13, f_0 captures the approximate information or "identity" of the function, whereas the function g_i captures the edges or spikes present in f of different strengths, as depicted in Figure 8.4.

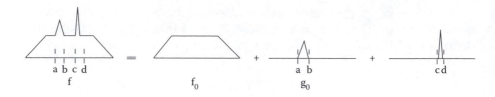

Figure 8.4   Multiresolution decomposition.

The following conditions on the sequence $\{h_n\}$ ensure [10] the properties such as stability, convergence, and orthogonality of the wavelet basis.

$$\sum_{k=-\infty}^{\infty} h_k = 2 \quad \text{(stability)}$$

$$\sum_{k=-\infty}^{\infty} (-1)^k k^m h_k = 0 \quad \text{(stability)} \tag{8.15}$$

$$\sum_{k=-\infty}^{\infty} h_k h_{k+2n} = 2\delta_{0,n} \quad \text{(orthogonality)}$$

The middle equation of Equation 8.15 holds for some suitable choice of integer m [10]. The bar over $\bar{h}_k$ represents the complex conjugate operation of h_k. The integer translates and dyadic scaling of ψ, i.e., $\psi(2^j x - k)$, generate a representation of a finite energy function. In particular, when the sequence $\{h_n\}$ is finite, the functions ϕ, ψ become zero outside some finite interval [10]. Ingrid Daubechies [10] has given a procedure for the construction of compactly supported, sufficiently regular, and orthonormal wavelets. The construction procedure of Daubechies' wavelets ensures that the length of the sequence $\{h_n\}$ determines the width of support, zero moment property of ψ, and the smoothness of the wavelet function.

A direct application of MRA is the fast discrete wavelet algorithm, called the *pyramid algorithm* [16]. The basic idea in the pyramid algorithm is the progressive reconstruction feature, which involves the successive addition of details to coarser approximations for better representation.

Using Equation 8.7 and Equation 8.9, the approximation and the detail coefficients at the jth level of resolution, denoted by $c^j = \{< f, \phi_{j,k} >\}$ and $d^j = \{< f, \psi_{j,k} >\}$, respectively, are computed via the following iterative decomposition formulas:

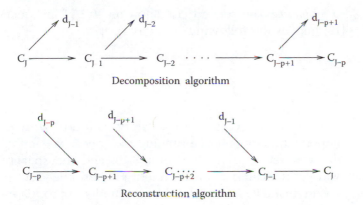

Decomposition algorithm

Reconstruction algorithm

Figure 8.5 Decomposition and reconstruction processes.

$$c_l^j = \sum_k \bar{h}_{k-2l} c_k^{j+1} = \left[\downarrow_2 (\bar{h} \star c^{j+1}) \right]_l$$

$$d_l^j = \sum_k \bar{g}_{k-2l} c_k^{j+1} = \left[\downarrow_2 (\bar{g} \star c^{j+1}) \right]_l$$

$$(8.16)$$

Here, the following notations are used: $h = \{h_n\}$, $g = \{g_n = (-1)^n h_{1-n}\}$, with $\bar{h}_n = h_{-n}$ and $\downarrow_2 \{h_n\} = \{h_{2n}\}$, called the *downsampling operation*. The *star* or * operation denotes the convolution operation. Conversely, the approximation coefficients at the $(j + 1)$th level are obtained via the reconstruction formula

$$c_k^{j+1} = \sum_l (\tilde{h}_{k-2l} c_l^j + \tilde{g}_{k-2l} d_l^j) = [(\uparrow_2 c^j) \star \tilde{h} + (\uparrow_2 d^j) \star \tilde{g}]_k \qquad (8.17)$$

The operation $\uparrow_2 h$ doubles the size of sequence h by inserting zeros in alternate positions and is called the *upsampling operation*. The decomposition and reconstruction processes are shown diagrammatically in Figure 8.5. Because of the involvement of convolution, upsampling, and downsampling operations, when we use finitely supported functions, different levels have different numbers of coefficients. In the following text, we summarize some of the properties of the wavelet transform:

> *Multiresolution framework:* As in the decimal system of represen-
> tation of numbers, in wavelet decomposition, details are added
> successively to coarser-level information, as in Equation 8.14.
> This progressive reconstruction feature is critical in many appli-
> cations, including the ones in IDS.

Zero moments: The second condition on $\{h_n\}_{n \in Z}$ in Equation 8.15 [10] implies the following property of ψ:

$$\int_{-\infty}^{\infty} x^m \psi(x) dx = 0. \tag{8.18}$$

This property reveals the oscillatory nature of ψ, which is an important factor [10] determining the speed of convergence of the wavelet series in Equation 8.13, and the sparsity in the wavelet domain of a function, etc. Higher-order zero moments ensure that data in wavelet domain (under appropriate smoothness conditions on data) can become sparse, i.e., many wavelet coefficients are negligibly small. This feature is useful in data reduction problems.

Stability: When the wavelet basis used is orthonormal, we have

$$\|f\|_2^2 = \sum_{j,k \in Z} |d_{j,k}|^2 \tag{8.19}$$

i.e., the energy of a function is the same as the energy of its wavelet coefficients. Thus, any small error in the input function results in a small error in wavelet coefficients and *vice versa,* justifying the stability of (orthonormal) wavelet bases.

Decorrelation of data: Another important property of wavelets is their ability to reduce temporal correlations in the wavelet domain. Hence, wavelets can be used to reduce the complex process in the time domain into a much simpler process in the wavelet domain. For example, the wavelet coefficients of a self-similar and LRD process form an SRD process [11].

Computational complexity: A vector matrix multiplication is an $O(N^2)$ procedure. Hence, the discrete Fourier transform is an $O(N^2)$ procedure that is achieved in $O(N \log_2 N)$ computations by fast Fourier transform. However, the fast wavelet algorithm [16] based on the pyramidal algorithm achieves the same in $O(N)$ computations [8]. Consequently, the complexity involved in wavelet computations varies linearly with the size of data (N).

Note 4: Brani Vidakovic [23] suggests that if the autocorrelation sequence of $\{h_n\}_{n \in Z}$ (shown in the third line of Equation 8.15 at $2n$) at 1 becomes 0, i.e., $\sum_{k=-\infty}^{\infty} h_k h_{k+1} = 0$, the corresponding scaling function ϕ is orthogonal not only to its integer shifts, but also to its immediate ½ shifts, i.e.:

$$\int_{-\infty}^{\infty} \phi\left(x - \frac{m}{2}\right)\phi\left(x - \frac{n}{2}\right) = \begin{cases} 1 & \text{when } m = n \\ 0 & \text{when } m \neq n \end{cases}$$

Besides being self-similar, it looks comparably "bad" at any resolution. The corresponding wavelet turns out to be good for estimating the Hurst exponent of monofractals with low regularity (H being close to zero) [23].

Acknowledgment

The authors are thankful to Arun K. Pujari, University of Hyderabad, Hyderabad, India, and Rao Vemuri, University of California, Davis, for their help and suggestions. The first author thanks the National Board for Higher Mathematics (NBHM), India, for its financial support (Grant No. FNO: 40/7/2002-R & D II/1124). The second author is also thankful to V.P. Gulati, Director IDRBT, India, for his constant encouragement, and to IDRBT for the research scholarship to pursue his research work. The author is associated with IDRBT as a research fellow.

References

1. Abramovich, F., Bailey, T., and Sapatinas, T. (2000), Wavelet analysis and its statistical applications, *JRSSD*, 48: 1–30.
2. Abry, P. and Veitch, D. (1998), Wavelet analysis of long-range dependent traffic, *IEEE Trans. Inform. Theory* 44: 2–15.
3. Abry, P., Flandrin, P., Taqqu, M.S., and Veitch, D. (2003), Self-similarity and long-range dependence through the wavelet lens, *Theory and Applications of Long-Range Dependence*, Doukhan, P., Oppenheim, G., and Taqqu, M.S. (Eds.), Birkhauser, pp. 526–556.
4. Allen, W.H. and Marin, G.A. (2003), On the self-similarity of synthetic traffic for the evaluation of intrusion detection systems, *Proc. of the IEEE/IPSJ International Symposium on Applications and the Internet (SAINT)*, Orlando, FL, pp. 242–248.
5. Allen, W.H. and Marin, G.A. (2004), The loss technique for detecting new denial of service attacks, *Proc IEEE South East Conference*, Greensboro, NC.
6. Barford, P. and Plonka, D. (2001), Characteristics of network traffic flow anomalies, *Proceedings of ACM SIGCOMM Internet Measurement Workshop IMW*.
7. Beran, J. (1994), *Statistics for Long-Memory Processes*, Chapman and Hall, New York.
8. Beylkin, G., Coifman, R., and Rokhlin, V. (1991), Fast wavelet transforms and numerical algorithms, *Comm. Pure and Appl. Math,* 44: 141–183.

9. Crovella, M. and Bestavros, A. (1997), Self-similarity in World Wide Web traffic: Evidence and possible causes, *IEEE-ACM Transactions on Networking*, 5: 835–846.

10. Daubechies, I. (1992), *Ten lectures on wavelets*, CBMS-NSF Series in Appl. Math., 61, SIAM Philadelphia.

11. Gilbert, A.C. (2001), Multiscale analysis and data networks, *Applied and Computational Harmonic Analysis*, 10: 185–202.

12. Huang, P., Feldmann, A., and Willinger, W. (2001), A non-intrusive, wavelet-based approach to detect network performance problems, *Proc of the First ACM SIGCOMM Workshop on Internet Measurement IMW'01*, San Francisco, California, pp. 213–227.

13. Lee, W. and Stolfo, S.J. (1998), Data mining approaches for intrusion detection, *Proc of the 7th USENIX Security Symposium (SECURITY-98)*, Usenix Association, January 26–29, pp. 79–94.

14. Liao, Y. and Vemuri, V.R. (2002a), Use of K-nearest neighbor classifier for intrusion detection, *Computers and Security*, 21(5): 439–448.

15. Li, T., Li, Q., Zhu, S., and Ogihara, M. (2002), A survey of wavelet applications in data mining, *SIGKDD Explorations*, 4(2): 49.

16. Mallat, S., *A Wavelet Tour of Signal Processing*, Academic Press, 1998.

17. Nash, D.A. and Ragsdale, D.J. (2001), Simulation of self-similarity in network utilization patterns, *Transactions of the IEEE Systems, Man, and Cybernetics*, part A, 31(4): 327–331.

18. Pong Chan, K. and Fu, A.W.C. (1999), Efficient time series matching by wavelets, *Proc ICDE*, pp. 126–133.

19. Rawat, S. and Sastry, Ch.S. (2004), Network intrusion detection using wavelet analysis, *Proc. of CIT, Hyderabad, India, 2004*, LNCS 3356, Springer-Verlag, pp. 224–232.

20. Rawat, S., Pujari, A.K., and Gulati, V.P. (2004), On the use of singular value decomposition for a fast intrusion detection system, *Proc. of the First International Workshop on Views on Designing Complex Architectures (VODCA 2004)*, ENTCS, Elsevier, pp. 59–71.

21. Sastry, Ch.S., Pujari, A.K., Deekshatulu, B.L., and Bhagvati, C. (2004), A wavelet based multiresolution algorithm for rotation invariant feature extraction, *Pattern Recognition Letters*, 25: 1845–1855.

22. Sheikholeslami, G., Chatterjee, S., and Zhang, A. (1998), WaveCluster: A multiresolution clustering approach for very large spatial databases, *Proc. 24th Int. Conf. Very Large Data Bases, VLDB*, pp. 428–439.

23. Vidakovic, B. (2004), An Open Problem or Easy Exercise, http://www.isye.gatech.edu/brani/wavelet.html.

24. Willinger, W., Taqqu, M., and Erramilli, A. (1996), A bibliographical guide to self-similar traffic and performance modeling for modern high-speed networks, *Stochastic Networks*, Kelly, F.P., Zachary, S., and Ziedins, I. (Eds.), Oxford University Press, Oxford, pp. 339–366.

25. Xia, X., Lazarou, G.Y., and Butler, T. (2004), Automatic scaling range selection for long-range dependent network traffic, Submitted to the *IEEE Communications Letters*.

Chapter 9

Application of Exploratory Multivariate Analysis for Network Security

Khaled Labib and V Rao Vemuri

Abstract

There are many ways to study, analyze, visualize, and detect network traffic anomalies. Some of these are quite successful. However, it is difficult to compare the results obtained from these studies and to define the merits and demerits of each method. This difficulty is exacerbated while comparing visualization methods. A primary reason for this difficulty is the heterogeneous nature of the development process of these methods; they do not use a common framework for development and testing. This study uses the S language for statistical computing and graphics as a unified framework for evaluating the applicability of seven exploratory multivariate analysis methods for anomaly detection and visualization. The methods are used to study, visualize, and possibly detect computer network attacks. The methods, namely, *k*-means, hierarchical clustering, self-organizing maps, principal component analysis (PCA), independent component analysis (ICA), stars plots, and mosaic plots, are used to analyze and visualize selected network attacks from the DARPA 1998 dataset. Visualization techniques associated with each method provide more in-depth

229

representation of the nature of the network traffic, with each method having its unique view of the data. Some of the results obtained may be used in identifying trends in the behavioral change in the traffic characteristics. Using this unified framework, a comparison of the performance, feature, graphical representation, and applicability of each method is possible.

9.1 Introduction

Several successful implementations of intrusion detection systems (IDSs) have resulted from recent research. Each of these implementations generally uses its own set of home-grown software tools, scripts, and programs to construct and validate every new IDS concept and method. The steps involved in developing and testing a new IDS method include data collection, preprocessing, algorithm development, data storage, and visualization. In addition, the research and development process typically spans multiple disciplines, including statistics, artificial intelligence (AI), mathematics, and visualization. However, there is a lack of a unified framework for developing and testing these systems. This results in difficulties in comparing the results. Moreover, the software components developed for one system are not reusable by another system that is under development, because of the lack of a common framework for reusability.

Another issue arises when trying to evaluate and compare visualization methods that are created through different computer programs. To be able to do a meaningful comparison, several tools must be set up, each having its own flavor of graphical representation. In addition, these tools may be designed to run on different platforms, making it even harder to compare these graphical representations.

It is also desired to graphically characterize the development of network traffic in general and the development of attack patterns in particular. This is an area in which little research has been done. Tracking behavioral changes in the characteristics of the network traffic across time can enable earlier detection of attacks. This approach of characterizing the development of network attacks is inspired by the work of Herman and Montroll [1] in characterizing the development of countries.

To address these issues, we propose in this chapter the use of the S language to provide a unified framework for studying, developing, testing, and comparing the results of various methods for the implementation of anomaly detection systems, with emphasis on visualization. As discussed earlier, seven exploratory multivariate analysis algorithms are studied, namely: the *k*-means, hierarchical clustering, self-organizing maps, PCA, ICA, stars plots, and mosaic plots. Using a single program, datasets can be loaded and postprocessed. Then, each method is applied to the datasets. The generated statistics are displayed, and graphical views of the data provide an intuitive visual approach for finding relationships amongst the different data elements.

A comparison of the results obtained from running different algorithms reveals that some methods are suitable for detecting certain anomalies, whereas the others provide for a more powerful visualization of the data.

The rest of the chapter is organized as follows: Section 9.2 provides a brisk summary of the problem of intrusion detection, to the extent relevant to the methods presented in this chapter. Section 9.3 introduces the S language and its environment. Section 9.4 provides an introduction to the multivariate analysis methods used in this study. Section 9.5 describes denial-of-service (DoS) and network probe attacks. Section 9.6 details the process of data collection and preprocessing and the creation of feature vectors. Section 9.7 discusses the results obtained and suggests a method of detecting intrusions using these results.

9.2 The Intrusion Detection Problem

Currently, three approaches to intrusion detection have gained some degree of popularity. The first, a signature-based method [2], creates a database of known intrusion signatures and compares all user signatures with this database. The disadvantage of this model is its inherent inability to detect new attacks or known attacks that have significantly changed their behavior, that is, the signature.

The second approach, referred to as *anomaly detection,* attempts to establish what the normal traffic patterns look like for a given network, and flags out any variations in traffic from this norm. Unlike signature-based detectors, anomaly detectors do not compare the traffic against any signature database; they rather attempt to identify anomalies in the traffic that suggest a possibility of an attack or intrusion that is taking place. The disadvantages of this model are high false-alarm rates and the lack of the ability to easily cope with normal changes in network activity. In addition, anomaly detectors can flag out abnormal behavior, but may not be able to specify the exact type of attack or its nature.

The third approach, referred to as *specification-based intrusion detection,* relies on manually specifying program behavioral specification that is used as a basis to detect attacks. It has been proposed as a promising alternative that combines the strengths of signature-based and anomaly-based detection [3].

The focus of this chapter is on evaluating the use of exploratory multivariate analysis methods as applied to anomaly detection with emphasis on visualization. Anomaly detection is a widely used method in the field of computer security, and there are many approaches that utilize it for detecting intrusions [4]. Various techniques for modeling normal and anomalous data have been developed for anomaly detection. A survey of these methods can be found in Reference 5.

Clustering methods have been used in many fields, including statistics [6], machine learning [7], and visualization. Some studies, summarized next, attempted to use clustering methods for anomaly detection.

Portony et al. [8] presents a method for clustering similar data instances together and uses distance metrics on clusters to determine an anomaly. The author makes two basic assumptions: First, data instances having the same classification should be close to each other in feature space under some reasonable metric, whereas instances with different classifications should be far apart. Second, the number of instances in the training set that represent normal traffic is overwhelmingly larger than the number of intrusion instances. Clusters were labeled automatically, and were later used to classify unseen network data instances. Both training and testing were done using subsets of KDD CUP 99 data [9]. On average, the detection rate was around 40 to 55 percent with a 1.3 to 2.3 percent false-positive rate.

There are a number of research projects that focus on using statistical approaches for anomaly detection.

Staniford-Chen et al. [10] address the problem of tracing intruders who obscure their identity by logging through a chain of multiple machines. They use PCA to infer the best choice of thumbprinting parameters from data. They introduce *thumbprints,* which are short summaries of the content of a connection.

Shah et al. [11] study how fuzzy data–mining concepts can cooperate in synergy to perform distributed intrusion detection. They describe attacks using a semantically rich language, reason over them, and subsequently classify them as instances of an attack of a specific type. They use PCA to reduce the dimensionality of the collected data.

There are some studies that attempt to apply self-organizing maps as a tool to address network intrusion detection in general and DoS attack detection in particular.

A system developed by Rhodes et al. [12] uses multiple self-organizing maps for intrusion detection. They use a collection of more specialized maps to process network traffic for each layered protocol separately. They suggest that each neural network becomes a kind of specialist, trained to recognize the normal activity of a single protocol.

Another approach that differs from anomaly detection and misuse detection considers human factors to support the exploration of network traffic [13]. The authors use self-organizing maps to project the network events on a space appropriate for visualization, and achieve their exploration using a map metaphor. The use of self-organizing maps, combined with *stars plots* as a visualization tool in this study, is motivated by the work of Herman and Montroll [1]. These authors attempted to characterize the temporal evolution of countries by the use of labor force distribution data on a multidimensional phase plot so that the development of a country is represented by an evolutionary track of a phase point.

In the works cited in the preceding text, a heterogeneous set of tools and software packages were used to develop and test each method, leading to difficulties in comparing the results obtained and in accurately assessing the method's performance. This issue is also common in other similar works in the field. Different tools generate different output formats, reports, and graphics, making it hard to compare their results. In addition, the preprocessing phase of data using different programs and techniques can lead to variable performance numbers among the different implementations, which makes the process of evaluating comparative performance difficult. Using the S language creates a unified framework for evaluating the results and associated performance of each method. In addition, the reusability of software components can become a much easier task when using a single framework.

Common to the implementation of these anomaly detection approaches is a set of tasks that are performed to achieve the desired goal of detecting intrusions. These tasks can be summarized as follows:

- *Data collection and processing:* For example, sniffing data off the network and processing it to extract the desired portions of packet data.
- *Application of detection algorithm:* The desired detection algorithm or method is applied to the data previously collected.
- *Evaluation of results:* This is done by generating reports and using advanced visualization to assess the results obtained.

In practice, each of these tasks may be implemented using one or more software segments. Many of the current projects evaluating new IDS concepts use a variety of different programs, ranging from scripts and compiled executables to third-party tools and perhaps certain portions of code from an older project. All these tasks can be achieved within a single framework by using S.

9.3 The S Language and Its Environment

The S environment is an integrated suite of software facilities for data analysis and graphical display. "The term *environment* is intended to characterize it as a planned and coherent system built around a language and a collection of low-level facilities, rather than the 'package' model of an incremental accretion of very specific, high-level, and sometimes inflexible tools" [14]. One of the strengths of S is that functions implementing new statistical methods can be developed on top of the low-level facilities.

For example, to create a single function to perform the three basic tasks of an IDS, as described in Section 9.2, the S code would look like:

```
evalIDS ← function(indata) {
  pd ← procData(indata);
  intrusion ← detectIntrusion(pd);
  evalResult ← evalResult(intrusion);
}
```

The top-level function evalIDS accepts one argument, indata, and calls three functions, namely, procData, detectIntrusion, and evalResult, representing the three basic tasks. Each of the three functions in turn calls other lower-level functions to implement their details. Specific examples of these functions will be discussed in detail in Section 9.7.

Using S, it is quite easy to play around with the design decisions made by the original implementers to explore new ideas. For example, an existing library function uses linear interpolation. This behavior can be changed to reflect a nonlinear model by rewriting the function. In the previous example, the function detectIntrusion could be made a library function with some default algorithm to detect intrusions. This default behavior could easily be modified, by modifying the library function source, to implement variations of the default algorithm or a completely new algorithm while maintaining the same structure of the rest of the program.

This flexibility is even more evident in the open-source R implementation, in which all the details of implementation are open for exploration. Indeed, R is used in this study to generate all results and graphics.

The commercial implementation of S, called *S-Plus,* has an extensive graphical user interface (GUI) that provides menus and dialogues for many simple statistical and graphical operations. A full-featured student edition is available at no cost for students at accredited universities. The open-source R package can be downloaded directly from the project Web site and is installable on many platforms including Windows and Linux. Almost all S scripts developed for S-Plus will run on R and *vice versa.* The main difference between S-Plus and R is that S-Plus, including the student edition, has a sophisticated GUI that is especially helpful for new users.

Both S-Plus (including the student edition) and open-source R implementations provide a command-line interface for entering S commands. Once the program is started, this command line allows the user to enter S commands, create variables, call functions, draw graphs, create and manipulate data tables, and save and print results. Because S is also a full programming language in its own right, it provides for assignment statements, control structures, arithmetical expressions, array and matrix operations, and calling conventions for functions, among other capabilities.

Some of the language features found in S are also found in other scientific analysis languages such as Matlab and Mathematica, but S provides for some key features that make it more applicable for use in intrusion detection research. First, S is designed to be a statistical analysis tool and, thus, many of the specialized statistical functions are already available in its libraries and need not be written from scratch. These functions are typically the core functions that are used to develop intrusion detection engines. On the other hand, Matlab is essentially a numerical simulation tool that is designed to do linear algebra computations and simulation. For example, implementing statistical models from Becker et al. [15] (commonly known as the blue book models) in Matlab is a chore, whereas, it is essentially a built-in feature in S-Plus and R.

Also, S's ability to run on many platforms makes it ideal for use in intrusion detection research, in which the hosts under study are running a variety of operating systems and hardware. For example, R is available for over 14 different processor architectures and operating systems, including the most common ones such as Linux, Windows, Mac OS, and many UNIX flavors. This is a key feature for distributed IDSs, in which detection sensor devices need to be installed on a network of hosts with different processor architectures that run different operating systems. In this case, each sensor binary executable (an R installation) can be built from sources according to the processor architecture used at each host. On the other hand, Matlab is available for five different platforms, and only in binary executables form.

Furthermore, S has a powerful object-oriented language structure that can implement quite complex algorithms and their variants. Finally, S-Plus student edition is free for use by students and the open-source R is free to everyone. Open-source software packages have proved to be very useful to research institutions that cannot afford costly software licenses.

Several speed and feature comparisons are available that compare S-Plus and R to other data analysis packages, including Matlab, which is one of the most common ones. A speed comparison between these three packages and several others can be found in Reference 16. A detailed comparison of the features available in these packages, including a comparison of the mathematical functionality, graphical functionality, programming environment functionality, data handling, available operating systems, and speed comparison, can be found in Reference 17.

Using S for intrusion detection enables a researcher to study and compare the results of several detection methods by using a single tool. Because S runs from a command-line interface, the processes of data collection, preprocessing, conversion to S objects (such as arrays and matrices), manipulation of data using a method of choice, generating the required statistics, and plotting the results can all be done using a single tool.

S comes with many preimplemented routines that can be used without being changed. These routines cover methods from exploratory multivariate analysis, including cluster analysis, factor analysis, and discrete multivariate analysis to classification methods, including discriminant analysis, neural networks, and support vector machines, to name a few. All the methods can be replaced or changed to explore newer ideas.

9.4 Introduction to Multivariate Analysis Methods

9.4.1 Exploratory Multivariate Analysis

Multivariate analysis is concerned with datasets that have more than one response variable for each observational unit. The datasets can be summarized by data matrices X with n rows and p columns, the rows representing the observations, and the columns, the variables. The main division in multivariate methods is between those that assume a given structure, for example, dividing the cases into groups, and those that seek to discover the structure from the evidence of the data matrix alone, also called *data mining*. In pattern recognition terminology, the distinction is between supervised and unsupervised methods. Most of the emphasis of this chapter is on unsupervised methods, with the assumption of no *a priori* knowledge of the structure of data.

9.4.2 Visualization Methods

A simple way to examine multivariate data is via a *pairs plot* or a *scatterplot matrix*. Pairs plots are sets of two-dimensional projections of a high-dimensional point cloud. However, a pairs plot can easily miss interesting structures in the data that depend on three or more variables, and genuinely multivariate methods explore the data in a less coordinate-dependent way. Many of the visualization methods can be viewed as projection methods for particular definitions of "interestingness." Feature vectors dimensions used in this study have $p = 12$ columns, therefore, several visualization techniques are applied that attempt to reduce the dimensionality of these vectors.

In the following subsections, a brief description of each of the methods used in this study is provided.

9.4.3 Clustering Methods

Cluster analysis is concerned with discovering groupings among the cases of an n by p matrix, where n is the number of observations, and p is the number of variables in each observation. A comprehensive general reference can be found in Reference 18.

Cluster analysis searches for groups (clusters) in data in such a way that objects belonging to the same cluster resemble each other, whereas objects in different clusters are dissimilar. In two or three dimensions, clusters can be visualized; with more than three dimensions, some kind of analytical assistance and simplified visualization are necessary.

Generally speaking, clustering algorithms fall into two categories [19]:

■ *Partitioning algorithms:* A partitioning algorithm describes a method that divides the dataset into k clusters, in which the integer k needs to be specified. Typically, the algorithm is run for a range of k-values. For each k, the algorithm carries out the clustering and also yields a quality index, which allows the selection of the best value of k afterward. The S functions `kmeans`, `pam`, `clara`, and `fanny` implement algorithms of this type.

■ *Hierarchical algorithms:* A hierarchical algorithm describes a method yielding an entire hierarchy of clustering for the given dataset. Divisive methods start by considering the whole dataset as one cluster, and then split up the clusters until each object is separate. Algorithms of this type are used in the S functions `diana` and `mona`. The seven functions `daisy`, `pam`, `clara`, `fanny`, `agnes`, `diana`, and `mona` make up the cluster library. Algorithms to implement these functions are described in Reference 20.

9.4.3.1 Partitioning Methods

Partitioning methods are based on specifying an initial number of groups and iteratively reallocating observations among groups until some equilibrium is attained.

9.4.3.1.1 k-means Clustering

One of the best-known partitioning methods is the *k*-means. In the *k*-means algorithm, the observations are classified as belonging to one of *k* groups. Group membership is determined by calculating the *centroid* for each group (the multidimensional version of the mean) and assigning each observation to the group with the closest centroid.

The *k*-means clustering algorithm chooses a prespecified number of cluster centers to minimize the within-class sum of squares of the vectors for those centers. Because the algorithm needs a starting point, it chooses the mean of the clusters identified by group-average clustering. The *k*-means needs access to the data matrix and uses Euclidean distance.

The *k*-means algorithm alternates between calculating the centroids based on the current group memberships and reassigning observations to groups based on the new centroids. Centroids are calculated using least-squares, and observations are assigned to the closest centroid based on least-squares. This use of a least-squares criterion makes *k*-means less resistant to outliers.

The S function `kmeans` performs *k*-means clustering. It is an older function that does not have a special plot or summary methods. The main arguments to `kmeans` are dissimilarities as produced by `daisy` or `dist` and the number of clusters. Alternatively, a matrix of starting centroids may be specified in place of the number of centroids. If starting values are not specified, the initial centroids are obtained using the hierarchical clustering algorithm in `hclust`.

9.4.3.2 Hierarchical Methods

The partitioning algorithms discussed in the previous subsection are based on specifying an initial number of groups and iteratively reallocating observations between groups until some equilibrium is attained. In contrast, hierarchical algorithms proceed by combining or dividing existing groups, producing a hierarchical structure displaying the order in which groups are merged or divided.

9.4.3.2.1 Divisive Clustering

Divisive analysis starts with one group and repeatedly divides the group to form many groups. The function `diana` implementation, of a divisive hierarchical method, is probably unique in computing a divisive hierarchy, because most other software for hierarchical clustering is agglomerative. Moreover, `diana` provides (a) the divisive coefficient, which measures the amount of "clustering structure," and (b) the banner plot.

In `diana`, the initial clustering (at step 0) consists of one large cluster containing all n objects. In each subsequent step, the largest available cluster is split into two smaller clusters, until finally all clusters contain but a single object.

9.4.4 Self-Organizing Maps

The self-organizing map (SOM) [21] is a neural network model for analyzing and visualizing high-dimensional data. It belongs to the category of competitive learning networks. The SOM is based on unsupervised learning to map nonlinear statistical relationships between high-dimensional input data into a two-dimensional lattice. This mapping is called *topology preserving*. This property means that points near each other in the input space are mapped to nearby map units in the SOM.

SOM is a family of algorithms with no well-defined objective to be optimized, and the results can be critically dependent on the initialization and the values of the tuning constants used. Despite this high degree of arbitrariness, the method scales well and often produces useful insights in datasets whose size is way beyond, for example, multidimensional scaling (MDS) methods.

If all the data is available at once, the preferred method is batch SOM. For a single iteration, assign all the data points to representatives, and then update all the representatives by replacing each by the mean of all data points assigned to that representative or one of its neighbors, possibly using a distance-weighted mean. The algorithm proceeds iteratively, shrinking the neighborhood radius to zero over a small number of iterations.

9.4.5 PCA

PCA [22] is a well-established technique for dimensionality reduction and multivariate analysis. Examples of its many applications include data compression, image processing, visualization, exploratory data analysis, pattern recognition, and time series prediction. A complete discussion of PCA can be found in textbooks mentioned as Reference 23 and Reference 24. The popularity of PCA comes from three important properties. First, it is the optimum (in terms of mean squared error) linear scheme for compressing a set of high-dimensional vectors into a set of lower-dimensional vectors and then reconstructing the original set. Second, the model parameters can be computed directly from the data — for example, by diagonalizing the sample covariance matrix. Third, compression and decompression are easy operations to perform, given the model parameters; they require only matrix multiplication.

A multidimensional hyperspace is often difficult to visualize. Summarizing multivariate attributes by two or three variables that can be displayed graphically with minimum loss of information is useful in knowledge discovery. Because it is hard to visualize multidimensional space, PCA is mainly used to reduce the dimensionality of p multivariate attributes into two or three dimensions.

PCA summarizes the variation in correlated multivariate attributes to a set of noncorrelated components, each of which is a particular linear combination of the original variables. The extracted noncorrelated components are called *principal components* (PCs) and are estimated from the eigenvectors of the covariance matrix of the original variables. Therefore, the objective of PCA is to achieve parsimony and reduce dimensionality by extracting the smallest number components that account for most of the variation in the original multivariate data and to summarize the data with little loss of information. The S function `princomp` calculates the PCs of a given data matrix.

9.4.6 ICA

ICA has become a hot topic in data visualization. It is a method for finding the underlying factors or components from multivariate (multidimensional) statistical data. What distinguishes ICA from other methods is that it looks for components that are both statistically independent and nongaussian.

ICA looks for rotations of sphered data that have approximately independent components. This will be true (in theory) for all rotations of samples from multivariate normal distributions; hence, so ICA is of most interest for distributions that are far from normal. The function `fastICA` performs ICA on a given data matrix.

9.4.7 Stars Plots

There is a wide range of ways to trigger multiple perceptions of a figure, and these can be used to represent each of a moderately large number of rows of a data matrix by an individual figure. Perhaps the best known of these is the *stars plots* as implemented in the function `stars`. This glyph plot does depend on the ordering of the variables and perhaps also their scaling, and it does rely on properties of human visual perception. So it has rightly been criticized as subject to manipulation, and one should be aware of the possibility that the effect may differ by viewer. Nevertheless, it can be a very effective tool for private exploration.

9.4.8 Mosaic Plots

Most works on visualization implicitly assume continuous measurements. However, large-scale categorical datasets are becoming more prevalent. There are some useful tools available for exploring categorical data, but it is often essential to use models to understand the data. Mosaic plots divide the plotting surface recursively according to the proportion of each factor in turn (so the order of the factors matters). For mosaic plots, the feature vectors created from the network traffic are viewed as categorical data to explore additional information in the data.

9.5 DoS and Network Probe Attacks

In a DoS attack, the attacker makes some computing or memory resource too busy or too full to handle legitimate users' requests. But before an attack is launched on a given site, the attacker typically probes the victim's network or host by searching these networks and hosts for open ports. This is done using a sweeping process across the different hosts on a network and within a single host for services that are up by probing the open ports. This process is referred to as *probe attacks*.

Table 9.1 summarizes the types of attacks used in this study. The attacks are described in more detail in the following text.

Smurf attacks, also known as directed broadcast attacks, are a popular form of DoS packet floods. Smurf attacks rely on directed broadcast to create a flood of traffic for a victim. The attacker sends a ping packet to the broadcast address for some network on the Internet that will accept and respond to directed broadcast messages, known as the *Smurf amplifier*. These are typically misconfigured hosts that allow the translation of broadcast IP addresses to broadcast medium access control (MAC) addresses. The attacker uses a spoofed source address of the victim. For

Table 9.1   Description of DoS and Probe Attacks

Attack Name	Attack Description
Smurf (DoS)	DoS ICMP echo reply flood
Neptune (DoS)	SYN flood DoS on one or more ports
IPsweep (Probe)	Surveillance sweep performing either a port sweep or ping on multiple host addresses
Portsweep (Probe)	Surveillance sweep through many ports to determine which services are supported on a single host

example, if there are 30 hosts connected to the Smurf amplifier, the attacker can cause 30 packets to be sent to the victim by sending a single packet to the Smurf amplifier [25].

Neptune attacks can make memory resources too full for a victim by sending a TCP packet requesting to initiate a TCP session. This packet is part of a three-way handshake that is needed to establish a TCP connection between two hosts. The SYN flag on this packet is set to indicate that a new connection is to be established. This packet includes a spoofed source address, such that the victim is not able to finish the handshake but has to allocate an amount of system memory for this connection. After sending many of these packets, the victim eventually runs out of memory resources.

IPsweep and Portsweep, as their names suggest, sweep through IP addresses and port numbers for a victim network and host, respectively, looking for open ports that could potentially be used later in an attack.

9.6 Data Collection and Preprocessing

9.6.1 Data Collection

The 1998 DARPA intrusion detection datasets were used as the source of all traffic patterns in this study. The training dataset includes traffic collected over a period of seven weeks and contains traces of many types of network attacks as well as normal network traffic.

This dataset has been widely used in intrusion detection research and has been used in the comparative evaluation of many IDSs. McHugh [26] presents a critical review of the design and execution of this dataset. Attack traces were identified using the time stamps published on the DARPA project Web site.

9.6.2 Data Preprocessing

Datasets were preprocessed by extracting the IP packet header information to create feature vectors. The resulting feature vectors were used to calculate the PCs and other statistics. The feature vector chosen has the format shown in Table 9.2.

This format represents the IP packet header information. Each feature vector has 12 components corresponding to the p columns in Section 9.4.1. The IP source and destination addresses are broken down to their network and host addresses to enable the analysis of all types of network addresses.

Seven datasets were created, each containing 300 feature vectors as described earlier. Four datasets represented the four different attack types, one for each shown in Table 9.1. The three remaining datasets represent

Table 9.2 Feature Vector Format

SIPx	Sport	DIPx	Dport	Prot	Plen

where
SIPx = Source IP address nibble, where x = [1–4]. Four nibbles constitute the full source IP address.
Sport = Source port number.
DIPx = Destination IP address nibble, where x = [1–4]. Four nibbles constitute the full destination IP address.
Dport = Destination port number.
Prot = Protocol type: TCP, UDP, or ICMP.

different portions of normal network traffic across different weeks of the DARPA datasets. This allows for variations of normal traffic to be accounted for in the experiment.

One of the motives in creating small datasets (i.e., 300 feature vectors each) for representing the feature vectors is to study the effectiveness of this method for real-time applications. Real-time processing of network traffic mandates the creation of small-sized databases that are dynamically created from real-time traffic presented at the network interface. Because DARPA data is only available statically, seven small datasets were created to mimic the case of dynamic real-time operation.

With each packet header being represented by a 12-dimensional feature vector, it is difficult to view this high-dimensional vector graphically and be able to extract the relationships between its various features. It is equally difficult to extract the relationship between the many vectors in a set. Therefore, the goal of using several methods in this study is to reduce the dimensionality of the feature vector by using various techniques. It is also important to be able to graphically show the distinctions between normal and attack traffic for each dataset.

9.7 Results

The seven multivariate analysis methods described in Section 9.4 were applied to the datasets also described in Section 9.5. The objective is to evaluate the ability of each method to separate the first 300 feature vectors (containing normal traffic) from the next 300 feature vectors (containing attack traffic) into a different cluster. If the method can isolate all attack feature vectors into one or more clusters consistently, then its graphical representation is compared to other methods in terms of overall visual detection ability and computational performance. The goal is to do all these steps within S.

Using S, the three common tasks discussed in Section 9.2 are performed as follows:

9.7.1 Data Collection and Processing

The following code snippet shows how the feature vector datasets are loaded into R, and how the different calls to the methods are made:

```
Library(cluster)
library(MASS)
library(class)
library(fastICA)

## Load Regular data frames
regular1 <- read.table("regular300.txt", row.names=NULL)

## Load Attack data frames
smurf      <- read.table("smurf300.txt", row.names=NULL)
ipsweep    <- read.table("ipsweep300.txt", row.names=NULL)
portsweep  <- read.table("portsweep300.txt", row.names=NULL)
neptune    <- read.table("neptune300.txt", row.names=NULL)
```

The first four lines load preinstalled R libraries, namely: cluster library, MASS library (which contains many datasets and a number of S functions), classification library, and a fast ICA library.

Next, data frames are created by reading their corresponding files from disk. The data frames are named by their type. A data frame is an S object normally used to store a data matrix.

9.7.2 Application of Multivariate Analysis Algorithms

9.7.2.1 k-means Clustering

k-means clustering is applied to each dataset of the different attack types after binding (combining) each of their data frames with the normal traffic data in `regular1` to form a new data frame called "master" with 600 rows and 12 columns. This binding process is used for the remaining datasets as well:

```
for (dataset in masterlist){
    master <- rbind (regular1, dataset)
    kmeansout <- kmeans(master[1:12], 2)
```

```
plot(kmeansout$cluster, type = "b",
   main=masterlistnames[counter] ,
   xlab="Packet Number", ylab="Cluster Number")
}
```

The function `kmeans` performs *k*-means clustering on the combined data frame. Two arguments are given to `kmeans`. First is the "master" data frame, which is the result of binding the attack dataset to the regular dataset. Second is the number of clusters required. In this case, `kmeans` will attempt to cluster the 600 feature vectors, given as its input, into two clusters without any other prior knowledge of the nature of the data.

The results of `kmeans` are then plotted using the "plot" function. The resulting four plots are shown in Figure 9.1. The function plots the assignment of each input vector to an output cluster. This information is stored in the `kmeansout$cluster` variable. Because the number of desired output clusters is two, each input feature vector is assigned to either

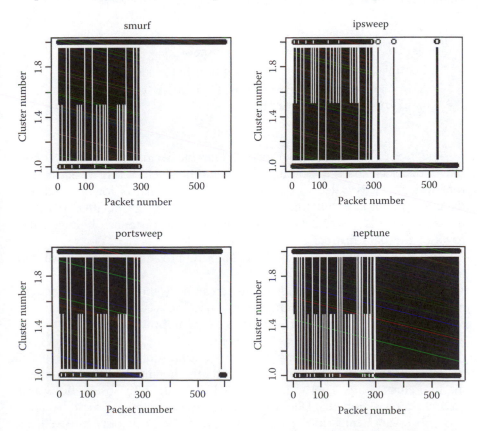

Figure 9.1 *k*-means clustering plot.

cluster one or two as shown in the figure. A line connects the output points on the graph to provide visual continuity. In the case of Smurf, all the attack feature vectors (301 to 600) were assigned to cluster two, whereas all normal feature vectors (0 to 300) were assigned to clusters one and two. Similar results can be seen for IPsweep, Portsweep, and Neptune datasets. For these sets, some of the attack vectors were clustered in a different cluster than the majority of the packets. Careful study of these packets shows that few normal instances of traffic existed in the midst of the attack.

By increasing the number of output clusters to four, some attacks were exclusively clustered in one cluster in which no normal instances were assigned, thereby giving better clustering results than using two clusters.

9.7.2.2 Hierarchical Clustering

Hierarchical clustering is applied to the datasets as follows:

```
for (dataset in masterlist){
    master <- rbind (regular1, dataset)
    hclustout <- hclust(dist(master[1:12]))
    plot(hclustout, main=masterlistnames[counter],
      xlab="PacketNumber")
}
```

The `hclust` function performs hierarchical clustering on the combined datasets. Prior to starting the hierarchical clustering process, the function `dist` is called to compute the distance matrix for the "master" dataset. The distance matrix is computed by using a specified distance measure, in this case Euclidean, to compute the distances between the rows of the data matrix.

The output "hclustout" is plotted using the plot function and is shown in Figure 9.2.

Figure 9.2 shows the dendrograms created by the `hclust` function. A *dendrogram* is a convenient method used to visualize the clustering results. It is a tree graph that is used to examine how clusters are formed in hierarchical cluster analysis. The vertical axis indicates a distance or dissimilarity measure. The height of a node represents the distance of the two clusters that the node joins. The greater the height, the more dissimilar the two clusters are. The horizontal axis lists all the 600 observations and their cluster assignments. Dendrograms have two limitations: First, because each observation must be displayed as a leaf, they can only be used for a small number of observations. This is clear in this figure, in which the

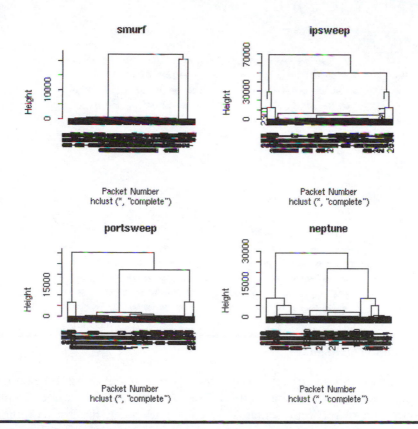

Figure 9.2   Hierarchical clustering plot.

text of the observations on the horizontal axis is not readable. Second, the vertical axis represents the level of the criterion at which any two clusters can be joined. Successive joining of clusters implies a hierarchical structure, meaning that dendrograms are only suitable for hierarchical cluster analysis [27].

9.7.2.3 SOM Clustering

SOM algorithm is applied to the combined datasets as follows:

```
for (dataset in masterlist){
    master <- rbind (regular1, dataset)
    gr <- somgrid(topo = "hexagonal")
    som.out <- SOM(master[1:12], gr)
    plot(som.out, main=masterlistnames[counter])
}
```

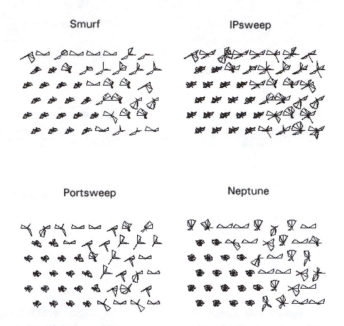

Figure 9.3   SOM plot.

The function `somgrid` records the coordinates of the grid to be used for `SOM,` and it has a plot method. The plot method for class SOM plots a stars plot of the representative at each grid point, thereby combining the output of SOM and stars plots together in a single diagram. A hexagonal topology is selected. The function `SOM` implements Kohonen's SOM algorithm and takes the "master" dataset as its input argument along with the grid output from the `somgrid` function. The stars plot output is plotted and shown in Figure 9.3. Stars plots may be used directly on the data as discussed in Section 9.7.2.6 or superimposed on the output of other functions as in the case of `somgrid`.

The results of Figure 9.3 reveal interesting features of the data. First, the distinction between normal and attack traffic is quite clear from the graphs in which the stars with longer and irregular segments are clustered in one area, whereas the remaining stars with shorter and more regular segments are clustered in another. The SOM algorithm plots stars from the bottom-left corner of the graph to the top and then goes back to the bottom, drawing the next star while maintaining the hexagonal structure. This reveals the fact that normal feature vectors are clustered first using stars with shorter and more regular segments, while attack feature vectors result in stars with longer and irregular spans. Second, this distinction can be used to study the evolution of network traffic. Using this combination of SOM and stars plots can provide an intuitive graphical approach to studying and identifying trends in the behavioral change in the traffic characteristics.

9.7.2.4 PCA

PCA is applied to the dataset as follows:

```
for (dataset in masterlist){
  master <- rbind (regular1, dataset)
  master.pca <- princomp(master[1:12], cor = T)
  master.pc <- predict(master.pca)
  eqscplot(master.pc[, 1:2], type = "p", main=
    masterlistnames[counter], xlab = "First principal
    component",ylab = "Second principal component")
  text(master.pc[,1:2], labels = as.character(master$V13),
    col = c("SkyBlue", "Orange") )
}
```

The function `princomp` performs PCA on the input numeric data matrix and returns the results as an object of class "princomp." The argument "cor" is a logical value indicating whether the calculation should use the correlation matrix or the covariance matrix. The function `predict` is a generic function for predictions from the results of various model-fitting functions. The function invokes particular methods, which depend on the "class" of the first argument. The function `eqscplot` is a version of the function `scatterplot` with scales chosen to be equal on both axes. This function is available in the MASS library. The resulting plot for PCA is shown in Figure 9.4.

In Figure 9.4 the distinction between normal and attack traffic is not clear. Perhaps there is a better way of marking the data on the graph, an issue that needs further experimentation. The PCA algorithm mapped each of the observations with p = 12 dimensions onto two components. For each observation, the value of each component is plotted on the x and y axes, respectively.

9.7.2.5 ICA

ICA is applied to the datasets as follows:

```
for (dataset in masterlist){
    master <- rbind (regular1, dataset)
    nICA <- 2
```

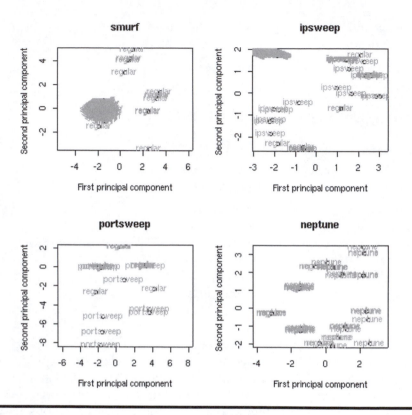

Figure 9.4   PCA plots.

```
master.ica <- fastICA(master[1:12], nICA)
plot(master.ica$S, main=masterlistnames[counter],
    xlab = "First ICA Component", ylab = "Second ICA
    Component", col = c("Black", "Red"))
text(master.ica$S, labels = as.character(master$V13),
    col = c("Black", "Red"))
}
```

The function fastICA is available from the FastICA library. It is an implementation of the fastICA algorithm of Hyvarinen et al. [28] to perform ICA and projection pursuit. The value nICA = 2 is the number of components to be extracted. The resulting plot for ICA is shown in Figure 9.5.

Figure 9.5 shows (similar to the results from PCA) that there is no clear distinction between normal and attack traffic. This may be due to the high dependency that exists among the columns of the dataset.

There are dependencies between the different nibbles of SIP*x* and DIP*x*. There are also dependencies between Sport, Dport, Plen, and Prot.

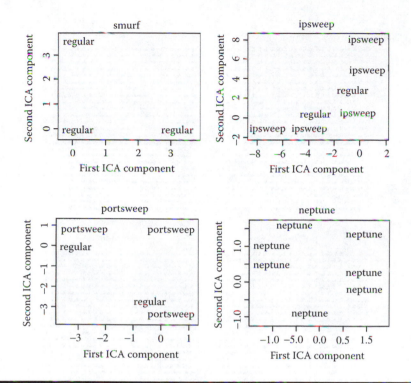

Figure 9.5   ICA plots.

9.7.2.6 Stars Plots

Stars plots are applied to the datasets as follows:

```
for (dataset in masterlist){
    master <- rbind (regular1, dataset)
    stars(master[1:12], full = FALSE, labels = NULL,
        main=masterlistnames[counter] )
}
```

The function `stars` draws star plots or segment diagrams of multivariate datasets. Also, with a single location, it draws spider (or radar) plots. The argument "full" is a logical flag: if TRUE, the segment plots will occupy a full circle. Otherwise, they occupy the (upper) semicircle only. Missing values are treated as zeros. Each star plot or segment diagram represents one row of the input *x*. Variables (columns) start on the right and wind counterclockwise around the circle. The size of the (scaled) column is shown by the distance from the center to the point on the star

smurf   ipsweep

portsweep   neptune

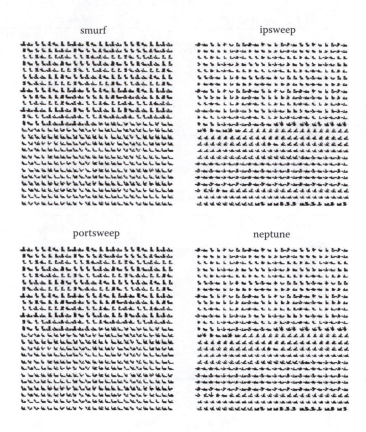

Figure 9.6   Stars plots.

or the radius of the segment representing the variable. The resulting stars plot is shown in Figure 9.6.

As shown in Figure 9.6, the graph of each attack type contains 25 rows and 24 columns, totaling 600 stars for each dataset. That is, each of the 600 observations is represented by one star. Each star has 12 segments corresponding to the $p = 12$ columns of the dataset.

A sample star is shown in Figure 9.7. Each of the 12 feature vector elements described in Section 9.6.2 is drawn as a segment of the semicircle. Comparing this sample star with the results obtained in Figure 9.6, a close look at the stars reveal that there is a relatively clear distinction between the normal traffic in the upper half of the graph and the attack traffic in the lower half. This method of analyzing multivariate data is clearly simple and effective.

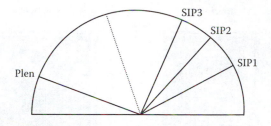

Figure 9.7   A sample star from the stars plot.

9.7.2.7 Mosaic Plots

Mosaic plots are applied to the datasets as follows:

```
for (dataset in masterlist){
    master <- rbind (regular1, dataset)
    names(master) <- c("Src1", "Src2", "Src3", "Src4",
        "Sport", "Dst1", "Dst2", "Dst3", "Dst4", "Dport",
        "Prot", "Plen", "TrafType")
    mosaicplot(master[1:12], color = T,
        main=masterlistnames[counter],
        xlab = "Packet Number", ylab = "Packet Fields")
}
```

The function `mosaicplot` plots a mosaic. Extended mosaic displays show the standardized residuals of a log-linear model of the counts by the color and outline of the mosaic's tiles. Standardized residuals are often referred to as *standard normal distribution*. Negative residuals are drawn in shades of red with broken outlines; positive ones are drawn in blue with solid outlines.

Mosaic plots can be seen as an extension of grouped bar charts in which the width and height of the bars show the relative frequencies of two variables; a mosaic plot simply consists of a collection of tiles whose sizes are proportional to the observed cell frequencies [29].

Sequential horizontal and vertical recursive splits are used to visualize the frequencies of more than two variables, each new variable conditional to the previously entered variables. A first extension uses a color coding of the tiles to visualize deviations (residuals) from a given log-linear model fitted to the table, that is, from the expected frequencies under independence. This approach works not only in two-way tables but also in log-linear models fitted to multiway tables.

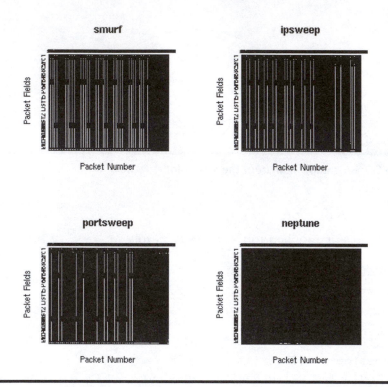

Figure 9.8   Mosaic plots.

In this extension, positive and negative signs of the residuals are coded by rectangles with solid and dashed borders, respectively. Furthermore, residuals exceeding an absolute value of 2 are shaded light blue and red, respectively; those that even exceed an absolute value of 4 are shaded with full saturation. The heuristic behind this shading is that the Pearson residuals are approximately standard normal, which implies that the highlighted cells are those with residuals individually significant at approximately the 5-percent and 0.01-percent levels. But the main purpose of the shading is not to visualize significance but the pattern of deviation from independence.

The input data should be a data frame or matrix containing the variables to be cross-tabulated. In this case, after possibly selecting a subset of the data as specified by the "subset" argument, a contingency table is computed from the variables given in "formula," and a mosaic is produced from this. Missing values are not supported unless "data" contains variables to be cross-tabulated when rows containing missing values are omitted. The resulting mosaic plots are shown in Figure 9.8.

The results shown in Figure 9.8 are not intuitively obvious. Further elaboration is necessary. First, a large number of observations are shown

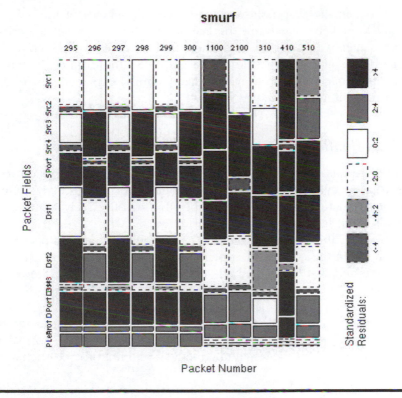

Figure 9.9 Mosaic plot for feature vectors 295 through 305 of the Smurf attack.*k*-means clustering plot.

in one graph. Second, four graphs are combined into one figure, resulting in loss of resolution needed for such graphs. To better illustrate the graph, a zoomed-in version of the Smurf results is shown in Figure 9.9. In this figure, only feature vectors at the border between normal and attack traffic are considered. More specifically, only feature vectors 295 through 305 are considered while adding a legend to the graph. This would capture six feature vectors of the normal traffic and five feature vectors of Smurf attack traffic. The legend shows the color coding used to mark both negative and positive residuals. It is easily seen that the normal traffic represented by the first six bars in the chart has very similar residual values. The facts that these residuals represent deviations from the standard distribution and that they look very much alike reflect some common properties of this data. On the other hand, the five remaining bars to the right that represent the attack traffic also have residual values that are quite different from those of the normal traffic.

In the light of these results, an analogous explanation can be given to the graphs of Figure 9.8. For the Smurf attack, the height and width of each bar in the graph show the relative frequencies of the variables. The attack packets, which are the last 300 feature vectors in the dataset, had a smaller width of the bars and, thus, were shown as compacted (black) blocks at the right side of the graph. So the distinction between normal and attack data is easily visualized. Similar explanations are given for the remaining three graphs.

9.7.3 Evaluation of Results

From the results obtained using the different methods as applied to the datasets, it is evident that each method gives an interestingly different view of the nature of the data. To be able to effectively compare the results, several factors should be considered.

First is the ability of each method to distinguish between normal and attack traffic in the context of explanatory multivariate analysis. It should be emphasized that these methods do not have any *a priori* knowledge of the data and that they are trained to know what the structure of the data is. These methods are comparable to unsupervised learning methods in the field of AI and soft computing. To this end, k-means, hierarchical clustering, and SOM provided a clear distinction between normal and attack traffic, whereas the remaining methods did not provide such a clear view.

Second is the effectiveness of each method in its visual presentation by conveying the underlying structure in the data. Several methods performed really well here, most notably, k-means, SOM, and mosaic plots. One of the compelling features of the graphical output of these methods is that the relationship between the original data and its final transformation is relatively clear. In the case of k-means, there is a direct relationship between the packet number and its cluster assignment. In the case of SOM and mosaic plots, the relationship between the packet number and its final representation is somewhat preserved. On the contrary, using the output from PCA and ICA, the relationship between the packet numbers and the final transformations is not clear.

The final factor is the time that each method takes to execute the algorithm. Table 9.3 shows the execution time of each algorithm. Three times are shown: *user time* indicates the time (in seconds) consumed for the user process, *system time* indicates the time consumed by the operating system, and the *elapsed time* indicates the total time consumed by the overall operation. The difference between user time and system time is that user time is the CPU time used while executing instructions in the user space of the calling process, whereas system time is the CPU time used by the system on behalf of the calling process. It should be noted that the times given include the time for applying the algorithms for all

Table 9.3   Algorithm Execution Times

Algorithm/Time	User (s)	System (s)	Elapsed (s)
k-means	0.31	0.04	0.42
Hierarchical	37.02	0.49	38.76
SOM	1.94	0.03	2.2
PCA	1.28	0.03	1.59
Fast ICA	1.07	0.02	1.36
Stars	9.56	0.4	12.18
Mosaic	224.32	2.73	243.46

four datasets, the time to generate the graphics related to the method, and finally, the time to write this information to the disk. From this perspective, k-means performed best. FastICA, PCA, and SOM were next. Star plots and hierarchical clustering used relatively high user time. Finally, mosaic plots performed very poorly in terms of user time.

It is clear from these results that the best overall performance and visualization are achieved using k-means and SOM. The remaining methods provide interesting insights into the data and may be used to supplement the results obtained through k-means and SOM. However, they have several performance and visual limitations, making them inappropriate for use as a primary method for analyzing network traffic anomalies.

Acknowledgment

Work reported in this paper is supported in part by AFOSR's grant, FA9550-04-1-0159.

References

1. Herman, R., Montroll, E., A manner of characterizing the development of countries. *Proceedings of the National Academy of Sciences U.S.A.*, No. 10, pp. 3019–3023, October 1972.
2. Han, H., Lu, X.L., Lu, J., Chen, B., and Yong, R.L., Data mining aided signature discovery in network-based intrusion detection systems. *ACM SIGOPS Operating System Review.* Vol. 36, Issue 4, October 2002.
3. Uppuluri, P. and Sekar, R., Experiences with specification-based intrusion detection. *Proceedings of the 4th International Symposium on Recent Advances in Intrusion Detection*, pp. 172–189, 2001.

4. Denning, D.E., An intrusion detection model. *IEEE Transactions on Software Engineering*, SE-13: 222–232, 1987.
5. Warrender, C, Forest, S., and Pearlmutter, B., Detecting intrusions using system calls. *Alternate Data Models*, 1999.
6. Schnell, P., A method for discovering data-groups. *Biometrica* 6: 47–48, 1964.
7. Rojas, R., *Neural Network: A Systematic Introduction*. Springer-Verlag, Berlin, 1996.
8. Portony, L., Eskin, E., and Stolfo, J. Intrusion detection with unlabeled data using clustering, *Proceedings of ACM CSS Workshop on Data Mining Applied to Security (DMSA-2001)*. Philadelphia, PA: November 5–8, 2001.
9. Knowledge Discovery and Data Mining competition, KDD99 CUP Data Set, 1999. http://kdd.ics.uci.edu.
10. Staniford-Chen, S., and Heberlein, L.T., Holding intruders accountable on the Internet. *Proceedings of the 1995 IEEE Symposium on Security and Privacy.*
11. Shah, H., Undercoffer, J., and Joshi, A., Fuzzy clustering for intrusion detection. *FUZZ-IEEE*, 2003.
12. Rhodes, B., Mahaffey, J., and Cannady, J., Multiple self-organizing maps for intrusion detection. *Proceedings of the NISSC 2000 conference,* Baltimore, MD, 2000.
13. Girardin, L., An eye on network intruder-administrator shootouts. *Proceedings of the Workshop on Intrusion Detection and Network Monitoring*, Santa Clara, CA, April 9–12, 1999.
14. Venables, W.N. and Ripley, B.D., *Modern Applied Statistics with S*, 4th ed., Springer-Verlag, New York, 2002.
15. Becker, R., Chambers, J., and Wilks, A., *The New S Language*, Chapman & Hall, London, 1988.
16. http://www.sciviews.org/other/benchmark1.htm.
17. http://www.scientificweb.com/ncrunch/ncrunch4.pdf.
18. Gordon, A.D., *Classification*, 2nd ed., Chapman & Hall, London, 1999.
19. *S-Plus: Guide to Statistics*, Vol. 2. Insightful Corporation, 2001.
20. Kaufman, L. and Rousseeuw, P.J., *Finding Groups in Data: An Introduction to Cluster Analysis*, John Wiley & Sons, New York, 1990.
21. Kohonen, T., *Self-Organizing Maps*. Springer-Verlag, New York, 1995.
22. Hotelling, H., Analysis of a complex of statistical variables into principal components. *Journal of Educational Psychology*, 24: 417–441, 1933.
23. Duda, R., Hart, P., and Stork, D., *Pattern Classification*. 2nd ed., John Wiley & Sons, New York, 2001.
24. Haykin, S., *Neural Networks: A Comprehensive Foundation*. 2nd ed. Prentice Hall, Englewood Cliffs, NJ, 1999.
25. Skoudis, E., *Counter Hack: A Step-by-Step Guide to Computer Attacks and Effective Defenses*. Prentice Hall, Englewood Cliffs, NJ, 2002.
26. McHugh, J., Testing intrusion detection systems: Critique of the 1998 DARPA intrusion detection system evaluations as performed by Lincoln laboratory. *ACM Transactions on Information and System Security*, Vol. 3, No. 4, November 2000, pp. 262–294.

27. Schonlau, M., The clustergram: a graph for visualizing hierarchical and non-hierarchical cluster analyses. *The Stata Journal*, 2002, 3, pp. 316–327.
28. http://www.cis.hut.fi/aapo.
29. Meyer, D., Zeileis, A., and Hornik, K., Visualizing independence using extended association plots. *Proceedings of the 3rd International Workshop on Distributed Statistical Computing*, Vienna, 2003.

Index